Politics in Mexico
The Decline of Authoritarianism

Third Edition

RODERIC AI CAMP

New York   Oxford
OXFORD UNIVERSITY PRESS
1999

Oxford University Press

Oxford   New York
Athens   Auckland   Bangkok   Bogota   Buenos Aires
Calcutta   Cape Town   Chennai   Dar es Salaam   Delhi
Florence   Hong Kong   Istanbul   Karachi
Kuala Lumpur   Madrid   Melbourne
Mexico City   Mumbai   Nairobi   Paris   São Paulo   Singapore
Taipei   Tokyo   Toronto   Warsaw

and associated companies in
Berlin   Ibadan

Copyright © 1993, 1996, 1999 by Oxford University Press, Inc.

Published by Oxford University Press, Inc.,
198 Madison Avenue, New York, New York 10016

Oxford is a registered trademark of Oxford University Press

Library of Congress Cataloging-in-Publication Data
Camp, Roderic Ai.
    Politics in Mexico : the decline of authoritarianism / Roderic Ai
  Camp.—3rd ed.
      p.   cm.
    Includes bibliographical references and index.
    ISBN 0-19-512412-X
    1. Mexico—Politics and government.   I. Title.
  JL1281.C35   1999
  306.2′0972—dc21   98-29058
                                                                  CIP

Printing (last digit): 9 8 7 6 5 4 3 2 1

Printed in the United States of America
on acid-free paper

To My Teachers

Contents

Acknowledgments

Anyone who has been in the business of teaching eventually writes a mental textbook, constantly revised and presented orally in a series of lectures. As teachers, however, we often dream of writing just the right book for our special interest or course. Such a book naturally incorporates our own biases and objectives. It also builds on the knowledge and experiences of dozens of other teachers. While still a teenager, I thought of being a teacher and, perhaps unusually, a college professor. Teachers throughout my life, at all levels of my education, influenced this choice. They also affected the way in which I teach, my interrelationship with students, and my philosophy of learning and life. To these varied influences, I offer heartfelt thanks and hope that this work, in some small way, repays their contributions to me personally and professionally and to generations of other students.

Among those special teachers, I want to mention Thelma Roberts and Helen Weishaupt, who devoted their lives to the betterment of young children, instilling worthy values and beliefs and setting admirable personal examples, and to Mrs. Lloyd, for numerous afternoon conversations at Cambridge School. I wish to thank Ralph Corder and Don Fallis, who encouraged my natural interest in history toward a more specific interest in social studies. Sharon Williams and Richard W. Gully, my toughest high school teachers, introduced me to serious research and to the joys of investigating intellectual issues; and Inez Fallis, through four years of Spanish, prompted my continued interest in Mexico. Robert V. Edwards and Katharine Blair stressed the importance of communication, orally and in writing, helping me understand essential ingredients in the process of instruction. My most challenging professor, Dr. Bergel, during a high school program at Chapman College, opened my eyes to Western civilization and to the intellectual feast that broad interdisciplinary teaching could offer.

For his humanity, advice, and skill with the English language, I remain indebted to George Landon. As a mentor in the classroom and a model researcher, Mario Rodríguez led me to the Library of Congress and to the joys of archival research. On my arrival in Arizona, Paul Kelso took me under his wing, contributing vastly to my knowledge of Mexico and the out-of-doors, sharing a rewarding social life with his wife, Ruth. I learned more about Latin America and teaching in the demanding classrooms of George A. Brubaker and Edward J. Williams. Both convinced me of the importance of clarity, teaching writing as well as substance. Finally, Charles O. Jones and Clifton Wilson set examples in their seminars of what I hoped to achieve as an instructor.

Indirectly, I owe thanks to hundreds of students who have graced my classrooms and responded enthusiastically, sometimes less so, to my interpretations of Mexican politics. I am equally indebted to Bill Beezley, David Dent, Oscar Martínez, and Edward J. Williams, devoted teachers and scholars, who offered many helpful suggestions for this book.

1

Mexico in Comparative Context

> The contours of political development in modern Mexico often appear clearer and more pronounced when viewed as the products of tension among three key ideological traditions—namely, corporatism, pluralism, and Marxism. For its advocates, corporatism offers a humanistic alternative to both interest group liberalism identified with the United States and other western democracies, and communism as practiced in China, Cuba, North Korea, or the former Soviet union.
>
> GEORGE W. GRAYSON, *Mexico: From Corporatism to Pluralism?*

An exploration of a society's politics is, by nature, all-encompassing. Political behavior and political processes are a reflection of a culture's evolution, involving history, geography, values, ethnicity, religion, internal and external relationships, and much more. As social scientists, we often pursue the strategies of the modern journalist in our attempt to understand the political news of the moment, ignoring the medley of influences from the past.

Naturally, each person tends to examine another culture's characteristics, political or otherwise, from his or her own society's perspective. This is not only a product of ethnocentrism, thinking of one's society as superior to the next person's, for which we Americans are often criticized, but also a question of familiarity. Although we often are woefully ignorant of our own society's political processes and institutions, being more familiar with the mythology than actual practice, we become accustomed to our way of doing things in our own country.[1]

I will attempt to explain Mexican politics, building on this natural proclivity to relate most comfortably to our own political customs, by drawing on implied as well as explicit comparisons with the United States. This comparison is further enhanced by the fact that Mexico and the United States have been joined together in a free-trade agreement since January 1994. We also are products of a more comprehensive Western European

1

civilization, into which other traditions are gradually making significant inroads. Although some critics suggest that we have relied too exclusively on Western traditions in our education, they are unquestionably the primary source of our political values. Thus our familiarity with political processes, if it extends at all beyond United States boundaries, is typically that of the western European nations and England.[2] For recent immigrants, of course, that heritage is different. Again, where possible, comparisons will be made with some of these political systems in order to place the Mexican experience in a larger context. Finally, Mexico is a Third World country, a category into which most countries fall, and hence its characteristics deserve to be compared with characteristics we might encounter elsewhere in the Third World.

WHY COMPARE POLITICAL CULTURES?

The comparison of political systems is an exciting enterprise. One reason that the study of politics in different societies and time periods has intrigued inquiring minds for generations is the central question, Which political system is best? Identifying the "best" political system, other than its merely being the one with which you are most familiar and consequently comfortable, is, of course, a subjective task. It depends largely on what you want out of your political system. The demands made on a political system and its ability to respond efficiently and appropriately to them are one way of measuring its effectiveness.

Throughout the twentieth century, perhaps the major issue attracting the social scientist, the statesperson, and the average, educated citizen is which political system contributes most positively to economic growth and societal development. From an ideological perspective, much of international politics since World War II has focused primarily on that issue. As Peter Klarén concluded,

> U.S. policymakers searched for arguments to counter Soviet claims that Marxism represented a better alternative for development in the Third World than did Western capitalism. At the same time U.S. scholars began to study in earnest the causes of underdevelopment. In particular scholars asked why the West had developed and why most of the rest of the world had not.[3]

The two political systems most heavily analyzed since 1945 have been democratic capitalism and Soviet-style socialism. Each has its pluses and minuses, depending on individual values and perspectives. Given recent events in eastern Europe and the breakup of the Soviet state, socialism is in decline. Nevertheless, socialism as a model is not yet dead, nor is it likely to be in the future. Administrators of the socialist model rather than the weaknesses inherent in the ideology can always be blamed for its failures. Furthermore, it is human nature to want alternative choices in every facet of life. Politics is just one facet, even if somewhat all-encompassing. The history of humankind reveals a continual competition between alternative political models.

In short, whether one chooses democratic capitalism, a fresh version of socialism, or some other hybrid ideological alternative, societies and citizens will continue to search for the most viable political processes to bring about economic and social benefits. Because most of the earth's peoples are economically underprivileged, they want immediate results. Often, politicians from less fortunate nations seek a solution through emulating wealthier (First World) nations. Mexico's leaders and its populace are no exception to this general pattern.

One of the major issues facing Mexico's leaders is the nature of its capitalist model, and the degree to which Mexico should pursue a strategy of economic development patterned after that of the United States. Since 1988 they have sought to alter many traditional relationships between government and the private sector, increasing the influence of the private sector in an attempt to reverse Mexico's economic crisis and stimulate economic growth. In fact, Mexico received international notice in the 1990s for the level and pace of change under President Carlos Salinas de Gortari.[4]

In public statements and political rhetoric, Salinas called for economic and political modernization. He explicitly incorporated political with economic change, even implying a linkage.[5] Thus, he advocated economic liberalization, which he defined as increased control of the economy by the private sector, more extensive foreign investment, and internationalization of the Mexican economy through expanded trade and formal commercial relationships with the United States and Canada. Simultaneously, Salinas advocated political liberalization, which he defined as including more citizen participation in elections, greater electoral competition, and integrity in the voting process—all features associated with the United States and European liberal political traditions.

Salinas's successor, Ernesto Zedillo, who took office on December 1, 1994, inherited a political system in transition and an economic situation that shortly turned into a major financial and political crisis. A combination of economic decisions and an unsettled political context led to capital flight and a significant decline in investor confidence in the Mexican economy. Accordingly, Mexico began pursuing a severe austerity program, exceeding even those in the 1980s during a time of severe recession. By 1997, however, Mexican economic indicators showed strong growth, even if those results were not translated into improved income levels for most Mexicans. Investor confidence in Mexico returned. Zedillo continued to pursue an economic liberalization strategy and increase the pace of political reforms compared to his predecessor. Strong doubts about neo-liberal economic policies remain from various quarters, however, generating some nationalistic, anti–United States sentiments.

It is hotly debated among social scientists whether a society's political model determines its economic success or whether its economic model produces its political characteristics. Whether capitalism affects the behavior of a political model or whether a political model is essential to successful capitalism leads to the classic chicken-and-egg argument. It may well be a moot point because the processes are interrelated in terms of not only institutional patterns but cultural patterns as well.[6]

The comparative study of politics reveals, to some extent, a more important consideration. If the average Mexican is asked to choose between more political freedom or greater economic growth, as it affects him or her personally, the typical choice is the latter.[7] This is true in other Third World countries too. People with inadequate incomes are much more likely to worry about bread-and-butter issues than about more political freedom. A country's political model becomes paramount, however, when its citizens draw a connection between economic growth (as related to improving their own standard of living) and the political system. If they believe the political system, and not just the leadership itself, is largely responsible for economic development, it will have important repercussions on their political values and their political behavior. If Mexicans draw such a connection, it will change the nature of their demands on the political leadership and system, and the level and intensity of their participation.[8]

The comparative study of societies provides a framework by which we can measure the advantages and disadvantages of political models as they affect economic growth. Of course, economic growth itself is not the only differentiating consequence. Some political leaders are equally concerned, in some cases more concerned, with social justice. Social justice may be interpreted in numerous ways. One way is to think of it as a means of redistributing wealth. For example, we often assume that economic growth—the percentage by which a society's economic productivity expands in a given time period—automatically conveys equal benefits to each member of the society. More attention is paid to the level of growth than to its beneficiaries. It is frequently the case that the lowest-income groups benefit least from economic growth. This has been true in the United States but is even more noticeable in Third World and Latin American countries. There are periods, of course, when economic growth produces greater equality in income distribution.[9] Per capita income figures (national in-

---

Social justice: a concept focusing on each citizen's quality of life and the equal treatment of all citizens.

---

come divided by total population) can be deceiving because they are averages. In Mexico, for example, even during the sustained growth of the 1950s and 1960s, the real purchasing power (ability to buy goods and services) of the working classes actually declined.[10] Higher-income groups increased their proportion of national income from the 1970s through the 1990s, decades of economic crisis, and that of the lower-income groups fell.[11] This pattern has been further exacerbated since early 1995. The importance of social justice to Mexicans, defined as redistribution of wealth, is illustrated by the fact that one-fourth of Mexicans surveyed in 1998 consider it to be the second most important task of democracy.[12]

Another way of interpreting social justice is on the basis of social equality. This does not mean that all people are equal in ability but that each person should be treated equally under the law. Social justice also implies a leveling of differences in opportunities to succeed, giving each person equal access to society's resources. Accordingly, its allocation of resources can be a measure of a political system.

The degree to which a political system protects the rights of all citizens is another criterion by which political models can be compared. In Mexico, where human rights abuses are a serious problem, the evidence is unequivocal that the poor are much more likely to be the victims than are members of the middle and upper classes. This is why the arrest of Raúl Salinas, brother of the former president, as the alleged mastermind of a political assassination, is such a dramatic departure from past practices. This also helps to explain why only a third of all Mexicans have any confidence in their court system.[13] The same can be said about many societies, but there are sharp differences in degree between highly industrialized nations and Third World nations.[14]

From a comparative perspective, then, we may want to test the abilities of political systems to eliminate both economic and social inequalities. It is logical to believe that among the political models in which the population has a significant voice in making decisions, the people across the board obtain a larger share of the societal resources. On the other hand, it is possible to argue, as in the case of Cuba, that an authoritarian model can impose more widespread, immediate equality in the distribution of resources, even in the absence of economic growth, while reducing the standard of living for formerly favored groups.

Regarding social justice and its relationship to various political models, leaders also are concerned with the distribution of wealth and resources *among* nations, not just within an individual nation. The choice of a political model, therefore, often involves international considerations. Such considerations are particularly important to countries that achieved independence in the twentieth century, especially after 1945. These countries want to achieve not only economic but also political and cultural independence. Although Mexico, like most of Latin America, achieved political independence in the early nineteenth century, it found itself in the shadow of an extremely powerful neighbor. Its proximity to the United States eventually led to its losing half of its territory and many natural resources.

A third means to compare political models is their ability to remake a citizenry. A problem faced by most nations, especially in their infancy, is building a sense of nationalism. A sense of nationalism is difficult to erase, even after years of domination by another power, as in the case of the Soviet Union and the Baltic republics, but it is equally difficult to establish, especially in societies incorporating diverse cultural, ethnic, and religious heritages.[15] The political process can be used to mold citizens, to bring about a strong sense of national unity, while lessening or dampening local and regional loyalties. The acceptability of a political model, its very legitimacy among the citizenry, is a measure of its effectiveness in developing national sensibilities. Mexico, which had an abiding sense of regionalism, struggled for many decades to achieve a strong sense of national unity and pride.[16] On the other hand, Mexico did not have sharp religious and ethnic differences, characteristic of other cultures such as India, to overcome.

Many scholars have suggested that the single most important issue governing relationships among nations in the twenty-first century will be that of the haves versus the have nots.[17] In fact, Mexico's linkage to the United States and Canada in a free-trade agreement highlights this point. One of the arguments against such an agreement was the impossibility of eliminating trade barriers between a nation whose per capita wage is one-seventh of the per capita wage of the other nation.[18] One of the arguments for such an agreement was that it could temper this disparity.

The dichotomy between rich and poor nations is likely to produce immense tensions in the future, yet the problems that both sets of nations face are remarkably similar. As the 1990 *World Values Survey* illustrates, an extraordinary movement in the coincidence of some national values is afoot, for example, in the realm of ecology. This survey, which covers forty countries, discovered that from 1981 to 1990 an enormous change in concern about environmental issues occurred in poor as well as rich nations. Other problems that most countries—regardless of their standard of living or political system—share include availability of natural resources, notably energy; production of foodstuffs, especially grains; level of inflation; size of national debt; access to social services, including health care; inadequate housing; and maldistribution of wealth.

Another reason that examining political systems from a comparative perspective is useful is personal. As a student of other cultures you can learn more about your own political system by reexamining attitudes and practices long taken for granted. In the same way a student of foreign languages comes to appreciate more clearly the syntax and structure of his or her native tongue and the incursions of other languages into its constructions and meanings, so too does the student of political systems gain. Comparisons not only enhance your knowledge of the political system in which you live but are likely to increase your appreciation of particular features.

Examining a culture's politics implicitly delves into its values and attitudes. As we move quickly into an increasingly interdependent world, knowledge of other cultures is essential to being well educated. Comparative knowledge, however, allows us to test our values against those of other cultures. How do ours measure up? Do other sets of values have applicability in our society? Are they more or less appropriate to our society? Why? For example, one of the reasons for the considerable misunderstanding between the United States and Mexico is a differing view of the meaning of political democracy. Many Mexicans attach features to the word *democracy* that are not attached to its definition in the United States.[19] As will be discussed later, for many Mexicans, democracy does not incorporate tolerance of opposing viewpoints. Problems arise when people do not realize they are using a different vocabulary when discussing the same issue.

Another reason for comparing political cultures is to dispel the notion that Western industrialized nations have all the solutions. It is natural to think of the exchange of ideas favoring the most technologically developed nations, including Japan, Germany, and the United States. But solutions do not rely on technologies alone; in fact, most rely on human skills. In other words, how do people do things? This is true whether we are analyzing politics or increasing sales in the marketplace. Technologies can improve the efficiency, quality, and output of goods and services, yet their application raises critical questions revolving around values, attitudes, and interpersonal relationships. For example, the Japanese have a management philosophy governing employee and employer relations. It has nothing to do with technology. Many observers believe, however, that the philosophy in operation produces better human relationships and higher economic productivity. Accordingly, it is touted as an alternative model in the workplace. The broader the scope of human understanding, the greater the potential for identifying and solving human-made problems.

Finally, as a student new to the study of other cultures, you may be least interested in the long-term contributions such knowledge can make for its own sake. Yet your ability to explain differences and similarities between and among political systems and, more important, their consequences, is essential to the growth of political knowledge. Although not always the case, it is generally true that the more you know about something and the more you understand its behavior, the more you can explain its behavior. This type of knowledge allows social scientists to create new theories of politics and political behavior, some of which can be applied to their own political system as well as to other cultures. It also allows—keeping in mind the limitations of human behavior—some level of prediction. In other words, given certain types of institutions and specific political conditions, social scientists can predict that political behavior is likely to follow certain patterns.

SOME INTERPRETATIONS OF THE MEXICAN SYSTEM

We suggested earlier that social scientists set for themselves the task of formulating some broad questions about the nature of a political system and its political processes. A variety of acceptable approaches can be used to examine political systems individually or comparatively. Some approaches focus on relationships among political institutions and the functions each institution performs. Other approaches give greater weight to societal values and attitudes and the consequences these have for political behavior and the institutional features characterizing a political system. Still other approaches, especially in the last third of the twentieth century, place greater emphasis on economic relationships and the influence of social or income groups on political decisions. Taking this last approach a step further, many analysts of Third World countries, including Mexico, concentrate on international economic influences and their effect on domestic political structures.

Choosing any one approach to explain the nature of political behavior has advantages in describing a political system. In my own experience, however, I have never become convinced that one approach offers an adequate explanation. I believe that an examination of political processes or functions entails the fewest prejudices and that by pursuing how and where these functions occur, one uncovers the contributions of other approaches.[20] An eclectic approach to politics, incorporating culture, history, structures, geography, and external relations, provides the most adequate and accurate vision of contemporary political behavior. Such an eclectic approach, combining the advantages of each, will be used in this book.

In general, the study of Mexican politics has provoked continued debate about which features have the greatest impact on political behavior and, more commonly, to what degree Mexico is an authoritarian model[21] It is important, as we begin this exploratory task, to offer some theories about the nature of Mexican politics.

Does Mexico have an authoritarian political system? The simple answer is yes. Is Mexican politics in the same authoritarian category as Cuba under Fidel Castro, China since the Communist revolution, or Russia before 1991? The answer is definitely no. Mexico can best be described as a semiauthoritarian political system—a hybrid of political liberalism and authoritarianism that gives it a special quality or flavor—that is well documented institutionally in its 1917 constitution, currently in effect. Since 1994, Mexico can be described as a system in transition, especially in its electoral structures and division of powers. Although it appears to be moving rapidly toward a more pluralistic model that includes features associated with democratic polities, it has not yet made a complete transition.

Mexico's unique authoritarianism sets it apart from many other societies, including Latin American countries that have passed through long periods of authoritarian control, especially in the 1970s and 1980s.[22] Normally, *authoritarian* refers to a political system in which fewer people have access to the decision-making process and fewer still are in a position to make important political choices and policies.

What sets Mexico's authoritarian system apart from many others is that it allows much greater access to the decision-making process, and more important, its decision makers change frequently.[23] Usually the advantage of a well-established authoritarian regime is continuity. Whereas it is fair

---

Authoritarian: in political terms, a system in which only a small number of people exercise and have access to political power.

---

to say that successive generations of Mexican leaders, with ties to their predecessors, have controlled the decision-making process, that has not led necessarily to continuity in policy. Furthermore, its leadership, in the hands of the executive branch, especially the president, is limited to a six-year term.

A second feature of the Mexican political model, integral to its hybrid authoritarianism, is a special feature found in many Latin American cultures: *corporatism.* Corporatism in this political context refers to how groups in society relate to the government or, more broadly the state; the process through which they channel their demands to the government; and how the government responds to their demands.[24] Perhaps no characteristic of the Mexican political model has undergone more change in the 1990s than corporatism. In the United States, any introductory course in U.S. politics devotes some time to interest groups and how they present their demands to the political system. Mexico, which inherited the concept of corporatism from Spain, instituted in the 1930s a corporate relationship between the state and various important interest or social groups, primarily under the presidency of General Lázaro Cárdenas (1934–1940). This means that the government took the initiative to

---

Corporatism: a formal relationship between selected groups or institutions and the government or state.

---

strengthen various groups, creating umbrella organizations to house them and through which their demands could be presented. The government placed itself in an advantageous position by representing various interest groups, especially those most likely to support opposing points of view. The state attempted, and succeeded over a period of years, in acting as the official arbiter of these interests. It generally managed to make various groups loyal to it in return for representing their interests. For example, it absorbed the largest groups in a government-sponsored political party, now called the Institutional Revolutionary Party (Partido Revolucionario Institucional, the PRI), giving them legitimacy and a role in party affairs. These included peasants, labor, and middle-class professional groups.

The essence of the corporatist relationship is political reciprocity. In return for official recognition and official association with the government or government-controlled organizations, these groups can expect some consideration of their interests on the part of the state. They can also expect the state to protect them from their natural political enemies. For example, labor unions hope the state will favor their interests over the interests of powerful businesses.[25]

The corporatist structure has made the state the all-powerful force in the society, and it is often patronizing in its relations with various groups.

Corporatism facilitated the state's ability to manipulate various groups in the state's own interest. In other words, Mexico's political leadership itself might be thought of as a separate interest group, but unlike all other interest groups, it is in control of the decision-making process.[26] The state's uncontested dominance has enabled its leaders to make some choices that benefit themselves rather than various social-class or group interests.

Mexico's political system is not only semiauthoritarian, while retaining some weak corporatist features, but it also allows the government and/or state to play a paramount role, a third distinguishing feature. State institutions have generally had far more prestige, resources, and influence than private, independent, or nonprofit organizations have had. The state's prestige has contributed to the perpetuation of its influence. Many of the best minds, regardless of profession or educational background, are attracted to lifetime careers with the state.[27] (This is also true elsewhere in Latin America and throughout Asia and Africa.) State dominance has contributed enormously to the growth and centralization of resources in the capital city and the Federal District, somewhat analogous to the District of Columbia in the United States. The power of the Mexican national state and the comparative weakness of local and provincial authorities contribute to a mentality of dependence on the state. The excessive dependence has engendered resentment as well, as various groups and geographic regions have sought to establish their autonomy from centralized state control.[28]

The dominance of the state within a semiauthoritarian, declining corporatist political structure contributes to a fourth political feature of the Mexican model: the centralization of authority in the executive branch. The Mexican model is unquestionably presidentially dominant, a phenomenon that Mexicans refer to as *presidencialismo* (presidentialism).[29] Americans think of their president as being tremendously influential. Of course, no other individual citizen or official can exercise the level of political influence that the U.S. president can. His influence is further exaggerated because he is seen as the, or a, major world leader. The Mexican president has no comparable international credentials—even though President Salinas

---

Presidencialismo: the concept that most political power lies in the hands of the president and all that is good or bad in government policy stems personally from the president.

(1988–1994) enhanced his domestic status considerably by virtue of his international reputation—but the president nevertheless exercises far more control over the Mexican political scene than does his American counterpart in the United States. The strength of the presidency specifically, and the executive branch generally, comes at the cost of an ineffectual legislative and judicial branch, or any other autonomous authority. Although early in his administration President Zedillo introduced important reforms in the judicial system, especially at the level of the supreme court, they have not yet influenced the decision-making process. On the other hand, the influence of the legislative branch, controlled by opposition parties, has grown markedly in the late 1990s. By 1998, a majority of Mexicans believed that Congress was more important than the president for a functioning democracy.

The importance of Mexican executive leadership and the dominance of the state have led to the development of a dynamic political elite whose careers are formed within the national governmental bureaucracy. The elite, which has never been characterized by ideological homogeneity, is relatively open but has recently taken on fairly homogeneous social, career, and educational characteristics.[30] Although entry into political leadership ranks is available to well-educated Mexicans, it is a self-designated group. That is, most important decision-making posts are appointive in nature, and those selecting the officeholders are themselves incumbents. These persons change over time, thus facilitating access to leadership positions and the alteration of policy goals, but they are not as responsive to constituencies as are U.S. officials.[31] In fact, fewer than one out of three Mexicans in 1998 believed they were well represented by their congressperson. Moreover, because a primary goal of politicians everywhere is to stay in power, Mexican politicians, lacking constituent responsibilities, have generally been pragmatic, doing whatever is necessary to remain in office rather than pursuing a committed, ideological platform.

The final structural feature of the Mexican model is the presence and level of influence exercised by international capital and, since the 1980s, international financial agencies. As was the case among so many of its fellow Latin American nations, the impact of foreign investment on macroeconomic policy, and on the lives of ordinary Mexican citizens, became paramount in the 1980s, and again to an even greater degree in 1995, when Mexico suffered its worst recession since the worldwide depression of the 1930s. The dependence of Mexico on outside capital and on foreign trade has exercised an important effect on policy making, if not to the same degree on how decisions are taken.[32] Such influences raise significant issues of national sovereignty and autonomy.

The structural features of Mexico's political model—semiauthoritarianism, declining corporatism, state dominance, centralization of authority, and a self-selecting elite—are complemented by a dual political heritage incorporated into the political culture. The political culture is neither democratic nor authoritarian. It is contradictory: modern and traditional. Mexico, as the late Nobel Prize winner Octavio Paz argued, is built from two different populations, rural versus urban and traditional versus modern.[33] It bears the burden of many historical experiences, precolonial, colonial, independence, and revolutionary. These experiences produced a political culture that admires essential democratic values, such as citizen participation, yet strongly favors intolerance of opposing points of view.[34] It is the cultural blend of contradictory values that explains Mexico's special authoritarian system. The contradictions in its political culture and historical experiences have also produced a set of policy goals, many incorporated in the constitution, that too are contradictory. On one hand, a strong state is favored; on the other, capitalism is the preferred tool for economic growth.

Place and historical experience have also contributed to another feature of mass political culture: a dependent psychology.[35] The proximity of the United States, which shares a border with Mexico nearly two thousand miles long, and the extreme disparities between the two in economic wealth and size tend to foster an inferiority complex in many Mexicans, whether they operate in the worlds of business, academia, technology, or politics. The economic, cultural, and artistic penetration of the United States into Mexico carries with it other values foreign to its domestic political heritage. Psychologically and culturally, Mexicans must cope with these influences, most of which are indirect, often invisible. A strong sense of Mexican nationalism, especially in relation to its political model, is expressed in part as a defensive mechanism against United States influences. The December 1994 devaluation of the peso and the perceived and real impact of the United States on Mexico's economic crisis have exacerbated this reaction. This level of nationalism has produced and sustained unique characteristics of the Mexican political model.

MEXICO'S SIGNIFICANCE IN A COMPARATIVE CONTEXT

From a comparative perspective, Mexico provides many valuable insights into politics and political behavior. The feature of Mexico that has most intrigued students of comparative politics is the stability of its political system.[36] Although challenged seriously by military and civilian factions in 1923, 1927, and 1929, its political structure and leadership have prevailed for most of this century, at least since 1930—an accomplishment un-

matched by any other Third World country. Even among industrialized nations like Italy, Germany, and Japan, such longevity is remarkable. The
phenomenon leads to such questions as What enables the stability? What
makes the Mexican model unique? Is it the structure of the model? Is it
the political culture? Does it have something to do with the country's proximity to another exemplar of political continuity? Or with the values and
behavior of the people?

We know from other studies of political stability that a degree of political legitimacy accompanies even a modicum of support for a political
model. Although social scientists are interested in political legitimacy and
political stability each for its own sake, they assume, with considerable evidence, that some relationship exists between economic development and
political stability. Although it is misleading to think that the characteristics of one system can be successfully transferred to another, it is useful to
ascertain which may be more or less relevant to accomplishing specific,
political goals.

Mexico has also attracted considerable international interest because
it is a one party–dominant system encountering only limited opposition
from 1929 through 1988, the year in which a splinter group from the official party ran a highly successful campaign. Mexico's system is unusual in
that the antecedent of the PRI, the National Revolutionary Party (Partido
Nacional Revolucionario, the PNR), did not bring the political leadership
to power. Rather, the leadership established the party as a vehicle to *remain* in power; the PRI was founded and controlled by the government bureaucracy. This had long-term effects on the nature of the party itself, and
on its importance to policymaking.[37] In this sense, the PRI is unlike the
Communist Party in the Soviet Union, whose death in 1991 spelled the end
of Communist leadership in the successor states. The PRI, because it does
not produce Mexico's leadership, as do the Democratic and Republican
parties in the United States, is much more tangential to political power and
consequently much more expendable. If the Mexican model continues to
evolve along democratic lines, then the party's function, and consequently
its importance, will grow significantly. This is already apparent in the internal race for the party's presidential nominee for 2000.

A third reason that Mexico's political system intrigues outside observers has been its ability to subordinate military authorities to civilian
control. Mexico, like most other Latin American countries, endured a century when violence became an accepted tool of the political game. Such
acceptance makes it extremely difficult, if not impossible, to eliminate the
military's large and often decisive political role. Witness many Latin American countries;[38] one has only to look at Argentina and Chile during the

1970s and 1980s. No country south of Mexico has achieved its extended *civilian* supremacy. Rather, in most Latin American countries where civilian leadership is once again in ascendancy, their dominance is tenuous at best.

Mexico, therefore, is a unique case study in Third World civil–military relations. What produced civilian supremacy there? Is the condition found elsewhere? A confluence of circumstances and policies gradually succeeded in putting civilian control incrementally in place. Some involve the special characteristics of the system itself, including the creation of a national political party. Some are historical, the most important of which is the Mexican Revolution of 1910, which led to the development of a popular army whose generals governed Mexico in the 1920s and 1930s and who themselves initiated the concept of civilian control.[39]

A fourth reason for studying Mexico is the singular relationship it has developed with the dominant religious institution, the Catholic Church. Throughout much of Latin America, the Catholic Church has been one of the important corporate actors. For significant historical reasons in the nineteenth and twentieth centuries, Mexico's leadership suppressed and then isolated itself from the Catholic hierarchy and even in some cases the Catholic religion.[40] The Catholic Church has often played a political role in Latin American societies and currently has the potential to exercise considerable political and social influence. A study of church–state relations in Mexico offers a unique perspective on how the church was removed from the corporatist structure and the implications of this autonomy for a politically influential institution.

A fifth reason for examining Mexico in a comparative political context is the opportunity to view the impact of the United States, a First World country, on a Third World country. No comparable geographic relationship obtains anywhere else in the world: Two countries that share a long border exhibit great disparities in wealth. Mexico provides not only a test case for those who view Latin America as dependent on external economic forces but also an unparalleled opportunity to look at the possible *political* and *cultural* influences and consequences of a major power.[41] The relationship is not one way but instead is asymmetrical.[42] The United States exercises or can exercise more influence over Mexico than vice versa. This does not mean that Mexico is the passive partner. It, too, exercises influence, and in many respects its influence is growing. Because of European civilization's influence on our culture, we have long studied the political models of England and the Continent. Our obsession with the Soviet Union exaggerated our focus on Europe. As Latino and other immigrant cohorts grow larger in the United States, our knowledge of the Mexican culture will become far more relevant to understanding *contemporary political behavior* in the United States than anything we might learn from contemporary Europe.

A sixth reason to explore the Mexican political model is its experiences since 1989 with economic liberalization. One of the issues that has fascinated social scientists for many years, but especially since the downfall of the Soviet Union and the emergence of new economic and political models in eastern Europe, is the linkage between economic and political liberalization. What does the Mexican case suggest about its strategy of concentrating on opening its markets, which then may create conditions favorable to political development? Indeed, is there a causal linkage between economic and political liberalization? If so, what lessons can be offered by the Mexican transition?[43]

Finally, a seventh reason Mexico may offer some useful comparisons is the transition taking place between national and local political authorities. Long dominated by a national executive branch in both the decision-making process and the allocation of resources, Mexico is witnessing, since the first opposition-party victory at the state level in 1989, an increasing pattern of decentralization and deconcentration of political control at the state and local level, as the National Action Party and the Democratic Revolutionary Party win more elections.[44] How has the dominant, national political leadership responded to these victories? How have they affected the process of governance, as distinct from electoral competition? The potential implications of such change from the bottom up offers many insights into structural political relationships in Mexico.

CONCLUSION

To summarize, then, approaching politics from a comparative perspective offers many rewards. It allows us to test political models against one another; it enables us to learn more about ourselves and our own political culture; it offers a means for examining the relationship between political and economic development and the distribution of wealth; and it identifies the common interests of rich and poor nations and what they do to solve their problems.

Scholars have interpreted Mexico's political system in different ways. This book argues that the system remains semiauthoritarian, with weakened corporatist features, but is in transition; is dominated by a declining state; is led by a bureaucratic elite and a centralized executive competing with a legislative branch growing in influence; is built on a contradictory political culture that includes authoritarian and liberal qualities; is characterized by international economic features embedded in its domestic structures; and is affected psychologically and politically by its proximity to the United States. Mexico offers unique opportunities for comparative study because of its political continuity and stability, one party–dominant system, civil–military relations, unique separation of church and state, and nearness to a powerful, wealthy neighbor.

In the next chapter, the importance for Mexico of time, place, and historical roots is examined in greater detail and contrasted with the experiences of other countries. Among these elements are its Spanish heritage, the role of the state, nineteenth-century liberalism and positivism, the revolution, and U.S.–Mexican relations.

NOTES

1. Gabriel Almond and Sidney Verba, *The Civic Culture* (Boston: Little, Brown, 1965), 59.

2. Compare, for example, the number of academic course offerings and textbooks available on Europe and European countries with those representing other, especially Third World, regions and societies.

3. Peter Klarén, "Lost Promise: Explaining Latin American Underdevelopment," in *Promise of Development: Theories of Change in Latin America*, ed. Peter Klarén and Thomas J. Bossert (Boulder, Colo.: Westview Press, 1986), 8.

4. See for example, the glowing statement in the *Washington Post*, that Salinas "has proved to be as radical in his own way as the revolutionaries who galloped over Mexico at the beginning of the century." May 17, 1991.

5. For Salinas's views in English, see the interview "A New Hope for the Hemisphere," *New Perspective Quarterly* 8 (Winter 1991): 8.

6. The clearest presentation of this argument, in brief form, can be found in Gabriel Almond, "Capitalism and Democracy," *PS* 24 (September 1991): 467–73.

7. In the World Values Survey (a collaborative survey of forty countries in 1981 and again in 1990, available in data format from the University of Michigan, Ann Arbor. Ronald Inglehart, Institute for Social Research, directed the North American project), 1990, data from Mexico show that approximately 60 percent of the population chose economic growth as most important, compared with approximately 25 percent who selected increased political participation. Similar results have been repeated in every major survey taken through 1998.

8. On a presidential level, most Mexicans have not yet made the connection, or if they have, it is not significant to their voting. See Jorge Domínguez and James McCann, "Whither the PRI? Explaining Voter Defection from Mexico's Ruling

Party in the 1988 Presidential Elections," paper presented at the Western Political Science Association meeting, March 1991, 23–24. They follow up this argument in "Shaping Mexico's Electoral Arena: The Construction of Partisan Cleavages in the 1988 and 1991 National Elections," *American Political Science Review* 89 (March 1995): 39–40, and in their *Democratizing Mexico, Public Opinion and Electoral Choices* (Baltimore: The Johns Hopkins University Press, 1996).

9. It has been argued, as a general rule, that as countries achieve advanced industrial economies, greater economic equality will be achieved. See Samuel P. Huntington, *Political Order in Changing Societies* (New Haven, Conn.: Yale University Press, 1968), 57. Also see Dan LaBotz's statement that real minimum wages for Mexicans declined 44 percent between 1977 and 1988, in *Mask of Democracy: Labor Suppression in Mexico Today* (Boston: South End Press, 1992), 19.

10. Roger D. Hansen, *The Politics of Mexican Development* (Baltimore: Johns Hopkins University Press, 1971), especially "Trends in Mexican Income Distribution," 72ff.

11. Sidney Weintraub, *A Marriage of Convenience: Relations Between Mexico and the United States* (New York: Oxford University Press, 1990), 36; and Wayne Cornelius, "Foreword," in *The Politics of Economic Restructuring, State-Society Relations and Regime Change in Mexico*, ed. Mario Lorena Cook, Kevin J. Middlebrook and Juan Molinar Horcasitas (La Jolla, Calif.: Center for U.S.–Mexican Studies, UCSD, 1994), xiv–xv.

12. Roderic Ai Camp, "Democracy Through Latin American Lenses," Hewlett Foundation, Pilot Study, Mexico, April, 1998.

13. Miguel Basáñez, Marta Lagos, and Tatiana Beltrán, *Reporte 1995: encuesta latino barómetro* (1996), np.

14. Of course, this is true worldwide. Unfortunately, the problems *seem* less severe when these groups are the primary victims. Americas Watch, *Human Rights in Mexico: A Policy of Impunity* (New York: Human Rights Watch, 1990), 53.

15. Karl W. Deutsch, *Nationalism and Social Communication: An Inquiry into the Foundations of Nationality*, 2d ed. (Cambridge: MIT Press, 1966), 156ff.

16. Frederick Turner, *The Dynamics of Mexican Nationalism* (Chapel Hill: University of North Carolina Press, 1968).

17. The classic argument for this was presented by Barbara Ward, *The Rich Nations and the Poor Nations* (London: Hamilton, 1962).

18. Jeff Faux, "No: The Biggest Export Will Be U.S. Jobs," *Washington Post Weekly Edition*, May 13–19, 1991, 8.

19. See one commissioner's statement that this is a source of bilateral problems in the blue-ribbon Report of the Bilateral Commission on the Future of United States-Mexican Relations, *The Challenge of Interdependence* (Lanham, Md.: University Press of America, 1989), 237; these findings are reinforced empirically in Roderic Ai Camp, "Democracy Through Latin American Lenses," 1998.

20. The most comprehensive explanation of various interpretations still is Carolyn Needleman and Martin Needleman, "Who Rules Mexico? A Critique of Some Current Views of the Mexican Political Process," *Journal of Politics* 31 (November 1969): 1011–34. Some of these issues have been reexamined by Diane E.

Davis, *Urban Leviathan, Mexico City in the Twentieth Century* (Philadelphia: Temple University Press, 1994); and Viviane Brachet-Márquez, "Explaining Sociopolitical Change in Latin America: The Case of Mexico," *Latin American Research Review* 27 (1992): 91–122.

21. For example, Susan K. Purcell, "Decision-Making in an Authoritarian Regime: Theoretical Implications from a Mexican Case Study," *World Politics* 26 (October 1973): 28–54.

22. José Luis Reyna and Richard Weinert, eds., *Authoritarianism in Mexico* (New York: ISHI, 1977).

23. Lorenzo Meyer, one of Mexico's foremost independent commentators, expressed it in this way: "Mexico's system does allow, however, for some limited political pluralism and a higher degree of institutionalization and accessibility than the authoritarian regimes that dominated Latin America's Southern Cone a decade ago." See his "Democratization of the PRI: Mission Impossible?" in *Mexico's Alternative Political Futures*, ed. Wayne A. Cornelius, Judith Gentleman, and Peter H. Smith (La Jolla, Calif.: Center for U.S.–Mexican Studies, UCSD, 1989), 333.

24. Ruth Spalding, "The Mexican Variant of Corporatism," *Comparative Political Studies* 14 (July 1981): 139–61.

25. An excellent analysis of this relationship can be found in Ruth Berins Collier, *The Contradictory Alliance, State-Labor Relations and Regime Change in Mexico* (Berkeley: University of California International and Area Studies, 1992).

26. For evidence of this view, see John W. Sloan, "State Power and Its Limits: Corporatism in Mexico," *Inter-American Economic Affairs* 38 (1984): 3–18.

27. For the state's relationship to professional development, see Peter Cleaves, *Professions and the State: The Mexican Case* (Tucson: University of Arizona Press, 1987); and David E. Lorey, *The Rise of the Professions in Twentieth-Century Mexico, University Graduates and Occupational Change Since 1929*, 2d ed. (Los Angeles: UCLA Latin American Center, 1994).

28. Edward J. Williams, "The Resurgent North and Contemporary Mexican Regionalism," *Mexican Studies* 6 (Summer 1990): 299–323, makes a strong case for northern regionalism.

29. Edmundo Gonález Llaca, "El presidencialismo o la personalización del poder," *Revista Mexicana de Ciencias Politicas* 21 (April-June 1975): 35–42, discusses this at length.

30. For some of these, see Roderic A. Camp, *Political Recruitment Across Two Centuries, Mexico 1884–1991* (Austin: University of Texas Press, 1995).

31. For detailed, long-term patterns of continuity and turnover, see Peter H. Smith, *Labyrinths of Power: Political Recruitment in Twentieth Century Mexico* (Princeton, N.J.: Princeton University Press, 1979), 159ff. For comparisons with other countries, see John D. Nagle, *System and Succession, the Social Bases of Political Elite Recruitment* (Austin: University of Texas Press, 1977), 23ff.

32. For current reactions to the intervention of the International Monetary Fund, see Rick Wills, "The IMF's Economic Role Causes Controversy," *El Financiero International Edition*, October 6, 1997, 8. Fifty-six percent of Mexicans believe that U.S. influence over Mexico is excessive. "Mexico's Economic Situa-

tion Survey," *El Norte/Reforma* poll of 1,100 urban Mexicans with a ±3 percent margin of error, 1995. See *Dallas Morning News*, November 5, 1995, 3.

33. Octavio Paz, *The Other Mexico: A Critique of the Pyramid* (New York: Grove Press, 1972), 45. Paz noted the existence of "one fundamental characteristic of the contemporary situation: the existence of two Mexicos, one modern and the other underdeveloped. This duality is the result of the Revolution and the development that followed it: thus, it is the source of many hopes and, at the same time, of future threats."

34. Enrique Alduncín, *Los valores de los mexicanos* (Mexico City: Fomento Cultural Banamex, 1986); Enrique Alduncín, *Los valores de los mexicanos, México en tiempos de cambio*, vol. 2 (Mexico: Fomento Cultural Banamex, 1991); Raúl Béjar Navarro, *El mexicano, aspectos culturales y psicosociales* (Mexico City: UNAM, 1981). The most comprehensive work in English is that by Rogelio Díaz Guerrero, *Psychology of the Mexican* (Austin: University of Texas Press, 1975).

35. See Octavio Paz's classic, *The Labyrinth of Solitude: Life and Thought in Mexico* (New York: Grove Press, 1961).

36. For an overview of these issues, see Kevin Middlebrook's review essay "Dilemmas of Change in Mexican Politics," *World Politics* 41 (October 1988): 120–41; for predictions about the future, see Roderic Ai Camp, ed., *Mexico's Political Stability: The Next Five Years* (Boulder, Colo.: Westview Press, 1986).

37. See Dale Story, *The Mexican Ruling Party, Stability and Authority* (New York: Praeger, 1986), 9ff; John J. Bailey, *Governing Mexico: The Statecraft of Crisis Management* (New York: St. Martin's Press, 1988).

38. This is nicely explained in Gary Wynia, *The Politics of Latin American Development*, 3d ed. (Cambridge: Cambridge University Press, 1990), 28ff.

39. For greater detail about the causes, see Roderic Ai Camp, *Generals in the Palacio: The Military in Modern Mexico* (New York: Oxford University Press, 1992).

40. Karl Schmitt, "Church and State in Mexico: A Corporatist Relationship," *Americas* 40 (January 1984): 349–76.

41. For some examples of noneconomic variables, see Clark W. Reynolds and Carlos Tello, *U.S.–Mexico Relations: Economic and Social Aspects* (Stanford, Calif.: Stanford University Press, 1983).

42. For various insights into this, from the points of view of an American and Mexican, see Robert A. Pastor and Jorge G. Castañeda, *Limits to Friendship: The United States and Mexico* (New York: Vintage Press, 1989).

43. For an extensive discussion of the Mexican case, see Riordan Roett, ed., *Political & Economic Liberalization in Mexico, at a Critical Juncture* (Boulder, Colo.: Lynne Rienner, 1993), 17–94.

44. See especially "The Politics of Public Administration," in *Opposition Government in Mexico*, ed. Victoria Rodríguez and Peter M. Ward (Albuquerque: University of New Mexico Press, 1995). The editors also provide an excellent case study in their *Policymaking, Politics, and Urban Governance in Chihuahua* (Austin: LBJ School of Public Affairs, University of Texas, 1992).

2

Political–Historical Roots: The Impact of Time and Place

> The political life of all those states which during the early years of the last century arose upon the ruins of the Spanish Empire on the American mainland presents two common features. In all those states, constitutions of the most liberal and democratic character have been promulgated; in all, there have from time to time arisen dictators whose absolute power has been either frankly proclaimed or thinly veiled under constitutional forms. So frequently has such personal rule been established in many of the states that in them there has appeared to be an almost perpetual and complete contradiction between theory and practice, between nominal and the actual systems of government.
>
> CECIL JANE, *Liberty and Despotism in Spanish America*

Understanding politics is not just knowing who gets what, where, when, and how, as Harold D. Lasswell declared in a classic statement years ago, but also understanding the origins of why people behave the way they do. Each culture is a product of its own heritage, traditions emerging from historical experiences. Many aspects of the U.S. political system can be traced to our English colonial experiences, our independence movement, our western frontier expansion, and our immigrant origins. Mexico has had a somewhat similar set of experiences, but the sources of the experiences and their specific characteristics were quite different.

THE SPANISH HERITAGE

Mexico's political heritage, unlike that of the United States, draws on two important cultural foundations: European and indigenous. Although large numbers of Indians were never absorbed into the conquering culture in New Spain, a vast integration process took place in most of central Mexico. Conversely, British settlers encountered numerous Native Americans in their colonization of North America, but they rarely intermarried with them and thus the two cultures never blended. Racially, African blacks played an important role in some regions; politically, this was a limited role because of the small numbers brought to New Spain, the colonial Spanish viceroyalty that extended from Central America to what is now the United States Midwest and Pacific Northwest.

Mexico's racial heritage, unlike that of the United States, has a mixed or *mestizo* quality. In the initial absence of Spanish women, the original Spanish conquerors sought native mistresses or wives. In fact, cohabiting with female royalty from the various indigenous cultures was seen as an effective means of joining the two sets of leaders, firmly establishing Spanish ascendancy throughout the colony. The Indian–Spanish offspring of these unions at first were considered socially inferior to Spaniards fresh from Spain and the Spanish born in the New World. Frank Tannenbaum describes the complex social ladder:

> With the mixture of races in Mexico added to by the bringing in of Negroes in sufficient numbers to leave their mark upon the population in certain parts of the country, we have the basis of the social structure that characterized Mexico throughout the colonial period and in some degree continues to this day. The Spaniard—that is, the born European—was at the top in politics, in the Church, and in prestige. The *criollo*, his American-born child, stood at a lower level. He inherited most of the wealth, but was denied any important role in political administration. The *mestizo* and the dozen different *castas* that resulted from the mixtures of European, Indian, and Negro in their various degrees and kinds were still lower.[1]

In the late nineteenth century, mestizos reached a new level of social ascendancy through their numbers and control over the political system.

Early Mexican political history involved social conflicts based on racial heritage. Moreover, large indigenous groups were suppressed, exploited, and politically ignored. The prejudice with which Indians were treated by the Spanish and mestizo populations, and the mistreatment of the mestizo by the Spanish contributed further to the sharp class distinctions that have plagued Mexico.[2] Social prejudice was transferred to economic status as well, with those lowest on the racial scale ending up at the bottom of the economic scale. The degree of social inequality ultimately contributed to the independence movement, as the New World–born Spanish (*criollos*) came to resent their second-class status relative to the Old

World-born Spanish (*peninsulares*). It contributed even more significantly to the Mexican Revolution of 1910, in which thousands of downtrodden mestizo peasants and workers and some Indians joined a broad social movement for greater social justice.

All societies have some type of social structure. Most large societies develop hierarchical social groups, but from one society to another the level of deference exacted or given varies. In the United States, where political rhetoric, beginning with independence, focused on greater social equality, class distinctions were fewer and less distinct.[3] In Mexico, in spite of its revolution, the distinctions remain much sharper, affecting various aspects of cultural and political behavior. For example, a major study of U.S. intellectuals found that 40 percent of the younger generation were from working-class backgrounds. By contrast, in Mexico, fewer than 5 percent fell into this social category.[4] In the political realm, lower-income groups, who are formally well represented in the official government party, the PRI, are little represented in policy or leadership roles.[5] In addition, lower-income groups have limited protection from abuses by governmental authorities and do not always receive equal treatment under the law. In the United States some differences exist in the legal treatment of rich and poor, but they are fewer, and the gap between them is much smaller than in Mexico.

The Spanish also left Mexico with a significant religious heritage: Catholicism. Religion played a critical role in the pre-Conquest Mexican indigenous culture and was very much integrated into the native political processes. In both the Aztec and Maya empires, for example, religion was integral to political leadership. The Spanish were no less religious. Beginning with the Conquest itself, the pope reached some agreements with the Spanish crown. In these agreements, known collectively as the *patronato real* (royal patronate), the Catholic Church gave up certain rights it exercised in Europe for a privileged role in the Conquest generally and in New Spain specifically. In return for being allowed to send two priests or friars with every land or sea expedition, and being given the *sole* opportunity to proselytize millions of Indians, the church gave up its control over the building of facilities in the New World, the appointing of higher clergy, the collecting of tithes, and other activities. In other words, Catholicism obtained a monopoly in the Spanish New World.[6]

The contractual relationship between the Catholic Church and the Spanish authorities in the colonial period established two fundamental principles: the concept of an official religion, that is, only one religion recognized and permitted by civil authorities; and the integration of church and state. In the United States, of course, a fundamental principle of our political evolution is the *separation* of church and state. Moreover, many of the settlers who came to the English colonies came in search of religious freedom, not religious monopoly. As Samuel Ramos suggested,

> It was our [Mexico's] fate to be conquered by a Catholic theocracy which was struggling to isolate its people from the current of modern ideas that emanated from the Renaissance. Scarcely had the American colonies been organized when they were isolated against all possible heresy. Ports were closed and trade with all countries except Spain was disapproved. The only civilizing agent of the New World was the Catholic Church, which by virtue of its pedagogical monopoly shaped the American societies in a medieval pattern of life. Education, and the direction of social life as well, were placed in the hands of the Church, whose power was similar to that of a state within a state.[7]

The consequences of Mexico's religious heritage have been numerous. It is important to remember that Catholicism was not just a religion in the spiritual sense of the word but extended deeply into the political culture, given the influence of the church over education and social organizations, such as hospitals and charitable foundations, and its lack of religious competition.

One of the consequences is structural. In the first chapter, the Mexican political system is referred to as corporatist. Corporatism extends back to the colonial period, when certain groups obtained special privileges from civil authorities, giving them preferred relationships with the state. Among these groups were clergy, military officers, and merchants. The most notable privileges received by the clergy were special legal *fueros*, or rights, allowing them to try their members in separate courts.[8] The Spanish established the precedent for favored treatment of specific groups. Once groups are thus singled out, they will fight very hard to retain their advantages. Much of nineteenth-century politics in Mexico became a battle between the church and its conservative allies on just this issue.

The monopoly of the church in New Spain was very jealously protected. No immigrants professing other beliefs were allowed in before Mexican independence. The church also took on another task for the state: ferreting out religious and political dissenters by establishing the Inquisition in the New World. The primary function of this institution was to identify and punish religious heretics, those persons who threatened religious beliefs as taught by church authorities, but in practice the Inquisition controlled publishing, assembled a book index that censored intellectual ideas from abroad, and fielded special customs inspectors.[9] Although these activities were not entirely successful, in general the church and the civil authorities were intolerant of any other religious and secular thought. The Inquisition has been described in this fashion:

> The belief that heretics were traitors and traitors were heretics led to the conviction that dissenters were social revolutionaries trying to subvert the political and religious stability of the community. These tenets were not later developments in the history of the Spanish Inquisition; they were inherent in the rationale of the institution from the fifteenth century onward and were apparent in the Holy Office's dealings with Jews, Protestants, and other heretics during the sixteenth century. The use of the Inquisition by the later eighteenth-century Bourbon kings of Spain as an instrument of regalism was not a departure from tradition. Particularly in the viceroyalty of New Spain during the late eighteenth century the Inquisition trials show how the Crown sought to promote political and religious orthodoxy.[10]

The heritage of intolerance plagued Mexico during much of its post-independence political history. It has been argued that because culturally there had been little experience with other points of view and in promoting respect for them, accommodation was not perceived as desirable. Some analysts suggest that the Catholic religion's continuation as a dominant presence in spite of religious freedom and the existence of other faiths encourages persistence of intolerance.

To carry out the conquest of New Spain, the Spanish relied on armed expeditions and missionaries. Typically, once an area was made "safe" by an exploratory expedition, a permanent settlement around a mission and a *presidio*, or fort, was established. Some of the settlements were sited along a route known as the *camino real* (king's highway), which today is the old California Highway 1. The original mission towns are now among the most important cities in the Southwest: San Francisco (Saint Francis), San Diego (Saint James), Santa Barbara (Saint Barbara), Albuquerque, Tucson, and Santa Fe.

Originally, the authorities used Spanish armed forces; in the colonial period, American-born Spaniards began filling officer ranks as the government came to rely more heavily on the colonial militia. Although the armed forces were called on from time to time to protect the coast from French and British attacks, the army was used primarily to suppress Indian rebellions and to keep internal order. It patrolled the highways to keep them free of bandits. Basically, then, it functioned as police, not as defenders against external enemies.

The military, like the clergy, received special *fueros* in New Spain. It too had its own courts for civil and criminal cases, but unlike the clergy, military officers were immune to civil prosecution.[11] Their favored status inevitably led to legal conflicts. Some historians have argued that one of the reasons for the disintegration of civil authority at the time of independence was declining respect caused by its inability to control military cases.

As in the case of the church, granting the military special privileges—which were passed on to the colonial militia before independence—created another powerful interest group. Their professional heirs in the nineteenth century wanted to retain the privileges. Furthermore, the close ties between military and civil authorities, and the unclear lines of subordination led to the blurring of distinctions in civil-military relations.[12]

In the nineteenth and early twentieth centuries, these patterns in civil-military relations and civil-church relations had a great impact on Mexico's political development. They complemented the corporatist heritage by establishing groups that saw their own interests, not those of society, as primary. These groups competed for political ascendancy, reinforcing the already-present social inequality by creating a hierarchy of interests and prestige.

To the legacies of corporatism, social inequality, special interests, and intolerance can be added the Spanish bureaucratic tradition. Critics tend to focus on the inefficiencies of the Spanish bureaucracy and the differences between legal theory and the application of administrative criteria.[13] In part, problems can be attributed to the distance between the mother country and the colonies, as well as to the distance between Mexico City, the seat of the viceroyalty of New Spain, established in 1535, and its far-flung settlements in Yucatán, Chiapas, and what is today the southwestern United States. A more important feature of Spanish religious and civil structures was their strongly hierarchical nature and centralization. Low-level bureaucrats lacked authority. Decisions were made only at the top of the hierarchy, with delay, inefficiency, and corruption as the outcome.[14]

The hierarchical structure of the Spanish state in the New World is no better illustrated than through the viceroy himself. The viceroy (*virrey*) was in effect the vice-king, a personal appointee of and substitute for the king of Spain. He had two sources of power: He was the supreme civil authority and also the commander in chief. In addition, he was the vice-patron of the Catholic Church, responsible for the mission policies in the colonization process. Remember, this individual, along with a second viceroy in Lima, Peru, governed all of Spanish-speaking Latin America and the southwestern United States.

Upon its independence, the viceregal structure left Mexico with two political carryovers. First, the individual viceroys became extremely important, some serving for many years, completely at the whim of the crown. This shifted considerable political legitimacy away from Spanish institutions to a single person. The personalization of power tended to devalue the institutionalization of political structures, thereby enhancing the importance of political personalities. It also left Mexico with an integrated

---

Personalism: political authority and loyalty that are given to an individual person rather than to an institutionalized office held by a leader.

---

civil and religious/cultural tradition, complemented by an equally blended, hierarchical indigenous tradition of executive authority. Justo Sierra, a Mexican historian, described the viceroy's power and the church-state relationship:

> The Viceroy was the king. His business was to hold the land—that is, to conserve the king's dominion, New Spain, at all costs. The way to conserve it was to pacify it; hence the close collaboration with the Church. In view of the privileges granted by the Pope to the Spanish king in America, it could be said that the Church in America was under the Spanish king: this was called the Royal Patronate. But the ascendancy that the Church had acquired in Spanish America, because it consolidated, through conversions, the work of the Conquest, made it actually a partner in the government.[15]

Spanish political authority was top-heavy, placing most of the power in the hands of an executive institution. The viceroy's decision-making authority had few restrictions. In many respects, the viceroy's self-developed political aura was equivalent to the *presidencialismo* described earlier. The Spanish did create an *audiencia*, a sort of quasi legislative–judicial body that acted as a board of appeals for grievances against the viceroy and could channel complaints directly to the crown, bypassing the viceroy. Also, the crown appointed its own inspectors, often secret, who traveled to New Spain to hear charges against a viceroy's abuse of authority. These *visitadors* were empowered to conduct thorough investigations and report to the crown.

The minor restrictions on viceregal powers did not mean there was a separation of powers, an independent judiciary, a legislative body, or decentralization. Some participation at the local level existed, but Mexico had no legislative heritage comparable to that found in the colonial assemblies of the British colonies. Thus, it is not surprising that although Mexico quickly established a legislative body after independence, it functioned effectively for only brief periods in the 1860s and 1870s and again in the 1920s, remaining ineffectual and subordinate throughout most of the twentieth century until the 1990s.

Finally, another important Spanish political heritage is the role of the

state in society. The strong authoritarian institutions in New Spain and the
size of the Spanish colonial bureaucracy established the state as the preeminent institution.[16] The only other institution whose influence came close
was the Catholic Church. Educated male Spaniards born in the New World
essentially had three career choices: the colonial bureaucracy, the clergy
(which appealed to only a minority), and the military. New Spain's private
sector was weak, underdeveloped, and closed. The crown permitted little
commercial activity among the colonies or with other countries. The mo-
nopolistic relationship between Spain and the colonies kept the latter from
developing their full economic potential. Michael Meyer and William Sherman characterized Spain's policies as

> protectionist in the extreme, which meant that the economy in New Spain
> was very much restricted by limitations imposed by the imperial system.
> Thus the natural growth of industry and commerce was significantly im-
> peded, because manufacturers and merchants in Spain were protected from
> the competition of those in the colony. In accord with the classic pattern, the
> Spanish Indies were to supply Spain with raw products, which could be made
> into finished goods in the mother country and sold back to the colonists at
> a profit. As a consequence, the character of the colonial economy in Mex-
> ico was essentially extractive.[17]

A long-term political consequence of a strong state and a weak private sector was the overarching prestige of the state, to the disadvantage
of the private sector. Economically, then, the state was in the driver's seat,
not because it controlled most economic resources, but because it provided
the most important positions available in the colonial world. The same mentality developed in the twentieth century in other colonial settings. For example, Indians came to believe that the British civil service was the preeminent institution in India and that government employment would grant
them great prestige.[18] In the same way, positions in the Mexican state bureaucracy were seen by many educated Mexicans as the ultimate employment, and so the competition for places was keen. One cultural theorist,
Glen Dealy, argues that "public power like economic wealth is rooted in
rational accumulation. Capitalism measures excellence in terms of accumulated wealth; *caudillaje* [Latin American culture] measures one's virtue
in terms of accumulated public power."[19] This way of life did not end with
the decline of the Spanish empire and Spain's departure from Mexico. Figures from the last third of the nineteenth century demonstrate that the government employed a large percentage of educated, professional men, suggesting again the limited opportunities in the private sector.

The Mexican state's importance can be explained by not only economic underdevelopment but also the status of the state in the New World. In other words, it was natural for Mexicans to expect the state to play an influential role. Not liking state intervention in their lives, similar to the feeling of most people in the United States,[20] Mexicans nevertheless came to depend on the state as a problem solver, in part because there was no institutional infrastructure at the local level or the same self-reliant thinking.

Spain bequeathed to Mexico an individualistic cultural mind-set. North Americans, although characterized by self-initiative and independence, exhibited a strong sense of community. That is, throughout the western expansion, U.S. settlers saw surviving together as in the interest of the group as well as in the interest of its members. Mexicans, on the other hand, exhibited a strong sense of self. This, combined with the sharper social-class divisions and social inequality, led to a preeminence of individual or familial preservation, unassociated with the protection of larger groups. The lack of communal ties reinforced the primacy of personal ties. It was a familiar phenomenon elsewhere in Latin America as well. In the political realm, it generally translates into *whom* you know rather than *what* you know. Although an almost universal truism, whom you know gains in importance where access to authority is limited.[21]

Finally, the structural arrangements of the Spanish colonial empire and the distances between the colonies and the mother country and between the colonies themselves made for considerable dissatisfaction with the rules imposed. The Spanish settlers, and later their mestizo descendants, increasingly disobeyed orders from overseas. Sometimes they could justifiably assert that a law no longer applied to the situation at hand. At other times they would flout a law they found inconvenient. The inefficiencies inherent in the transatlantic management of possessions in two continents, built-in social inequalities, and the gap between Old World theory and New World reality meant the marginalization of Spain's laws in the Western Hemisphere. A lack of respect for the law and the primacy of personal and familial interests were fundamental factors in Mexico's political evolution from the 1830s through the end of the twentieth century.

NINETEENTH-CENTURY POLITICAL HERITAGE

Shortly after its independence Mexico experimented briefly with a monarchical system, but the rapid demise of the three-hundred-year-old colonial structure left a political void. The only legitimate authority, the crown, and its colonial representative, the viceroy, disappeared. Intense political conflict ensued as various groups sought to legitimize their political philosophies. The battle for political supremacy affected the goals of the antagonists and influenced the process by which Mexicans settled political disputes. By the 1840s Mexico had fluctuated between a political model advocating federalism, the decentralization of power similar to that practiced in the United States, and centralism, the allocation of more decision-making authority to the national government.

As was true of many Latin American countries, Mexico was caught between the idea of rejecting its centralized, authoritarian Spanish heritage and the idea of adopting the reformist U.S. model. The obstinacy of their proponents kept political affairs in constant flux. Violence was a frequent means for settling political disagreements, which enhanced the presence and importance of the army as an arbiter of political conflicts, and consumed much of the government budget that might otherwise have been spent more productively.

By the mid-nineteenth century two mainstreams of political thought confronted Mexicans: conservatism and liberalism. Mexican liberalism was a mixture of borrowed and native ideas that largely rejected Spanish authoritarianism and tradition and instead drew on Enlightenment ideas from France, England, and the United States. Some of its elements included such basic U.S. tenets as guarantees of political liberty and the sovereignty of the general will. Among its principles were greater citizen participation in government, free-speech guarantees, and a strong legislative branch. Liberals complemented these principles with a concept known as Jeffersonian

---

Mexican liberalism: an amalgam of basic concepts of political liberty and nineteenth-century laissez-faire economic principles.

---

agrarian democracy. Jefferson had advocated encouraging large numbers of small landholders in the United States. His rationale was that people with property constitute a stable citizenry; having something to lose, they would vigorously defend the democratic political process. The liberals also believed in classic economic liberalism, the philosophy pervading England and the United States during the same period. Economic liberalism of this period referred to the encouragement of individual initiative and the protection of individual property rights.[22]

Mexican conservatives held to an alternative set of political principles. Whereas an examination of Liberal ideas reveals that most of them were borrowed from leading thinkers and political systems foreign to Mexico's experience, the Conservatives praised the reform-minded Bourbon administration of the Spanish colonies prior to independence and emphasized a strong central executive. They argued for a strong executive because it would follow naturally after centuries of authoritarian colonial rule, and because the postindependence violence in the 1830s, 1840s, and 1850s seemed to be part of a larger struggle between anarchy and civilization in Latin America. Without forceful leadership, Mexico would succumb to disorder and remain underdeveloped economically.[23]

The conservatives favored policies promoting industrialization, stressing light manufacturing rather than expansion of the small-landholder class. Mexico desperately needed capital, much of which had fled after independence and during the chaotic political period that followed. Both conservatives and liberals looked approvingly on foreign investment and encouraged policies that would attract outside capital, particularly to mining and struggling industries such as textiles.[24]

Neither the conservatives nor the liberals gave much attention to the plight of the Indians. Because the thinkers in both camps generally were *criollos* of middle- and upper-middle-class background, their primary concerns were the maintenance of social order and the interests of their classes. Although the conservatives essentially ignored the Indians, the liberals sought to apply their philosophy of economic individualism to the Indian system of communal property holding, believing it to be an obstacle to development.

Liberals and conservatives clashed most violently on the role of the Catholic Church. The liberals believed, and correctly so, that the church, as an integral ally of the Spanish state, conveyed support for the hierarchical, authoritarian, political structure.[25] Essentially, it was the church's control of education and nearly all aspects of cultural life that permitted its influence. The conservatives, on the other hand, saw the church as an important force and worked toward an alliance with it.

Because the liberals viewed the church as a staunch opponent and as the conservatives' political and economic supporter, they wanted to reduce or eliminate altogether its influence. They introduced the Ley Lerdo (Lerdo law) on June 1, 1856, essentially forcing the church to sell off its large landholdings, which at that time accounted for a sizable portion of all Mexican real estate. But the law did not have its intended consequences: The church traded land for capital, thereby preserving a source of economic influence and at the same time enlarging the already substantial estates of the buyers.[26] The liberals also attacked the church's special privileges, which had been left inviolate by the 1824 constitution immediately after independence. They eliminated its legal *fueros* and placed cemeteries under the jurisdiction of public authorities.[27]

From this brief overview, we can see that each side had something useful to offer. Yet their unwillingness to compromise and the intensity with which they held their opinions led to a polity in constant disarray. The battles between conservatives and liberals culminated in the War of the Reform (1858–1861), in which the victorious liberals imposed, by force, their political views on the defeated conservatives. These views are well represented in the constitution of 1857, a landmark political document that influenced its revolutionary successor, the constitution of 1917.

The issue of church versus state, or the supremacy of state over church, was a crucial element of the conservative–liberal battles and a focus of nineteenth-century politics. The leading liberals of the day saw the classroom as the chief means of social transformation and the church's control in that arena as undesirable and so decided to establish secular institutions. To implement this concept, President Benito Juárez appointed in 1867 a committee under Gabino Barreda, an educator who set down some basic principles for public education in the last third of the nineteenth century. Although the liberals hoped to replace church-controlled schools with free, mandatory public education, their program was never fully implemented. Most important, they introduced a preparatory educational program, a sort of advanced high school to train future leaders in secular and liberal ideas.

Although by 1869 the liberals succeeded in defeating the conservatives' forces, their unwillingness to compromise and their introduction of even more radical reforms—particularly those associated with suppressing the Catholic Church, and incorporated into the 1857 constitution—impelled the conservatives and their church allies to take the unusual step of seeking help from abroad. This ultimately led to the French intervention of 1862–1867, and an attempt to enthrone a foreign monarch, Austrian archduke Ferdinand Maximilian. Although the liberals were nearly defeated during this interlude, under Benito Juárez's leadership they ultimately won and executed the archduke.

The liberals reigned from 1867 to 1876. This brief period is important because it gave Mexicans a taste of a functioning liberal political model. The legislative branch of government exercised some actual power. The successors to Benito Juárez lacked the political skills and authority to sustain the government, and their experiment came to an end with the successful revolt of Porfirio Díaz, a leading military figure in the liberal battles against the French.

Díaz's ambition and his overthrow of Juárez's collaborators introduced a new generation of liberals to leadership positions. These men, most of whom were combat veterans of the liberal–conservative conflicts and the French intervention, were *moderate* liberals, distinct from the radical orthodox liberals of the Juárez generation. Díaz and the moderate liberals paved the way for the introduction of a new political philosophy into Mexico: positivism. As described by historian Charles Hale,

> Scientific or positive politics involved the argument that the country's problems should be approached and its policies formed scientifically. Its principal characteristics were an attack on doctrinaire [radical] liberalism, or "metaphysical politics," an apology for strong government to counter endemic revolutions and anarchy, and a call for constitutional reform. It drew upon a current of European, particularly French, theories dating back to Henri de Saint-Simon and Auguste Comte in the 1820s, theories that under the name of positivism had become quite generalized in European thought by 1878. Apart from the theoretical origins of their doctrine, the exponents of scientific politics in Mexico found inspiration in the concrete experience of the contemporary conservative republics of France and Spain and in their leaders.[28]

The motto for many positivists in Mexico and elsewhere in Latin America was liberty and progress through peace and order. The key to Mexican positivism, as it was implemented by successive administrations under Profirio Díaz, who ruled Mexico from 1877 to 1880 and 1884 to 1911, was order. After years of political instability, violence, and civil war, these men saw peace as a critical necessity for progress. Their explanation for the disruptive preceding decades centered on the notion that too much of Mexico's political thinking had been based on irrational or "unscientific" ideas influenced by the spiritual teachings of the church and that alternative political ideas were counterproductive.

Building on the philosophy of their orthodox liberal predecessors, the Díaz administrations came to believe that the most effective means for conveying rational positivist thought, or this new form of moderate liberalism, was public education. Education therefore became the essential instrument for homogenizing Mexican political values. It would turn out a new generation of political, intellectual, and economic leaders who would guide Mexico along the path of material progress and political development. Preeminent among the public institutions was the National Preparatory School in Mexico City, which enrolled children of regional and national notables. Its matriculation lists read like a roll of future national leaders.[29]

The acceptance of positivist ideas by the moderate liberals ultimately led to the dominance of order over liberty and progress. Indeed, it can be argued that after decades of civil conflict, positivism became a vehicle for reintroducing conservative ideas among Mexico's liberal leadership. Díaz increasingly used the state's power to maintain political order, allowing economic development to occur without government interference. His government encouraged the expansion of mining and made generous concessions to foreigners to obtain investment.

The Porfiriato, as the period of Díaz's rule is known in Mexico, had significant consequences that led to the country's major social upheaval of the twentieth century, the Mexico Revolution of 1910, and numerous political and social legacies. Díaz attacked two important social issues: the relationship between church and state and the role of Indians in the society.

Ironically, the Catholic Church regained considerable influence during the liberal era. Even Benito Juárez realized after Maximilian's defeat that pursuit of radical antichurch policies would only generate further resistance and disorder. Díaz pursued a pragmatic policy of reconciliation in the 1870s, separating church and state, but permitting the church to strengthen its religious role as long as it remained aloof from secular and political affairs.[30] Thus, the two parties achieved a modus vivendi, although the state remained in the stronger position, and the 1857 constitution retained repressive, antichurch provisions.

Díaz's attitude toward the Indians was also significant because it reflected a broader attitude toward social inequality. He and his collaborators, as did the original liberals, saw the Indians as obstacles to Mexican development. They applied the provisions of the law forcing the sale of church property to the communal property held by Indian villages, accelerating the pace of sales begun by the orthodox liberals in the 1860s. But the positivists were not satisfied with this economic measure. Many of them accepted the notion, popular throughout Latin America at the time, that Indians were a cultural and social burden and were racially inferior.[31] To overcome this racial barrier, they proposed introducing European immigration, in the hope of wiping out the indigenous culture and providing a superior economic example for the mestizo farmer.

To ensure that immigration would take place, the Mexican government passed a series of colonization laws in the 1880s that granted generous concessions to foreigners who would survey public lands. By 1889 foreigners had surveyed almost eighty million acres and had acquired large portions of the surveyed acreage at bargain-basement prices. For the most part, however, these people were not typical settlers; rather, they, like the Mexicans who purchased church and Indian lands, were large landholders. Two million acres of communal Indian lands went to them and to corporations. Hence, the colonization laws not only increased the concentration of land in the hands of wealthy Mexicans and foreigners but antagonized small mestizo and Indian farmers, who became a force during the Mexican Revolution.

Although Díaz implemented policies that improved the country economically, the primary beneficiaries were the wealthy at home and abroad. The laboring classes, primarily mestizo in origin, benefited little from the politics of peace. Díaz focused on a small group of supporters and ignored the plight of most of his compatriots. Even middle-class mestizos, who rose to the top of the ladder politically by 1900, were limited in their abilities to share in the economic goods of the Díaz era. As two recent historians of Mexico suggested,

> The structure of Mexican society during the Porfiriato consisted of a number of levels that must be noted in order to understand the social dynamics of the era. Large holders of commercialized agriculture land constituted the top of the pyramid. Land provided the economic core as well as status. From this base large landholders diversified into manufacturing, mining, or other profitable activities. An elite, allied with national and regional political groups, with business and personal connections to foreign capitalists and investors, formed an interlocking socioeconomic and political directorate. They used their political, economic, and social influence to reinforce their position. Economic concessions, contracts, and other forms of political patronage fell to this group. They negotiated among themselves for a share of the political power and economic fruits of modernization.[32]

To understand Mexican politics in the twentieth century, in the postrevolutionary era, it is even more important to explore the political heritage left by Díaz and his cronies. In the first place, although church and state were separate and the lines were more firmly drawn between secular and religious activities, Díaz maintained fuzzier relationships between the state and two other important elements, the army and the private sector.

In effect, Díaz established the pattern for civil–military relations that characterized Mexico until the 1940s. Because he himself was a veteran of so many civil conflicts, it was only natural that he recruited many of his important collaborators, on both the national and state level, from among fellow officers.[33] Military men occupied many prominent positions. Although the presence of career officers in the top echelon declined across Díaz's tenure as they were replaced by younger civilian lawyers, no clear relationship of subordination between civil and military authorities was established (see Table 2-1). Díaz left a legacy of shared power and interlocking leadership.[34]

The unclear lines between military and civilian political power were duplicated between politicians and the business elite. Although it is the na-

Table 2-1 Career Military Officers in National Politics

Presidential Administration	Military Officers (%)	Presidential Administration	Military Officers (%)
Díaz		Portes Gil	14
1884–1889	54	Ortiz Rubio	41
1889–1893	46	Rodríguez	33
1893–1897	32	Cárdenas	27
1897–1901	16	Avila Camacho	19
1901–1905	11	Alemán	8
1905–1910	9	Ruiz Cortines	14
1910–1911	35	López Mateos	15
De la Barra	27	Díaz Ordaz	7
Madero	26	Echeverría	11
Huerta	61	López Portillo	6
Carranza	49	De la Madrid	4
Obregón	40	Salinas	6
Calles	30		

ture of a capitalist system to have an exchange of leaders between the economic and political spheres, as in the United States, such linkages in an authoritarian political structure, where access to power and decision making is closed, can produce potentially significant consequences. Díaz, who had control over most of the important national political offices, used appointments to reward supporters or as a means to co-opt opponents. At no time since 1884 has any administration had stronger elite economic representation in political office than under Díaz. Approximately a fifth of all national politicians from 1884 to 1911, with the peak in 1897, were businessmen. For most of the twentieth century they made up fewer than 10 percent of Mexico's public figures.[35] Giving these positions, especially at the provincial level, to members of prominent families further closed paths of upward social mobility to less-favored groups, especially the mestizo middle class.[36]

By the time Díaz began his third term as president in 1888, he had succeeded in controlling national elections, although he had not created a national electoral machine similar to that of the Partido Nacional Revolucionario (PNR) and its successors. He continued to hold elections to renew the loyalty of the people to his leadership and to allow him to reward his faithful supporters with sinecures as federal deputies (congressmen) and senators. His control was so extensive that occasionally he chose the same person for more than one elective office.

Building on the original conservative philosophy and the colonial heritage, Díaz reversed the tenuous decentralization trend begun under President Juárez. He accomplished this structurally by decreasing the powers of the legislative and judicial branches, making them subordinate to the executive branch and to the presidency specifically. He also strengthened the presidency as distinct from the executive branch.

Díaz went beyond aggrandization of political authority in the executive branch and the presidency by strengthening the federal government or state generally. He did this by expanding the federal bureaucracy. Between 1876 and 1910 the government payroll grew some 900 percent. In 1876 only 16 percent of the middle class worked for the government; by 1910 the figure was 70 percent.[37] As in the colonial period, the private sector was not incorporating new generations of educated Mexicans; rather, their careers were being pursued within the public sector, notably the federal executive. Díaz provided the twentieth century with a dominant state, an apparatus that most successful Mexicans would want to control because it was essential to their economic future.

Because Díaz held the presidency for some thirty years, a personality cult developed around his leadership. His collaborators conveyed the message that progress, as they defined it, was guaranteed by his presence. His indispensability enhanced his political maneuverability. On the other hand, Díaz put in place a political system that was underdeveloped institutionally. In concentrating on his personality, political institutions failed to acquire legitimacy. Even the stability of the political system itself was at stake because continuity was not guaranteed by the acceptability of its institutions but by an individual person, Díaz.

The Porfiriato also reinforced the paternalism handed down from the political and social culture of the precolonial and colonial periods. Díaz's concessions to favored people, providing them with substantial economic rewards, encouraged dependence on his personal largesse and the government generally. This technique, which he used generously to pacify opponents and reward friends, produced corruption at all levels of political life. It encouraged the belief that political office was a reward to be taken advantage of by the officeholder rather than a public responsibility. The political cultures of many other countries are similarly characterized to a greater or lesser degree.

Against his most recalcitrant foes, Díaz was willing to use less ingratiating techniques. Toward the end of his regime, press censorship became widespread. As a whole, he favored a controlled, complimentary press to counter criticism from independent sources. If threats or imprisonment were not sufficient to deter his opponents, he resorted to more severe measures. Typically, lower social groups were the victims of violent suppression. A notorious example of this policy was the treatment of the Yaqui Indians in northwestern Mexico, who rebelled after influential members of the Díaz administration began seizing their lands. The Yaquis were subjected to brutalities and were forced into what were in effect concentration camps, and many were deported to Yucatán, where most perished in forced labor on the henequen plantations in the hot tropical climate.[38]

As Mexico emerged from the first decade of the twentieth century, it acquired a political model that drew on Spanish authoritarian and paternal heritages. Like the viceroys before him but without reporting to any other authority, Díaz exercised extraordinary power. He built up a larger state apparatus as a means of retaining power, and although he strengthened the role of the state in society, he did not legitimize its institutions. While he did succeed in building some economic infrastructure in Mexico, he failed to meet social needs and maltreated certain groups, thereby continuing and intensifying the social inequalities existing under his colonial predecessors. His favoritism toward foreigners caused resentment and contributed to the rise of nationalism after 1911. The lack of separation between civilian and military leadership left Mexicans unclear about the principle of civilian supremacy and autonomy, an issue that would confront his successors. Finally, although the moderate liberals/converted positivists replaced orthodox liberals and, in many cases, substituted conservative principles for their original political ideas, the excluded liberal followers who remained faithful to the cause rose up once again after 1910.

THE REVOLUTIONARY HERITAGE:
SOCIAL VIOLENCE AND REFORM

It can never be forgotten that contemporary Mexico is the product of a violent revolution that lasted, on and off, from 1910 through 1920. The decimation of its population—more than a million people during the decade—alone would have left an indelible stamp on Mexican life. The revolution touched all social classes, and although it did not affect all locales with the same intensity, it brought together the residents of villages and cities to a degree never achieved before or since. In the same way that World War II altered life in the United States, the revolution brought profound changes to Mexican society.

The causes of the revolution have been thoroughly examined by historians. The causes are numerous, and their roots can be found in the failures of the Porfiriato. Among the most important to have been singled out are foreign economic penetration, class struggle, landownership, economic depression, local autonomy, the clash between modernity and tradition, the breakdown of the Porfirian system, the weakness of the transition process, the lack of opportunity for upward political and social mobility, and the aging of the leadership.[39] Historians do not agree on the primary causes nor on whether the 1910 revolution was a "real" revolution, that is, whether it radically changed the social structure.[40]

In my own view, the revolution introduced significant changes, although it did not alter social structures to the degree one expects of a major social revolution on a par with the Soviet or Chinese revolutions.[41] Nevertheless, to understand Mexican political developments in the twentieth century, it is necessary to explore the ideology of the revolution and the political structures that emerged in the immediate postrevolutionary era.

Ideologically, one of the best ways to understand the diverse social forces for change is to trace the constitutional provisions of 1917 to the precursors and revolutionary figures. Among the most important precursors, Ricardo Flores Magón and his brothers offered ideas leading up to the revolution and revived the legitimacy of orthodox liberalism by establishing liberal clubs throughout Mexico.[42] This provided a basis for middle-class participation in and support for revolutionary principles. Flores Magón and his adherents published a newspaper in exile in the United States, *La Regneración*, banned in Mexico. Many prominent political figures in the revolution, including General Alvaro Obregón, cited its influence on their values. Perhaps more than in any other area, Flores Magón offered arguments in support of workers' rights, establishing such principles as minimum wage and maximum hours in strike documents and Liberal Party platforms.[43] He also advocated the distribution of land, the return of communal (*ejido*) properties to the Indians, and the requirement that agricultural land be productive.

Politically, the most prominent figure in the pre- and revolutionary eras was Francisco I. Madero, son of wealthy Coahuilan landowners in northern Mexico, who believed in mild social reforms and the basic principles of political liberty. He founded the Anti-Reelectionist Party to oppose Porfirio Díaz. A product of his class, he did not believe in structural change but did believe in equal opportunity for all.[44] His *Presidential Succession of 1910*, the Anti-Reelectionist Party platform, and his revolutionary 1910 Plan of San Luis Potosí advocated three important political items: no reelection, electoral reform (effective suffrage), and revision of the constitution of 1857. The most important of Madero's social and economic ideas concerned public education; he believed, as did the orthodox liberals, that education was the key to a modern Mexico.

More radical social ideas were offered by such revolutionaries as Pascual Orozco, who later turned against Madero; Francisco Villa; and Emiliano Zapata. Orozco, who expressed many popular social and economic views, some complementary to those of Flores Magón, also called for municipal autonomy from federal control in response to Díaz's centralization of political authority. Villa, from the northern state of Chihuahua, did not offer a true ideology or program, but the policies he implemented in the regions under his control reflected his radical social philosophy. In Chihuahua, for example, he nationalized large landholders' properties outright and, because of his own illiteracy (he learned to read only late in life), instituted a widespread primary school program. Zapata, who came from the rugged state of Morelos just south of Mexico City, fought largely over the issue of land. His ideology, expressed by his collaborators, appeared in his famous Plan de Ayala.[45]

With the exception of Madero, these men offered few specific political principles. Consequently, the political ideology of the revolution, with the possible exception of effective suffrage and no reelection, emerged piecemeal, either in the constitutional debates at Querétaro, before the writing of the 1917 constitution, or from actual experience.

One of the most important of these themes was Mexicanization, a broad form of nationalism. Simply stated, Mexico comes first, outsiders second. In the economic realm, it can be seen in placing Mexicans instead of foreigners in management positions, even if the investment is foreign in origin. An even more important expression of economic nationalism occurred in regard to resources: the formalization of Mexican control. With few exceptions, at least 51 percent of any enterprise had to be in the hands of Mexicans. But after 1988, desperate for foreign investment, the government loosened up many restrictions in certain economic sectors.

Mexicanization spread to cultural and psychological realms. On a cultural level, the revolution gave birth to extraordinary productivity in art, music, and literature, in which methodology was often as important as the content. In the visual fields, the Mexicans revived the mural, an art form that could be viewed by large numbers of Mexicans rather than remain on the walls of private residences or inaccessible museums.[46] Political cartoons during and after the revolution blossomed. In literature, the social protest novel—the novel of the revolution—came to the fore. Often cyni-

---

Mexicanization: a revolutionary principle stressing the importance of Mexicans and Mexico, enhancing their influence and prestige.

---

cal or highly critical, these works castigated not only the failures of the Porfiriato but the apparent failures of the revolutionaries too.[47] Musicians paid attention to the indigenous heritage, even composing the classical *Indian Symphony*, whose roots lie in the native culture. Ballads and popular songs flourished throughout Mexico as each region made its contributions.[48]

Mexicanization also affected a line of intellectual thought known as *lo mexicano*, which was concerned with national or cultural identity, and pride in Mexican heritage. Henry Schmidt, one of the most insightful students of the Mexican cultural rebirth, assessed its impact:

> The 1910 Revolution generated an unprecedented expansion of knowledge in Mexico. At the same time as it lessened the tensions of an unresponsive political system, it ushered in a new age of creation. If the post-Revolutionary political development cannot always be viewed favorably, the efforts to reorient thought toward a greater awareness of national conditions at least merit commendation. Thus the 1920's is known as the period of "reconstruction" and "renaissance," when the country, having undergone its most profound dislocation since the Conquest, attempted to consolidate the gains its people had struggled for since the waning of the Porfiriato.[49]

Another important theme of the revolution was social justice. Economically, although not expressed specifically in the constitution, this included a fairer distribution of national income. Socially, and called for by nearly all revolutionary and intellectual thinkers, it involved expanded public education. Madero wanted to improve access. Many others promoted education as an indirect means to enhance economic opportunity, particularly for the Indians, whose integration into the mainstream mestizo culture could thereby be accomplished. A leading intellectual, José Vasconcelos, who made significant contributions to Mexican education, praised a coming "Cosmic race," suggesting that a racial mix would produce a superior, not inferior, culture.[50]

The revolution did not react adversely to a strong state. Instead, building on the administrative infrastructure created under the Porfiriato, postrevolutionary regimes contributed to its continued expansion. Yet unlike Díaz, the revolution heralded a larger state *role*, giving the state responsibilities not expected of a government before 1910. According to Héctor Aguilar Camín and Lorenzo Meyer, the construction of a new state incorporated "the first bold attempts at developing the state as an instrument of economic, educational, and cultural action and regulation."[51] For example, as a consequence of Mexicanization, the state gained control over subsoil resources and eventually became the administrator of extractive enterprises. The phenomenal growth in the value of the nation's oil in the 1970s cast the state in an even more important role. When the state nationalized foreign petroleum companies in 1938, it established national and international precedents elsewhere.[52] In later periods, the state came to control such industries as fertilizers, telephones, electricity, airlines, steel, and copper. In the mid-1980s the trend gradually began to be reversed.

The revolution stimulated the political liberalism that had lain dormant under the ideology of positivism during the last twenty years of the Porfiriato. Freedom of the press was revived during the revolution. The media underwent a regression in the 1920s, and although censorship continued to raise its head, the conditions under which the media operated were much improved. The most important principle of political liberalism— increased participation in governance expressed through effective suffrage—was given substance in Madero's election in 1911, probably Mexico's freest, but never returned to that level until 1997.[53]

The political mythology of the revolution, "Effective Suffrage, No Reelection," was stamped on official government documents until the 1970s. Effective suffrage is still only an ideal, however, not yet achieved in practice. On the other hand, no reelection, with but a few exceptions in the 1920s and 1930s, has become the rule. When General Alvaro Obregón tried to circumvent it in 1928 by forcing the congress to amend the constitution to allow him to run again after a four-year hiatus, he was elected but then assassinated before taking office. No president since has tried the maneuver. No elected executive, including mayors and governors, repeats officeholding, consecutively or otherwise. Legislators may repeat terms, but not consecutively, a concept introduced in the 1930s.

The revolution also had an extraordinary influence on Mexico's political leadership after 1920. Half the national political leaders born between 1870 and 1900 had participated in this violent event. Among those who held national office for the first time, 47 percent had fought on the side of the revolutionaries, 9 percent in opposition to these forces, and 2 percent on both sides. Presidents Alvaro Obregón (1920–1924) and Plutarco Elías Calles (1924–1928), as well as Díaz, recruited many of their wartime cronies. Through 1940, the presidents who succeeded them were, with one exception, generals who had fought in these battles, often under these two predecessors. As the data in Table 2-2 illustrate, veterans continued to dominate Mexican administrations from 1914 through 1934. As might be expected, the 1910 revolution introduced a different type of politician as well, one whose social origins were quite distinct from those of his noncombatant contemporary. In effect, the revolution reintroduced the importance of working-class origins among Mexico's leadership, since 72 percent of the public figures who were combat veterans were from working-class families, compared with only 34 percent who had middle- and upper-class backgrounds.

Table 2-2 Revolutionary Experiences of National Politicians

Presidential Administration	Experience (%)				
	Revolutionary	Antirevolutionary	Both	None	Total
Madero, 1911–1913	28	4	4	64	100
Huerta, 1913–1914	5	48	8	39	100
Convention, 1914–1915	77	0	0	23	100
Carranza, 1914–1920	71	0	0	29	100
Obregón, 1920–1924	61	1	1	37	100
Calles, 1924–1928	56	1	1	42	100
Portes Gil, 1928–1930	58	0	0	42	100
Ortiz Rubio, 1930–1932	54	0	0	46	100
Rodríguez, 1932–1934	56	0	0	44	100

Another revolutionary outcome was the changed relationship between church and state. Once again, the seeds of orthodox liberalism appeared in the constitutional debates. Many of the revolutionaries eyed the church with severe distrust and reinstituted many of the most restrictive provisions advocated by the early liberals. Until 1992 these provisions could be found, unchanged, in the constitution. They include removing religion from primary education (Article 3), taking away the church's right to own real property (Article 27), and secularizing certain religious activities and restricting the clergy's potential political actions (Article 130). No clergy of any faith were permitted in their capacity as ministers to criticize Mexican laws or even to vote.

The breakup of large landholdings is also a primary economic and social product of revolutionary ideology. As part of the redistribution of land in Mexico after 1915, the government made the Indian *ejido* concept (village-owned lands) its own, distributing land to thousands of rural villages to be held in common for legal residents, who obtained use rights, not legal title, to it.[54] In effect, the government institutionalized the indigenous land system that the liberals and positivists had attempted to destroy. This structure remained unchanged until 1992.

The revolution also introduced a change in attitude toward labor. For the first time, strikes were legalized, and the right to collective bargaining was sanctioned. Provisions regarding hours and wages, at least for organized labor, were introduced. The 1917 constitution was the first to mention the concept of social security, although it was not implemented until 1943. Organized labor helped General Obregón defeat president Venustiano Carranza in the last armed confrontation of the revolutionary decade.

Finally, although this list is incomplete, the revolution gave greater emphasis to a sense of constitutionalism. In a political sense, constitutionalism provides legitimacy for a set of ideas expressed formally in the national document. It is not only a reference point for the goals of Mexican society after 1920, as a consequence of the revolution, but it also identifies the basic outline of political concepts and processes. The constitution of 1917 itself took on a certain level of prestige. Although many of its more radical social, economic, and political provisions are observed more in abeyance than reality, its contents and its prestige together influenced the values of successive generations.[55]

THE POLITICS OF PLACE:
INTERFACE WITH THE UNITED STATES

The proximity of the United States has exercised an enormous influence on Mexico. As I argue, "The United States constitutes a crucial variable in the very definition of Mexico's modern political culture."[56] Beginning with independence, the political leaders who sought solutions emphasizing federalism, and later the decentralizing principles of liberalism, borrowed many of their concepts from U.S. political thinkers and documents. In fact, the intellectual ideas provoked by U.S. independence from England provided a fertile literature from which independence precursors could also borrow.

The destiny of the two countries became intertwined politically in more direct ways as a consequence of the annexation of Texas, a northern province of New Spain. Immediately after Mexico won independence, large numbers of Americans began to settle in Texas, quickly outnumbering the Mexicans there. The differences within Texas between Mexicans and Americans and between Texas and the Mexican government led to armed conflict. The Mexican army under General Antonio López de Santa Anna lay siege to the Alamo in February 1836 but was routed from Texas later that year. Texas remained independent of Mexico until 1845, when the United States, by a joint congressional resolution, annexed it. This provoked another conflict, one with even more serious repercussions.[57]

Desirous of more territory, President James Polk used several incidents as a pretext for war. In 1846 U.S. troops drove deep into Mexico's heartland and, in addition to occupying outlying regions of the former Spanish empire in New Mexico and California, seized the port of Veracruz and Mexico City. In the Treaty of Guadalupe Hidalgo, signed on February 2, 1848, Mexico ceded more than half its territory to the United States. Seven years later, the Mexican government, again under Santa Anna, sold the United States a strip of land (in what is now southern Arizona and southern New Mexico), known as the Gadsen Purchase, although this time it was not done under duress.

The war left a justifiably bitter taste in the mouths of many Mexicans. As has been suggested, "The terms of the Treaty of Guadalupe Hidalgo are among the harshest imposed by a winner upon a loser in the history of the world."[58] More than any single issue, the terms established a relationship of distrust between the two nations. Physical incursion from the north took place twice more. Voices in the United States always seemed to call for annexations. Even as late as the first decade of the twentieth century, California legislators publicly advocated acquiring Baja California.

During the Mexican Revolution the United States repeatedly and directly or indirectly intervened in Mexican affairs. The intense personal prejudices or interests of its emissaries often determined U.S. foreign policy decisions. Henry Lane Wilson, ambassador during the Madero administration (1911–1913), played a role in its overthrow and in the failure to ensure the safety of Madero and his vice-president, who were murdered by counterrevolutionaries led by Felix Díaz and Victoriano Huerta. Huerta established himself in power, and the violent phase of the revolution began in earnest. President Woodrow Wilson removed the U.S. ambassador and sent personal emissaries to evaluate Huerta. He decided to channel funds to the Constitutionalists, revolutionaries who had remained loyal to Madero and to constitutional government. But after a minor incident involving U.S. sailors in the port of Tampico, Wilson used it as a pretext to order the occupation of the port of Veracruz, resulting in the deaths of numerous Mexicans.[59]

Wilson's high-handedness produced a widespread nationalistic response in Mexico that nearly brought Wilson's intention—to oust Huerta from the presidency—to naught. Mexicans alive at the time of the occupation recall discontinuing classes in English, switching back to Mexican cigarettes, and throwing away their Texas-style hats in symbolic protest. Young men as far away as Guadalajara, in western Mexico, readily joined voluntary companies to go fight the Americans.[60] But Huerta fell, and the North Americans did not invade and, indeed, soon left Veracruz.

After the Constitutionalists' victory under Carranza, rebel chieftains began to bicker among themselves. They divided into two major camps: one led by Francisco Villa and Emiliano Zapata and the other by Álvaro Obregón and Carranza. After several major battles, Obregón defeated Villa's forces. In March 1916, after remnants of Villa's forces moved north and attacked Columbus, New Mexico, Wilson ordered a punitive expedition under General John "Black Jack" Pershing against Villa. The U.S. forces battled the Constitutionalists, never caught Villa, and remained in Mexico until 1917.[61]

From this necessarily brief selection of historical examples, it is clear that Mexicans have reason to distrust the United States and to have created an extremely strong sense of nationalism, especially directed toward its northern neighbor. The economic, political, and cultural exchanges between the two countries, especially since the 1920s, have given rise to issues common to Mexico's relations in all parts of the world, as well as others peculiar to relations between Mexico and the United States. The geographic proximity of two such culturally and economically different societies has had numerous consequences for domestic politics and their respective national security agendas. These issues will be examined in a broader perspective in a later chapter. For now, I just want to emphasize that Mexico's nearness to the United States has noticeably affected its political and economic history and development.

CONCLUSION

Throughout its recent history, Mexico, as both a colony and an independent nation, established patterns that have contributed heavily to the development of its political model. Some of the more important remnants from the Spanish colonial period are the conflicts of social class, exacerbated by sharp social divisions. Catholicism, introduced as the official religion of the Spanish conquerors, has been equally significant. Its monopoly encouraged a cultural intolerance of other ideas or values and enabled a symbiotic, profitable relationship between the state and the church. The Spanish also fostered a strong sense of special interests, granting privileges to other selected groups, including the military, and ultimately contributing to a particularized civil–military relationship. These elements led to corporatism, a sort of quasi-official relationship between important occupational groups or institutions and the state. The Spanish, through their own political structure, especially the viceroy, imposed three hundred years of authoritarian, centralized administration. Great powers accrued to the executive, to the neglect of other government branches. Restrictive economic policies discouraged the growth of a strong colonial economy, thus shoring up the role of the state versus that of an incipient private sector. The state's power and prestige attracted New Spain's most ambitious citizens.

Many features of the colonial period were further enhanced after independence. The conflicts between the liberals and conservatives, driven by an intolerance of counterviews, produced ongoing civil war and anarchy. Although Mexico experimented briefly with a more decentralized form of government, authoritarian qualities were back in the saddle by the end of the nineteenth century. The presidency replaced the viceroyship in wielding power, and President Díaz expanded the size and importance of the executive branch, thereby continuing to enhance the state's image. Although Díaz introduced political stability and some economic development, he perpetuated the social inequalities inherited from the Spanish period. He also made sure that the military would have a large voice in the political system, leaving unresolved the matter of military subordination to civilian authority. And the Spanish paternal traditions remained.

The revolution reactively introduced changes but in many respects retained some of the basic features from the previous two periods. One important innovation was Mexicanization, an outgrowth largely of Mexico's exploitation by foreigners and especially its proximity to the United States. Mexicanization strengthened Mexican values and culture as well as political nationalism. The revolution altered Mexicans' political rhetoric and social goals of legitimizing the needs and interests of lower-income groups and Indians. Yet instead of reducing the role of the state, it made the state into an even more comprehensive institution. The revolution also revived important principles of orthodox liberalism, including political liberties, suppression of the church's secular role, and decentralization of authority, but a decade of civil violence and the need for effective leadership in the face of successive rebellions in the 1920s discouraged implementation of a federal, democratic system. Instead, the revolution left Mexico with a heritage of strong, authoritarian leadership, of military supremacy. Even so, it established the importance of constitutionalism, even if many of the constitution's liberal provisions were never enforced. The legitimacy of its concepts provided the basis for political liberalization under Presidents Salinas and Zedillo.

Finally, Mexico's long, troublesome relationship with the United States has implications for its political evolution and the functioning of its model. The level of the United States's economic influence in Mexico and the United States seizure of more than half of Mexico's national territory, prompted Mexican nationalism and anti-Americanism. Mexico has had to labor under the shadow of its internationally powerful neighbor, a psychological as well as a practical political burden. Historical experience and geographic proximity influenced many domestic policy decisions and perhaps subtly encouraged a strong, even authoritarian regime that could prevent the kind of instability and political squabbling that had left Mexico open to territorial depredation.

NOTES

1. Frank Tannenbam, *Mexico: The Struggle for Peace and Bread* (New York: Knopf, 1964), 36.

2. For an extensive discussion of racial relations in Mexico and elsewhere in Latin America, see Magnus Morner's classic study *Race Mixture in the History of Latin America* (Boston: Little, Brown, 1967).

3. Interestingly, this is even true when comparing the United States with its colonizer, England. See Richard Rose, *Politics in England*, 5th ed. (Boston: Little, Brown, 1989), 69.

4. Charles Kadushin, *American Intellectual Elite* (Boston: Little, Brown, 1974), 26.

5. Judith Hellman, *Mexico in Crisis*, 2d ed. (New York: Holmes & Meier, 1983), 40–46.

6. For background, see Robert Ricard, *The Spiritual Conquest of Mexico* (Berkeley and Los Angeles: University of California Press, 1966).

7. Samuel Ramos, *Profile of Man and Culture in Mexico* (Austin: University of Texas Press, 1962), 27.

8. Nancy Farris, *Crown and Clergy in Colonial Mexico, 1759–1821* (London: University of London Press, 1968).

9. For a fascinating account of the importance of imported books in the colonies, see Irving A. Leonard, *Books of the Brave* (Cambridge, Mass.: Harvard University Press, 1949).

10. Richard Greenleaf, "Historiography of the Mexican Inquisition," in *Cultural Encounters, the Impact of the Inquisition in Spain and the New World*, ed. Mary Elizabeth Perry and Anne J. Cruz (Berkeley and Los Angeles: University of California Press, 1991), 256–57.

11. Lyle McAlister, *The "Fuero Militar" in New Spain, 1764–1800* (Gainesville: University of Florida Press, 1967).

12. Edwin Lieuwen, *Mexican Militarism* (Albuquerque: University of New Mexico Press, 1968).

13. Henry Bamford Parkes, *A History of Mexico* (Boston: Houghton Mifflin, 1966), 87. For an excellent discussion of some of the consequences of the Spanish bureaucratic system, see Colin M. MacLachlan, *Spain's Empire in the New World* (Berkeley and Los Angeles: University of California Press, 1991), 34ff.

14. For background, see Charles Gibson, *Spain in America* (New York: Harper & Row, 1967); Clarence Haring, *The Spanish Empire in America* (New York: Oxford University Press, 1947); Lillian Fisher, *Viceregal Administration in the Spanish American Colonies* (Berkeley and Los Angeles: University of California Press, 1926).

15. Justo Sierra, *The Political Evolution of the Mexican People* (Austin: University of Texas Press, 1969), 107.

16. *La formación del estado mexicano* (Mexico City: Porrúa, 1984); Juan Felipe Leal, "El estado y el bloque en el poder en México," *Revista Mexicana de Ciencias Políticas y Sociales* 35 (October–December 1989): 12ff.

17. Michael Meyer and William Sherman, *The Course of Mexican History* (New York: Oxford University Press, 1991), 168.

18. Edward A. Shils, *The Intellectual Between Tradition and Modernity: The Indian Situation* (The Hague: Mouton, 1961).

19. Glen Dealy, *The Public Man: An Interpretation of Latin American and Other Catholic Cultures* (Amherst: University of Massachusetts Press, 1977), 8.

20. In his examination of the heartland, William Least Heat Moon reported that rural Kansas still strongly opposes any project representing federal government intervention. See his *PrairyErth* (New York: Houghton Mifflin, 1991).

21. For an excellent discussion of this in contemporary Mexico, see Larissa Lomnitz, "Horizontal and Vertical Relations and the Social Structure of Urban Mexico," *Latin American Research Review* 17 (1982): 52.

22. For the views of a leading theoretician, and the larger context of liberalism in Mexico, see Charles A. Hale's *Mexican Liberalism in the Age of Mora, 1821–1853* (New Haven, Conn.: Yale University Press, 1968).

23. For many interesting interpretations of the origins of authoritarianism, see John H. Coatsworth, "Los orígenes del autoritarismo moderno en México," *Foro Internacional* 16 (October–December 1975): 205–32; and Lorenzo Meyer, "The Origins of Mexico's Authoritarian State, Political Control in the Old and New Regimes," in *Authoritarianism in Mexico*, ed. Luis Reyna and Richard Weinert (Philadelphia: ISHI, 1977), 3–22.

24. For examples, see David M. Pletcher, *Rails, Mines, and Progress: Seven American Promoters in Mexico, 1867–1911* (Ithaca, N.Y.: Cornell University Press, 1958).

25. For the long-term consequences of this relationship, see Karl Schmitt, "Church and State in Mexico: A Corporatist Relationship," *Americas* 40 (January 1984): 349–76.

26. Robert J. Knowlton, "Some Practical Effects of Clerical Opposition to the Mexican Reform," *Hispanic American Historical Review* 45 (1965): 246–56, provides concrete examples.

27. Jan Bazant, *Alienation of Church Wealth in Mexico: Social and Economic Aspects of the Liberal Revolution, 1856–1857* (Cambridge: Cambridge University Press, 1971).

28. Charles A. Hale, *The Transformation of Liberalism in Late Nineteenth Century Mexico* (Princeton, N.J.: Princeton University Press, 1989), 27.

29. *Inscripciones*, Universidad Nacional Autónomo de Mexico, Escuela Nacional Preparatoria, official registration records.

30. Karl Schmitt, "The Díaz Conciliation Policy on State and Local Levels, 1867–1911," *Hispanic American Historical Review* 40 (1960): 513–32.

31. Martin S. Stabb, "Indigenism and Racism in Mexican Thought, 1857–1911," *Journal of Inter-American Studies and World Affairs* 1 (1959): 405–23.

32. Colin MacLachlan and William H. Beezley, *El Gran Pueblo, A History of Greater Mexico* (Englewood Cliffs, N.J.: Prentice Hall, 1994), 131.

33. For evidence of this, see the officer promotion lists from various battles in the published records of the Secretaría de Guerra y Marina, *Escalafón general de ejército* (Mexico City, 1902, 1911, 1914). For his collaborators, see Roderic Ai Camp, *Mexican Political Biographies, 1884–1934* (Austin: University of Texas Press, 1994).

34. For background and the long-term consequences of this relationship, see Roderic Ai Camp, *Generals in the Palacio: The Military in Modern Mexico* (New York: Oxford University Press, 1992).

35. Roderic Ai Camp, *Political Recruitment Across Two Centuries, Mexico 1884–1991* (Austin: University of Texas Press, 1995), 132.

36. For excellent case studies of these interlocking economic–political families, see Mark Wasserman, *Persistent Oligarchs: The Political Economy of Chihuahua, Mexico* (Durham, N.C.: Duke University Press, 1993); and Gilbert Joseph and Allen Wells, "Yucatán: Elite Politics and Rural Insurgency," in *Provinces of the Revolution: Essays on Regional Mexican History, 1910–1929*, ed. Thomas Benjamin and Mark Wasserman (Albuquerque: University of New Mexico Press, 1990).

37. See Francisco Bulnes, *El verdadero Díaz y la Revolución* (Mexico City: Editorial Hispano–Mexicana, 1920), 42. This latter figure is probably exaggerated but indicates the bureaucracy's importance.

38. For a firsthand view of some of these methods, see John Kenneth Turner's muckraking, autobiographical account in *Barbarous Mexico* (Austin: University of Texas Press, 1969); or Evelyn Hu-Dehart, "Development and Rural Rebellion: Pacification of the Yaquis in the Late Porfiriato," *Hispanic American Historical Review* 54 (1974): 72–93.

39. This latter variable has been strongly emphasized. However, more careful empirical examination suggests the following conclusion: "Future analysis of continuity and turnover in Mexico and elsewhere needs to examine the interrelationship between generational and individual political mobility to determine which, if either, is a more useful variable of political upheaval. I am suggesting that *intra-generational* mobility, measured by access to political office for the first time, may be far more significant in explaining political stability and instability than *generational* access to power, measured by age cohort alone." See my *Political Recruitment Across Two Centuries*, 45.

40. An excellent but brief discussion of these arguments can be found in Paul J. Vanderwood, "Explaining the Mexican Revolution," in *The Revolutionary Process in Mexico: Essays on Political and Social Change, 1880–1940*, ed. Jaime E. Rodríguez (Los Angeles: UCLA Latin American Center, 1990), 97–114.

41. Support for this view can be found in John Womack Jr., "The Mexican Revolution, 1910–1920," in vol. 5 of *The Cambridge History of Latin America*, ed. Leslie Bethell (Cambridge: Cambridge University Press, 1986), 74–153.

42. For background on Flores Magón and other precursors, see James Cockcroft's excellent *Intellectual Precursors of the Mexican Revolution, 1900–1913* (Austin: University of Texas Press, 1968).

43. These can be found in Jesús Silva Herzog, *Breve historia de la revolución mexicana, los antecedentes y la etapa maderista* (Mexico City: Fondo de Cultura Económica, 1960), annexes.

44. Stanley R. Ross, *Francisco I. Madero: Apostle of Mexican Democracy* (New York: Columbia University Press, 1955).

45. See John Womack Jr., *Zapata and the Mexican Revolution* (New York: Knopf, 1968); Michael Meyer, *Mexican Rebel: Pascual Orozco and the Mexican Revolution, 1910–1915* (Lincoln: University of Nebraska Press, 1967).

46. Jean Charlot, *The Mexican Mural Renaissance, 1920–1925* (New Haven, Conn.: Yale University Press, 1967), provides an overview of this movement. For its influence on United States culture, see Helen Delpar, *The Enormous Vogue of Things Mexican, Cultural Relations Between the United States and Mexico, 1920–1935* (Tuscaloosa: University of Alabama Press, 1992).

47. See John Brushwood's, *Mexico in Its Novel: A Nation's Search for Identity* (Austin: University of Texas Press, 1966), 173ff.

48. For wonderfully revealing examples of popular appraisals of various revolutionary figures, see Merle E. Simmons, *The Mexican Corrido as a Source for Interpretive Study of Modern Mexico, 1879–1950* (Bloomington: Indiana University Press, 1957).

49. Henry C. Schmidt, *The Roots of Lo Mexicano: Self and Society in Mexican Thought, 1900–1934* (Austin: University of Texas Press, 1978), 97.

50. José Vasconcelos, *La raza cósmica: Misión de la raza iberoamericana* (Paris: Agencia Mundial de Librerías, 1925).

51. Héctor Aguilar Camín and Lorenzo Meyer, *In the Shadow of the Mexican Revolution, Contemporary Mexican History, 1910–1989* (Austin: University of Texas Press, 1993), 78.

52. Paul Sigmund, *Multinationals in Latin America: The Politics of Nationalization* (Madison: University of Wisconsin Press, 1980), 81.

53. The August 1994 presidential elections could be said to have been the most successful in the level of participation and the degree of integrity on election day. However, the larger electoral setting in which these elections occurred left much to be desired, especially since the conditions were favorable to the government party. An excellent discussion of this can be found in "Mexico's Electoral Aftermath and Political Future," *Memoria* of the papers presented at a binational conference, University of Texas, Austin, September 2–3, 1994 (Austin: Mexican Center, Institute of Latin American Studies, 1994).

54. For an account of these developments, see Eyler N. Simpson's classic, *The Ejido: Mexico's Way Out* (Chapel Hill: University of North Carolina Press, 1937); Nathan Whetten, *Rural Mexico* (Chicago: University of Chicago Press, 1948), the most comprehensive picture of land-tenure conditions; Paul Lamartine Yates, *Mexico's Agricultural Dilemma* (Tucson: University of Arizona Press, 1981). In 1992, the Mexican government introduced radical reforms in the *ejido* land structure. See Claire Poole, "Land and Life," *Forbes*, April 29, 1991, 45–46, and *El Financiero International*, March 30, 1992, 11.

55. The best discussion of this consequence can be found in Frank Branden-

burg, *The Making of Modern Mexico* (Englewood Cliffs, N.J.: Prentice-Hall, 1964), 10–11.

56. John H. Coatsworth and Carlos Rico, eds., *Images of Mexico in the United States* (La Jolla, Calif.: Center for U.S.–Mexican Studies, UCSD, 1989), 10.

57. For background, see Karl M. Schmitt, *Mexico and the United States, 1821–1973: Conflict and Coexistence* (New York: Wiley, 1974), 51ff.

58. Josefina Váquez Zoraida and Lorenzo Meyer, *The United States and Mexico* (Chicago: University of Chicago Press, 1985), 49.

59. Robert E. Quirk, *An Affair of Honor: Woodrow Wilson and the Occupation of Veracruz* (New York: Norton, 1962), 95ff.

60. Interview with Ernesto Robles Levi, Mexico City, May 21, 1985.

61. For a firsthand account of this experience by a U.S. officer on the expedition, see Colonel Frank Tompkins, *Chasing Villa* (Harrisburg, Pa.: Military Service Publishing Company, 1934).

3

Contemporary Political Culture: What Mexicans Value

> What is problematic about the content of the emerging world culture is its political character. Although the movement toward technology and rationality of organization appears with great uniformity throughout the world, the direction of political change is less clear. But one aspect of this new world political culture is discernible: *it will be a political culture of participation* [italics added]. If there is a political revolution going on throughout the world, it is what might be called the participation explosion. In all the new nations of the world the belief that the ordinary man is politically relevant—that he ought to be an involved participant in the political system—is widespread. Large groups of people who have been outside of politics are demanding entrance into the political system. And the political elites are rare who do not profess commitment to this goal.
>
> GABRIEL ALMOND AND SIDNEY VERBA, *The Civic Culture*

The political culture of any society is partially a product of its general culture. Culture incorporates all the influences—historical, religious, ethnic, political—that affect a society's values and attitudes. The political culture is a microcosm of the larger culture, focusing specifically on those values and attitudes having to do with a person's *political* views and behavior.[1]

In the Mexican society, as in many societies, the intensity with which someone holds certain values is related to religion, level of education, income, age, gender, place of residence, and other variables. Their impacts will be examined in the following chapter and are important to understand. Equally important for comparative purposes is to evaluate the beliefs that may influence Mexico's politics and Mexican attitudes toward the system.

LEGITIMACY: SUPPORT FOR THE
POLITICAL SYSTEM AND SOCIETY

One of the most significant explanatory variables regarding a political system's stability is its legitimacy in the eyes of the society. Of course, any political model consists of a variety of institutions, some of which have been accorded greater respect than others. Level of respect permits a comparison of the standing of political and other types of institutions.

When Mexicans evaluate their institutions, it is apparent that those most closely associated with the state are held in lowest regard (see Table 3-1). Only three institutions are widely esteemed: family, church, and schools.[2] The selection of family is not surprising because a culture with strong values generally ranks family and tradition highly. Of course, if loyalty to family is excessive, it makes transferring loyalty to governmental institutions difficult. This appears to be the case in Mexico, for Mexicans express some serious reservations about the trustworthiness of *governmental* institutions and institutions as a whole. The same pattern is found in Japan, where levels of trust in institutions is lower than in Mexico.[3]

The confidence Mexicans have in the church and schools is signifi-

Table 3-1 Legitimacy of the State in England, United States, and Mexico: Confidence of Citizens in Institutions

Institution	England	United States	Mexico 1988	Mexico 1996
		Percentage of Respondents Giving Positive Evaluation		
Family	—	—	84	—
Church	56	85	62	73
Schools	53	82	60	—
Television[a]	—	—	37	45
Law	—	—*	32	—
Army	79	86	32	50
Newspaper/media	38	69	25	45
Business	55	84	22	52
Congress/parliament	52	83	16	39
Unions	29	52	14	42
Political parties	—	—	—	39
Police	80	88	12	27

Sources: Este País, August 1991, 5; Laurence Parisot, "Attitudes About the Media: A Five-Country Comparison," *Public Opinion* 10 (1988): Table 1; Marta Lagos, "Actitudes económicas y democracia en Latinoamérica," *Este País* (January 1997): Table 16.
[a]For England and the United States, included under newspapers.

cant. In the first place, as suggested in the previous chapter, both the liberal tradition and the revolution encouraged anti-church sentiment. Nevertheless, although we will discover that Mexicans developed sentiments supporting the separation of church and state, secular criticism has not done away with respect or sympathies for the Catholic Church, particularly in a society in which at least 85 percent of the members are Catholic. Regard for the church as an institution may be a partial reaction to state suppression. It may also follow from the church's being one of the most autonomous institutions in the society, operating outside the control of the state despite severe constitutional restrictions. And it may well be that the church largely earned its standing among Mexicans by its deeds. When Mexicans are asked to rank the most estimable persons in their society after their parents, priests and schoolteachers are well above any others.

It is noteworthy that Americans also give high marks to the church as an institution, indicating both their respect and, implicitly, the importance of religion and religious values in the U.S. culture. In England, on the other hand, where religion's influence is less controversial and less encompassing, churches are held in high esteem but closer to that found in Mexico.[4]

Mexican attitudes toward education, borne out in survey after survey, are usually quite positive. The significance of this for the legitimacy of the political system is perhaps more important for Mexico than for the United States and England, where schools are also viewed very positively, especially in the former. The school system in Mexico is largely public, although Catholic schools do play an important role. Unlike in the United States, however, public schools until the 1990s were operated by the regional government, and so the teachers were its employees. Today, financial control is in the hands of state governments. Although they may not be perceived as doing so, they could serve as a positive, indirect means of reinforcing the state's legitimacy—especially because texts in elementary schools are selected by the government. Most important, Mexicans' satisfaction with the school system is one of the few consistent pluses for the government.

Mexicans' confidence in other institutions is not prepossessing. What one notices immediately when comparing it with that of Americans is the generally lower levels of favorability. The weaker positive responses are not necessarily an indication of extreme frustration with the Mexican system; rather, Mexicans are likely to have lower expectations of their institutions, given their institutions' past performances, than Americans have. Nevertheless, the fact that police, politics, and congress tail off in the rankings indicates a lack of confidence in as well as alienation from these institutions. In fact, in a 1987 study with additional categories, only 23 percent of Mexicans gave government bureaucrats a favorable rating. And in 1995, only one in three Mexicans rated government as trustworthy.[5]

Attitudes toward the police are an important indication of basic trust in government. On the local level, police are the most likely representatives of government to come in contact with the citizenry. Therefore, a good opinion of the police is generally seen as an important grassroots indicator of trust in government. A sense of personal security is often a variable in one's evaluation of government performance. In both England and the United States the police achieved the highest level of confidence; in state and local surveys throughout Mexico, the police consistently rank lowest. Explanations usually include the perception that they are dishonest, often involved in criminal activities, and abuse their authority, especially among lower-income and rural groups. Given the rapid increase in crime in the 1990s—it increased 36 percent from 1994 to 1995, for example—and the widespread involvement of police as criminals, confidence remains low.[6]

The connection between services and specific institutions in society is shown in Table 3-2. When Mexicans are asked about the quality of specific government services, they point most often to education and health care. Generally speaking, they are most concerned on the local level, with education, health care, transportation, and sanitation. Agencies associated with the government render services that win widespread approval, thus contributing to the legitimacy of the government and, as in the case of the police and the security apparatus, offer services that the average Mexican views as inadequate. For example, during the Salinas administration (1988–1994), most Mexicans believed that the quality of their educational system improved. Specifically, by 1994, 48 percent thought that it was better; 29 percent believed that it was the same; and only 17 percent felt that it had become worse. In contrast, in regard to personal security, as the Sali-

Table 3-2 Legitimacy of the Mexican State: The Case of Public Services

Service	Percentage of Respondents with Favorable Image
Schools	67
Medical	55
Trash disposal and sanitation	41
Telephone	40
Security	32
Police	24

Source: Este País, August 1991, 4.

nas administration completed its term, precisely the reverse proportions of Mexicans viewed security in a negative light, with 46 percent describing it as worse, 32 percent as the same, and only 19 percent as improved.[7] The government connection is not the deciding variable in the evaluative process.

Mexicans' assessment of their most prominent institutions is unflattering as a rule, with the exception of church and school. Unlike Americans, Mexicans do not highly regard private-sector institutions. This is partly because private-sector values and the business community have not received positive attention in the schools or from public leaders. Indeed, businessmen are often denigrated. As one private-sector notable remarked, many Mexicans "use terms related to business, businessman, and entrepreneurs in a pejorative sense."[8] The ratings given to the private sector and to other institutions in 1991 are lower than in the mid-1980s, but the rank order is unchanged. The distrust is manifest.

The attitude toward institutions may be explained in part by the grim economic and social conditions of Mexican life in the 1980s. A study in the early 1960s showed that urban Mexicans felt little pride in government institutions.[9] Yet the 1980s were a decade of economic ups and downs, and confidence in government fell in many countries. In fact, if Canada, Mexico, and the United States are compared in this regard, it is the United States that experienced a major drop (see Table 3-3).

Although Mexicans' confidence in their government is half that of Americans and Canadians in their respective governments, its decline is minimal relative to the extent of economic crisis and the economic conditions Mexicans faced during the 1980s. In 1986, 50 percent of Mexicans told interviewers they thought a revolution might occur by 1991. Nearly half also described their own economic situation in a mid-1980s *New York Times* poll as bad, and 11 percent as very bad. Nine of ten respondents believed the national economy was bad or very bad, and more than half

Table 3-3 Confidence in Government in Mexico, United States, and Canada

Country	Percentage of Respondents Expressing Confidence in Government	
	1981	1990
Mexico	20	18
United States	50	36
Canada	38	34

Source: World Values Survey, 1990.

thought it would not recover. Mexican attitudes toward government have remained remarkably stable. That confidence slipped no more than it did might be attributed to the initial high level of popularity achieved by President Salinas by 1990, reversing somewhat the decline in legitimacy of his predecessors' administrations. In other words, confidence in governmental institutions probably dropped below its 1990 level at some point between 1981 and 1990.

Although Mexicans faced a number of political crises in the last year of the Salinas administration—beginning with the uprising of indigenous groups in Chiapas in January 1994, followed by the assassination of the government party's presidential candidate, Luis Donaldo Colosio in March—confidence in the country overall continued to remain relatively stable. But the assassination of Colosio, an unprecedented event in recent Mexican politics, did begin to initiate some doubts about both their personal economic future and their governmental institutions. Then, a few months after Ernesto Zedillo took office in December 1994, their confidence as a whole began to erode dramatically with the economic devaluation and harsh austerity policies—combined with an untested cabinet and president. In February 1995, just two months into the Zedillo administration, 46 percent of urban Mexicans agreed that the cabinet changes suggested administrative incompetence. By the end of 1995, 80 percent described their economic situation as worse than the previous year, and only 15 percent thought economic recovery would occur in a year's time. In 1997, 30 percent considered their personal economic situation to be bad.

Mexicans expressed a much more favorable opinion of society in general than they did of specific institutions, governmental or otherwise, indicating a much higher level of trust in societal responses to problems. Scholars cite the 1985 earthquake in Mexico City as an example.[10] Although criticism abounds of government efforts to save persons trapped in the rubble, neighborhood volunteers' efforts are looked upon as exemplary. The same pattern was repeated in 1992 in the aftermath of a devastating explosion in Guadalajara's storm sewers.

The government's inadequacies after the quake produced a groundswell of popular movements that together pressed demands on the government. One analyst had this to say about their cooperation:

> In the aftermath of the disastrous Mexico City earthquake in 1985, a coalition of urban organizations successfully forced the Mexican government and the World Bank to alter housing relief plans, accelerate the process of reconstruction, and reverse several fundamental urban policies. The coalition achieved this by uniting scores of neighborhood organizations. Hundreds of thousands of earthquake victims joined other urban poor to wrest concessions through deft media manipulation and political bartering.[11]

Another explanation for the government's faring poorly in the minds of most Mexicans is their perception of its goals. Asked in a survey in the late 1980s if government officials were working for their own interests or the interests of the majority, nearly two-thirds of the respondents said the former was the case. Cynicism characterized the replies.

Mexicans believe their society's qualities to be equal or superior to those of the U.S. society but are less certain concerning people. According to a recent comparison of Mexican views of their political system between 1959 and 1991, positive evaluations of their model actually increased.[12] For example, in 1981 Mexicans had little confidence in their fellow human beings, about one-third that of Americans and Canadians (see Table 3-4). When asked if one could trust the majority of people, fewer than one in five said yes.[13]

Interestingly, Mexicans' confidence in their fellow human beings almost doubled during the 1980s. (A slight increase also was found among Americans and Canadians.) It is difficult to know to what this can be attributed. Dynamic social, economic, and political changes in recent years obviously influenced Mexicans' trust in different ways: trust in institutions, especially political institutions, declined; trust in society remained stable; and trust in individual people surged.

In terms of political behavior, trust in people is an important measure of the potential for democratic political institutions. Mexicans have expressed greater interest in democratizing their political institutions, sharing in the wave of democratization occurring elsewhere. To survive, democratic institutions rely on the high levels of personal trust necessary to ef-

Table 3-4 Confidence in Society and in People, Mexico, United States, and Canada

Country	1981	1990
	Percentage of Respondents Expressing Confidence in Civil Society	
Mexico	47	48
United States	46	40
Canada	40	35
	Percentage of Respondents Expressing Confidence in People	
Mexico	18	33
United States	45	50
Canada	49	52

Source: World Values Survey, 1990.

fect compromise and operate within the rules of the political game. On a personal level Mexico has moved in that direction.

PARTICIPATION: ACTIVATING THE ELECTORATE

Trust in institutions and in fellow citizens is also related to political interest and participation. At least since the early 1960s, interest in political affairs in urban Mexico has been lower than in the United States and England. Today, according to much better survey data, interest in politics remains relatively low. In 1986, 30 percent of all Mexicans expressed no interest in politics; 34 percent, little interest; and 36 percent, some or much interest. In 1995, those figures remained remarkably unchanged, given the intense electoral revisions, at 24 percent, 42 percent, and 32 percent. Differences between Mexico and the United States might be explained by differences in media, communications systems, and political competitiveness.

People generally move from an interest in politics to political activism when they believe they can affect outcomes in the system. One way to test peoples' attitudes toward outcomes is to examine *political efficacy.* This measures the degree to which a person believes he or she can participate in politics and the responsiveness of the system to their involvement. When Americans were asked whether or not they have a say in what government does, somewhere between 33 and 41 percent, from 1980 to 1988, replied that they do.[14] A similar but more specific question was posed to Mexi-

---

Political efficacy: the belief in one's ability to participate in or influence political affairs.

---

cans: When asked whether they could do something about election fraud, 56 percent thought not (see Table 3-5). It is not surprising that more than half of all Mexicans believe they cannot affect the outcome of government policy; they have lived under a semiauthoritarian political model in which control over decision making is concentrated at the top. After all, if a third of all Americans described themselves as ineffectual politically in a system where honest elections are the norm and competition is regularized, the higher Mexican response should be expected.

Most citizens in political systems where elections occur become involved through voting. Therefore, their ability to affect the outcome of government policy is influenced by their perception of the integrity of the vot-

Table 3-5 Political Efficacy of Mexicans

Response to Statement "Can do nothing about electoral fraud"	Percentage of Respondents
Definitely true	8.9
True	47.3
False	31.5
Definitely false	4.0
Not sure	5.6
No answer	2.7

Source: Los Angeles Times poll, August, 1989.

ing process. Mexico has had a long history of voter fraud in the twentieth century. Disputes over electoral results have occurred after every presidential election since 1920, and at the state and local levels as well. In 1929, 1940, and 1988 large numbers of Mexicans believed that the opposition candidate for president actually won the election.[15]

Before 1988 the accusations of wrongdoing were based solely on observation and political commentary,[16] but shortly before the presidential elections that year Mexicans were asked for the first time in a nationwide poll if their vote would be respected (see Table 3-6). More than half the interviewers thought their votes would not be counted honestly. Only a fourth believed in the integrity of the electoral process, and an equal number were unsure.

The question was repeated shortly before the off-year elections in August 1991, when many governors, half the senate, and all congresspersons were elected. Although the "don't knows" remained the same, those who viewed the elections as honest increased by 83 percent. Despite intense election battles and evidence of election fraud since 1989, the government successfully allayed the doubts of some Mexicans in the 1991 elections. By the spring of 1994, after several political crises had led to a number of

Table 3-6 Mexicans' Views of Elections

Responses to Question "Will Your Vote Be Respected?"	Percentage of Respondents				
	1988 Elections	Percentage of Change	1991 Elections	Percentage of Change	1994 Elections
Yes	23	83+	42	12−	37
No	53	40−	32	6+	34
Don't know	24	8+	26	12+	29

Source: Este País, August 1991, 6; *Este País*, weekly poll, urban voters only, May 25, 1994. In a much larger poll, conducted by Alianza Cívica, of 9,507 voters in twenty locations, 47 percent believed that the elections might be fraudulent.

structural reforms in the electoral process, including the presence of inter-national observers, Mexicans again were asked if they thought the forth-coming presidential elections would be fair. Their response, which had fluc-tuated considerably throughout 1994, remained fairly consistent with the 1991 responses. Two weeks before the election, in mid-August, a nation-wide poll revealed that 41 and 17 percent, respectively, thought the elec-tions would be clean or reasonably clean. Only 30 percent thought that fraud would be considerable or widespread.[17] Yet a year after the 1994 elections, four out of five Mexicans considered elections generally to be fraudulent.

To test the assumptions about the relationship between citizens' per-ception of fraud and their willingness to vote, Mexicans were asked in 1989 their reasons for not voting. In Mexico, as in the United States, a person cannot vote unless he or she is registered before the election. Approxi-mately half of all Mexicans eligible to vote were not registered. Although the government attempted to increase the number of registered voters by means of a voter identification card system instituted before the 1991 elec-tions, many remained unregistered. The same situation obtains in the United States: In 1988, 33 percent of all persons eligible to vote were unregis-tered.[18] By August 1994, the government had succeeded in registering the largest percentage ever of eligible voters. What was even more surprising to analysts is that a record 78 percent of the voters actually cast their bal-lots, the highest percentage ever recorded.[19]

The second most common reason that Mexicans offer for not voting is that they forgot or were too busy (see Table 3-7). Using the sample in the *Los Angeles Times* August 1989 poll, if we exclude the percentages of persons not voting because they were unregistered or forgot to vote and then collapse the percentages directly pertaining to the integrity of the elec-

Table 3-7 Mexicans' Reasons for Not Voting

Reasons for Not Voting	Percentage of Respondents[a]
Not registered	45.7
Too busy or forgot	14.3
Fraud	7.4
Never vote	6.7
Don't trust process	5.4
To protest election/candidate	5.2
Too difficult	2.2
Too complicated	1.6
Don't want to be involved	1.4
Ill	1.4

Source: Los Angeles Times poll, August 1989.

toral process (fraud, don't trust the process, and to protest election/candidate), the latter percentages would constitute 57.5 percent of the responses. In 1993, however, only 32 percent gave fraud as an excuse, and 19 percent were not registered. The largest group, 40 percent, were not interested.[20] It is also possible that a large percentage of those who never vote refrain because they believe that casting a ballot is meaningless. Indeed, according to a 1994 poll published in *etcétera*, only 41 percent of Mexicans responding believed their vote to be very important.[21]

People's proclivity to participate in the electoral process is affected to some extent not only by confidence in their political efficacy or by the integrity of the institutions and the process itself but also by their level of activism in general. Mexicans' involvement in organizations is not high. Among the most important organizations are religious organizations and unions, followed by charitable and youth groups. Fifty-eight percent of all Mexicans belong to no organization. With the exception of unions, membership is voluntary, which is a measure of level of interest in involvement. Slightly over half of all Mexicans who belong to organizations belong to voluntary groups. Only 2 percent of Mexicans in the late 1980s belonged to political parties or political organizations, suggesting a relatively low level of interest in politics.[22] By the mid-1990s, 6 percent of Mexicans had worked for a political party or a candidate.

The simplest form of political participation is voting, if it is one of the characteristics of the political model. A somewhat higher level of participation is indicated by membership in political organizations. Political organizations in Mexico have been constrained by the characteristics of the dominant government-party system and its control over the electoral process. In other words, most organizations expressing political goals or affiliated with a political party, especially at the national level, have ties to the political establishment. Two-thirds of all Mexicans do not belong to any political organization. Most of them belong to unions and professional organizations that are automatically incorporated into the Institutional Revolutionary Party (PRI) (Table 3-8). The most important of these are the party's sectorial organizations representing labor, peasants, and professional groups. Thus, working-class Mexicans are most likely to belong to the Mexican Federation of Labor (CTM) and the National Peasant Federation (CNC), and professionals and white-collar workers to the National Front of Organizations and Citizens (FNOC). Others belong to such PRI organizations as youth or women's groups. Among Mexican activists who join political organizations, government employees account for 86 percent.

Given the fact that in Mexico, government-controlled unions and professional organizations have been part of the corporatist political structure,

Table 3-8 Mexicans' Membership in Political Organizations

Organizational Affiliation	Percentage of Respondents
Mexican Federation of Labor (CTM)	8.6
National Peasant Federation (CNC)	3.8
National Front of Organizations and Citizens (FNOC)	4.5
Other PRI organizations	7.0
Independent (not government controlled)	4.0
None	66.7
Don't know	3.8
No answer	1.6

Source: Los Angeles Times poll, August 1989.

it is not surprising that the government workers dominate political organization membership and that membership is high. Few Americans are members of strictly political organizations. For example, a member of the AFL–CIO (a major labor confederation) is not automatically a member of either major party, although each party attempts to obtain labor's support for its candidates and programs.

If we move higher up the ladder of political participation, from membership in an organization to some type of action, it is possible to obtain a good sense of citizens' attitudes toward political involvement and of their level of commitment to direct political participation. One way to measure such participation is to ask citizens about their attitudes toward modes of political action. In other words, to test receptivity to greater political involvement, people are asked whether or not they favor such highly visible and committed activities as boycotting, legal demonstrations, illegal demonstrations, and occupation of buildings or factories. Comparison of attitudes in Mexico, the United States, and Canada appear in Table 3-9.

As confidence in the institutions of government has declined in Mexico, the United States, and elsewhere, the legitimacy of other forms of political behavior has risen. People favor these actions because they believe them to be effective means to convey political demands and, more important, that the regular channels are inadequate. In the past decade, in the United States and Canada, roughly a 70 percent increase occurred among those favoring less orthodox actions. Mexico experienced an even more remarkable upsurge in that Mexicans traditionally have not favored such activity. By 1995, at least one-third of all Mexicans claimed to have participated in a demonstration. Among the many explanations of their quiescence is that their more authoritarian system would not be likely to respond to the activity or that it might respond repressively. Over time, the political culture came to see such activity as unacceptable and illegitimate.

Table 3-9 Dispositions Toward Political Action in Mexico, United States, and Canada

Country	1981	1990	Percentage of Change
		Percentage of Respondents Favoring Political Action[a]	
Mexico	7	24	242+
United States	15	26	73+
Canada	18	30	67+
		Percentage of Respondents Actually Engaged in Political Action[a]	
Mexico	2	16	700+
United States	7	12	71+
Canada	9	16	78+

Source: World Values Survey, 1990.
[a]"Political action" includes boycotts, legal demonstrations, illegal demonstrations, and occupation of buildings or factories.

Whatever the explanation, only half as many Mexicans as Americans and Canadians favored such approaches in 1981, but the numbers approximated one another a decade later. In fact, when Mexicans were asked in 1994 if they thought that demonstrations were a good response to electoral fraud in the presidential elections, an overwhelming 70 percent agreed.

The dramatic increase among Mexicans accepting unorthodox political activity is indicative of the weakness of the Mexican system in coping with important demands, its loss of legitimacy, and perhaps its increased tolerance of such demands and its response to them. The percentage of change in actual *engagement* in the unorthodox political activity is even more remarkable for the change it suggests in Mexican behavior. There has been a substantial increase of those willing to involve themselves directly in political activity in all three countries, even though the overall numbers remain small, fewer than one of six citizens. Still, Mexico's 700 percent gain is extraordinary. What explains this behavior, and what does it mean?

The greater competitiveness of the national political game in Mexico beginning with local elections in 1985 and culminating in the national elections of 1997 had major repercussions on the nature of political activism. During the twelve-year period, public opposition to electoral fraud reached new highs.[23] It was given legitimacy in the media through announcements and advertisements by intellectuals and leading clergy. In fact, the clergy threatened after northern elections in 1986 to cease celebrating masses, something that had not happened since the 1920s if a recount did not take place.[24] The claims of fraud attracted international attention, and the U.S. media helped legitimize the claims of the domestic opposition. The rise of

Mexican participation in unorthodox political activity to a level beyond that found in the United States suggests a major change in the political culture and in political efficacy. Although most Mexicans still think of themselves as ineffective politically, far greater numbers than before think they can induce change through non-government-controlled channels.

Another provocative explanation was offered in recent research on Mexican political stability. Linda Stevenson and Mitchell Seligson presented the hypothesis that "over the past sixty years, negative memories of the Mexican Revolution of 1910 have sparked fear of a return to the violence of that period, which in turn inhibited the willingness of Mexicans engaged in anti-system political actions."[25] They believe that this collective memory has faded with the passage of time and that the surviving generation of the revolution has passed from the scene, thus eliminating an important source of inhibitions toward high-risk political actions, which they predicted would increase after 1994. The uprising of the Chiapan Indians in early 1994 sparked sympathy movements throughout Mexico, and in early 1995, within weeks of imposing austerity measures, thousands of Mexicans, including numerous middle-class professionals, demonstrated in front of federal agencies in the capital their anger toward government policies.[26] Citizen participation in unconventional political activities has continued to increase.

One of the most imaginative Mexican leaders of this new set of political techniques is "Superbarrio," a masked version of superman who is a wrestler. Sheldon Annis described him as "a colorful good guy sworn to oppose the bureaucracy, greedy landlords, and political hacks. Dressed in yellow tights, red cape, and mask emblazoned with 'SB,' Superbarrio led tens of thousands of people in street protests over renters' rights, housing codes, construction credit, and low-cost housing."[27] Collectively, among the most interesting and active organizations which emerged from the changing electoral process in the 1990s, and performed a crucial role in the 1994 elections, was Acción Democrática (AD), an umbrella organization of civic organizations designed to observe and publicly certify elections. Although not engaging in partisan politics, AD provided national coordination to dozens of civic groups, developing stronger linkages among various social organizations, and demonstrating the potential for exercising policy influence, national and internationally, to its thousands of affiliated members. Organizations like AD, through their involvement in the day to day process of participatory politics, expand the potential pool of Mexican activists.[28] (see Table 3-10)

Most Mexicans, as do most Americans, however, participate politically through voting. Most Mexicans, on the other hand, do not support a

Table 3-10 Participation in the Federal District, 1997

Type of Organization	Percentage of Mexicans Who Are Members
Others	18
Sports	17
Religious	14
Neighborhood	10
Unions	10
Educational	9
Political party	4
Women	3
None	13

Source: Este País, February, 1998, 9. Interviews with 1,225 residents,
September 22–25, 1997, margin of error ±3 percent.

political party. In fact, more than half of all Mexicans are what Americans label independent or uncommitted. In the United States in 1988, only 37 percent of all Americans considered themselves independent or uncommitted; 35 percent, Democrats; and 28 percent, Republicans. The higher percentage of Americans affiliated with a party is a consequence of a higher level of knowledge about the two major parties, which have operated during the entire century, and the fact that both parties have controlled both branches of government.[29] Among Mexicans, 44 percent sympathized with specific parties in 1991, and 57 percent did in 1994 (see Table 3-11).

Most analysts describe the ideology of the three major parties as follows: PAN, right of center; PRI, center right; and PRD, left of center. PRI would not always have received such a label. The breadth of its centrist posture allowed it to incorporate fairly radical populist views and presidents, such as Lázaro Cárdenas (1934–1940), as well as more conservative positions. Ideologically speaking, within their respective political systems, the United States and Mexico share certain similarities. Mexicans have been

Table 3-11 Party Sympathy in Mexico

Party	Percentage of Respondents	
	1991	1994
No party	56	43
Institutional Revolutionary Party (PRI)	28	23
National Action Party (PAN)	6	19
Democratic Revolutionary Party (PRD)	6	12
Other	4	3

Source: Este País, August 1991, 3; *Este País*, June 1, 1994, 3.

more conservative politically, as has the United States electorate. But Mexicans are more strongly in the center ideologically than are Americans. Whereas 45 percent of Americans described themselves as conservatives, 38 percent of Mexicans are sympathetic to the right. Mexico has a large group in the center, 44 percent; 31 percent of Americans placed themselves in this category. Liberals, who would not correspond precisely to Mexicans who lean to the left, account for 23 percent of the American electorate but only 18 percent of Mexicans (see Table 3-12).[30]

Ideologically, people tend to select parties and other groups that reinforce their political views. For example, nearly half of all American conservatives are Republican, and half of all liberals are Democrats. Thirty-eight percent of all Mexicans are conservatives, and nearly two-thirds identify with the PRI; more than half of those professing leftist views favor the PRD, the left-of-center party.

Although citizens tend to vote for political parties that they believe subscribe to their views, often ideology is not an important determinant of why people vote for a candidate. In fact, candidate ideology or program has very little to do with Mexicans' reasons for voting. Most Mexicans are interested in a particular candidate because they believe he or she will change things. One study concluded that large numbers of Mexicans could not distinguish, in terms of policy issues, among the three major candidates in the 1988 elections. The same author also noted that such issues, including the voter's economic welfare, affected partisanship only when the econ-

Table 3-12 Relationship Between Ideology and Party, Mexico and the United States

Country and Ideology	Party Identification			Total
United States	Democratic	Independent	Republican	
Liberal	12	8	3	23
Center	11	13	7	31
Conservative	9	14	22	45
Mexico	Institutional Revolutionary Party (PRI)	Democratic Revolutionary Party (PRD)	National Action Party (PAN)	
Left	5	10	3	18
Center	25	7	12	44
Conservative	24	3	11	38

Sources: William Flanigan and Nancy Zingale, *Political Behavior of the American Electorate*, 17th ed. (Washington, D.C.: Congressional Quarterly Press, 1991), 107; World Values Survey, 1990, courtesy of Miguel Basáñez.

omy's future was tied explicitly to the fate of the PRI.[31] The candidate's party is not important except for how the voter might perceive it as having a bearing on the candidate's ability to bring about change. In order of importance in supporting a candidate, Mexicans' reasons ranked as follows in 1989: to change things, 46.6 percent; ability, 14.7 percent; party, 8.4 percent; ideology, 8.0 percent; and other, 6.7 percent.[32]

POLITICAL MODERNIZATION:
AUTHORITARIANISM OR DEMOCRACY?

If ideology is not very important to how Mexicans vote, how their values related to other issues plays a critical role in the country's political development. Many Mexicans have long desired a more competitive political process, hoping to democratize the system. Desire, alone, of course, is not the only prerequisite of democracy. Democratization implies the importance of certain values. Some observers have remained skeptical because

> though there are few (and small) instances and spaces that are truly democratic in Mexico, these are exceptions to the overall trait of political life. The political culture, from its precedents in the Aztec world and through the times of the Spanish colonial period, is characterized by values of subordination and authoritarianism. In the structure of the prototypical Mexican family, the father figure is authoritarian; children develop in an environment of domination that goes well beyond the natural figure of authority of parents over children in any family. These values are reproduced at the work place, at school, in the unions, in businesses, in political parties. In each and every realm of life, the individual members often criticize the authoritarianism of the government, even though they behave the same way in their own firms; unions complain about the hierarchical structures of firms and the government, though it would be hard to find a more hierarchical scheme of domination top-down than the corporatist structures of the labor sector. Most cases in which individuals carry out negotiations and transactions—which can be properly termed political—tend to be characterized by schemes of an authoritarian nature where there is always an implicit structure of domination.[33]

One of the most essential of these democratic values is a commitment by more than half of all Mexicans to expanding the role of opposition in Mexico (see Table 3-13). Only one in four Mexicans believes the PRI should remain strong, about the same proportion that identifies themselves as firm supporters of the PRI. Other than PRI diehards, then, the typical Mexican is open to opposition-party growth. Although shortly before the

Table 3-13 Attitudes Toward Increased Political Opposition in Mexico

Answers to Question "Do you believe parties other than the governing party should increase their strength?"	Percentage of Respondents
Yes	55.1
Only the Institutional Revolutionary Party (PRI) should remain strong	24.5
Not sure	13.2
No answer	7.2

Source: Los Angeles Times poll, August 1989.

1994 presidential election a majority of Mexicans believed the PRI could better institute change, 55 percent thought that an opposition party could win.

Although the desire to see an expansion of opposition in Mexico is essential to political reform, an even more central feature of the actual *functioning* of a democratic political culture—as distinct from the institutions necessary to make it possible—is support for democratic liberties. Although not much research has been done on this variable in political liberalization, some comparative data are available (see Table 3-14).

A 1978 survey of *urban* Mexicans and New Yorkers suggested that

Table 3-14 Political Authoritarianism: Support or Rejection of Democratic Liberties Among Urban Mexicans and New Yorkers

	Mean Score (Scale 1–10)[a]	
Question and Response	Mexico	New York
Widespread Participation. Approve of		
Participating in petition signing	8.0	8.3
Participating in legal demonstration	8.2	8.1
Working for party, candidate, campaign	7.3	8.5
Support for Dissent. Approve of critics of Mexican government's having the right to		
Vote	6.3	7.1
Hold peaceful demonstrations	7.6	7.0
Run for public office	4.7	5.7
Opposition to Suppression of Democratic Liberties. Approve of government's prohibiting critics of the Mexican political system from		
Holding public demonstrations	6.3	8.3
Holding meetings	6.4	8.1
Expressing views	6.4	7.8
Expressing views in media	6.4	8.3

Source: Adapted from John Booth and Mitchell Seligson, "The Political Culture of Authoritarianism in Mexico," Latin American Research Review 19 (1984): 113. Table 1.
[a]1–5 = authoritarian; 6–10 = democratic.

although Mexicans' beliefs in democratic values were not, in most cases, at the level of New Yorkers', they did strongly support most of the values. The researchers examined three variables important to rejecting authoritarianism and supporting democracy: participation, political liberties, and dissent.[34] Not surprisingly, they found levels of support for participation, such as petition signing and demonstrating equal to those found among New Yorkers. The findings anticipated those discovered in the *World Values Survey* reported in Table 3-9, in which Mexicans reached a level of support for such activities similar to that found in the United States. Regarding defense of political liberties, Mexicans scored in the democratic range, although not nearly as high as New Yorkers did. In other words, Mexicans were not yet as tolerant of critics of the system. The most interesting results of this survey appear in connection with dissent.[35] The ultimate test of a democratic system is allowing a critic to run for public office. Neither New Yorkers nor Mexicans scored well on this measure.

When Americans were asked in another survey if everyone should have an equal right to hold public office, 91 percent replied yes.[36] But when they were asked in still another survey if Communists, with whom most Americans disagree intensely, should have an equal right to speak, only 64 percent said yes.[37] Although precisely the same questions have not been posed to Mexicans, one study asked whether they would be bothered by someone's having different values and beliefs, and 87 percent said no. But when asked whether they would like a leftist living near them, the response indicated much less tolerance.[38]

In terms of political values, Mexicans share attitudes that are both conducive and resistant to democratization. Although some aspects of democratization may become integrated effectively into the culture, others are likely to be more difficult. Nevertheless, survey data do suggest a trend in Mexican values shifting strongly in a direction supportive of democratic behavior since the 1980s.

CONCLUSION

Values play a significant role in the evolution of a political system and the behavior of its citizens. Political values, as a component of general cultural values, are most important. In particular, three categories are central to the interrelationship between societal values and political behavior: legitimacy, participation, and authoritarianism.

Mexicans have high levels of respect for and trust in certain institutions, especially churches and schools, but Mexicans have very low levels of respect for political institutions of any sort and the persons associated with them, such as bureaucrats and police. Their appraisals reflect a general lack of trust in government. This may be explained by their belief that most government agencies, and their representatives, are corrupt. Indeed, they believe corruption is the single most important obstacle to achieving democracy in Mexico. Mexicans are unusual, compared with Americans, for the low levels of respect they give to most societal institutions. This is likely to change as their own involvement in and respect for civic and social organizations grow.

Although governmental institutions receive lower levels of support, and therefore have less legitimacy in Mexico than in the United States, the universal decline in governmental legitimacy in most nations during the 1980s was less sharp in Mexico. It is likely that Mexicans reached an even lower level of support for institutions in the mid-1980s and, through the efforts of President Salinas, who personally achieved high levels of popularity in the early 1990s, recovered from that level, thus considerably reducing the overall decline in government legitimacy before 1994. Serious political and economic events throughout 1994 and the first half of 1995 reversed this pattern, destroying gains in legitimacy and bringing perceptions of the presidency and governmental institutions to new lows.

Mexicans also expressed less trust than did Americans or Canadians in their fellow human beings. Although their confidence in others rose dramatically during the 1980s, it is still substantially below that found in the United States. Nevertheless, Mexicans' remarkable increase in trust in one another is significant for their desire to increase participation and expand democratic institutions.

Other changes have also taken place in how Mexicans view their political efficacy. Although many are cynical about the election process and consequently their ability to influence government policy or leadership, a considerable shift occurred between 1988 and 1991 in the number of Mexicans who see the integrity of the process positively, stabilizing by 1994. Although more Mexicans view the election process as an accurate measure of their demands, the principal reasons for not participating, other than not being registered, relate to election fraud and lack of interest.

Not many Mexicans are highly active in voluntary social organizations. Even fewer are involved in political parties or organizations. Most of those who are politically involved are members of official party organizations—this is not surprising, given the politically interwoven corporatist structures discussed earlier. Of some surprise is Mexicans' increasing tolerance of informal channels of political participation. Not only do they favor, to a much greater degree than in 1981, direct and unorthodox political actions on par with the level of support found in the United States, but their actual involvement in such actions also jumped 700 percent in the past decade. As the legitimacy of the government fades, support for these alternatives is likely to increase toward the end of the century.

The average Mexican, however, is not in favor of radical social and economic change but prefers a peaceful, incremental approach. For example, poll after poll demonstrated public sympathy for the goals of the Zapatista National Liberation Army (EZLN), but few agreed with its original methods, specifically violence. In a 1996 poll in the newspaper *Reforma*, two-thirds of urban Mexicans surveyed did not favor the use of violence to achieve political change.[39] In fact, most Mexicans consider themselves moderate or conservative ideologically. Ideology itself is not an important determinant of party choices. Mexicans are more concerned about a candidate's willingness to improve conditions and his or her ability to do so.

Mexico is also part of a universal cultural shift described by Ronald Inglehart, Neil Nevitte, and Miguel Basáñez:

> [A] change from a world in which most people are absorbed in the tasks of sheer survival, to a world in which concern for the quality of life is becoming increasingly important. As we might expect, the peoples of Canada and the United States are well ahead of the Mexican public on this dimension, but during the 1980s, all three publics showed substantial shifts toward increasing emphasis on Postmaterialist concerns.[40]

If Mexicans incorporate increased participation and the integrity of the political process in their definition of postmaterialist values, further interest in politics is likely.

Finally, many Mexicans are interested in democratizing their political system, including increasing the competitiveness of the electoral process. There is considerable evidence of support for greater political opposition. Less evidence is available regarding Mexican attitudes toward liberty, a crucial value in appraising the potential for successful democratization. A fifth of all Mexicans today believe liberty is an essential component of democracy. Available data do suggest, however, the presence of many of the attitudes necessary for successful democratic behavior. They also show that Mexicans are still relatively intolerant of opposing views and of allowing persons holding with such views to participate politically and hold office. The crucial question remains, however, whether a delegitimized government can cope with the increasingly chaotic growing pains of political liberalization, economic deprivation, and familial and social insecurity.

President Ernesto Zedillo, who demonstrated the ability of his party to recover from a serious crisis—brought on by the assassination of its presidential candidate—has not demonstrated an equivalent capacity to govern Mexico. His image as a weak president and the perception of his cabinet— and therefore the executive branch—as uncoordinated and divided do not bode well for a gradual, peaceful political transition.

NOTES

1. For a more comprehensive definition, see Walter A. Rosenbaum, *Political Culture* (New York: Praeger, 1975), 3–11.

2. In a comparative survey of Canada, Mexico, and the United States, Ronald Inglehart, Neil Nevitte, and Miguel Basáñez found that Mexico demonstrated greater levels of "strong" confidence in *nongovernmental* institutions. See *Convergencia en norte américa, comercio, política y cultura* (Mexico City: Siglo XXI, 1994), Figure 4-3. Church and schools continued to rank strongest among Mexicans in 1997, with the police and political parties engendering the least trust. See *Este Pais*, April 1998, 27.

3. Ibid., Figure 4-2. Mexicans have also found it difficult to transfer loyalty to modern corporate forms in business, thus maintaining extensive family control. See Lavissa Lomnitz and Marisol Pérez-Lizaur, *A Mexican Elite Family, 1820–1980: Kinship, Class, and Culture* (Princeton, N.J.: Princeton University Press, 1987).

4. Richard Rose, *Politics in England: Change and Persistence* (Boston: Little, Brown, 1989), 158.

5. Alberto Hernández Medina and Luis Narros Rodríquez, eds., *Cómo somos los mexicanos* (Mexico City: CREA, 1987), 110; Miguel Basáñez, Marta Lagos, and Tatiana Beltrán, *Reportaje 1995: encuesta latino barometro* (August 1996), a survey of 1,200 urban Mexicans.

6. *Mexico Business* (March 1996), 6.

7. "Mexico 1994, A National Poll of the Mexican Electorate" (Washington, D.C., August 10, 1994), a survey of 1,526 Mexicans in all regions and sizes of communities.

8. Roderic A. Camp, *Entrepreneurs and Politics in Twentieth Century Mexico* (New York: Oxford University Press, 1989), 40.

9. Gabriel Almond and Sidney Verba, *The Civic Culture* (Boston: Little, Brown, 1965), 64.

10. Carlos B. Gil, *Hope and Frustration: Interviews with Leaders of Mexico's Political Opposition* (Wilmington, Del.: Scholarly Resources, 1992), 48–57.

11. Sheldon Annis, "Giving Voice to the Poor," *Foreign Policy*, no. 84 (Fall 1991): 100.

12. James A. McCann and Jorge I. Domínguez, "Norms of Mexican Citizenship: Are Mexicans 'Democrats' "?, Unpublished manuscript, 1995.

13. Alberto Alvarez Gutiérrez, "Cómo se sienten los mexicanos?" in *Cómo somos los mexicanos*, ed. Alberto Hernández Medina and Luis Narro Rodríguez (Mexico City: CREA, 1987), 81.

14. William H. Flanigan and Nancy H. Zingale, *Political Behavior of the American Electorate*, 7th ed. (Washington, D.C.: Congressional Quarterly, 1991), 180.

15. For discussion of each of these, see John Skirius, *José Vasconcelos y la cruzada de 1929* (Mexico City: Siglo XXI, 1978), for 1929; Albert Michaels, "The Mexican Election of 1940," Special Studies No. 5, Council on International Studies (Buffalo: State University of New York, 1971), for 1940; Edgar Butler and Jorge Bustamante, eds., *Sucesión Presidencial: The Presidential Election of 1988* (Boulder, Colo.: Westview Press, 1991), for 1988.

16. For a brief discussion of polls and elections, see Miguel Basáñez, "Elections and Political Culture in Mexico," in *Mexican Politics in Transition*, ed. Judith Gentleman (Boulder, Colo.: Westview Press, 1987), 181–84.

17. "Mexico 1994, A National Poll of the Mexican Electorate."

18. Harold W. Stanley and Richard G. Niemi, *Vital Statistics on American Politics*, 3d ed. (Washington, D.C.: Congressional Quarterly Press, 1992), 88.

19. "Algunas consideraciones sobre el proceso federal electoral de 1994," Secretaria de Gobernación, September 12, 1994, 17.

20. "La limpieza electoral en duda," "Enfoque," *La Reforma*, January 1994, 22.

21. Gabinete de estudios de opinión, S.C., reported in *etcétera*, February 17, 1994, 16–20.

22. Alvarez Gutiérrez, "Cómo se sienten los mexicanos?" 87. Specifically, in order of response, Mexicans' organization memberships were religious groups, 17.6 percent; unions, 10.3 percent; charities, 7.8 percent; educational or artistic organizations, 4.1 percent; youth groups, 3.4 percent; professional associations, 2.9 percent; ecology organizations, 2.6 percent; parties or political groups, 1.9 percent; consumer advocacy groups, 1.7 percent; human rights organizations, 1.5 percent.

23. For background on this period, see Judith Gentleman, ed., *Mexican Politics in Transition* (Boulder, Colo.: Westview Press, 1987); Arturo Alvarado Mendoza, ed., *Electoral Patterns and Perspectives in Mexico* (La Jolla, Calif.: Center for U.S.–Mexican Studies, UCSD, 1987).

24. Javier Conteras Orozco, *Chihuahua, trampa del sistema* (Mexico City: Edamex, 1987); Jaime Pérez Mendoza, "Por peteción de Bartlett, el Vaticano ordenó que hubiera misas en Chihuahua," *Proceso*, August 4, 1986, 6–13.

25. Linda Stevenson and Mitchell Seligson, "Fading Memories of the Revolution: Is Stability Eroding in Mexico?" in *Polling for Democracy: Public Opinion and Political Liberalization in Mexico*, ed. Roderic A. Camp (Wilmington, Del.: Scholarly Resources, 1996), 59–80.

26. See the numerous examples cited in Carmina Danini, "Chiapas Uprising

Apparently Inspires Demands Elsewhere," *Fort Worth Star-Telegram*, February 18, 1994, 3G.

27. Annis, "Giving Voice to the Poor," 101.

28. For examples of activities and member groups among one of Mexico's leading civic umbrella organizations, see the bulletin of the Movimiento Ciudadano por la Democracia (MCD), *Movimiento democrático*, March 1994, 15.

29. Flanigan and Zingale, *Political Behavior of the American Electorate*, 52.

30. Ibid., 107; *New York Times* poll, 1986, courtesy of Miguel Basáñez.

31. Jorge I. Domínguez and James A. McCann, "Shaping Mexico's Electoral Arena: The Construction of Partisan Cleavages in the 1988 and 1991 National Elections," *American Political Science Review* 89 (March 1995): 46; and James A. McCann, "The Mexican Electorate in a North American Context: Assessing Patterns of Political Engagement," in *Polling for Democracy: Public Opinion and Political Liberalization in Mexico*, ed. Roderic A. Camp (Wilmington, Del.: Scholarly Resources, 1996), 81–106.

32. *Los Angeles Times*, August 1989.

33. Luis Rubio, "Economic Reform and Political Liberalization," in *The Politics of Economic Liberalization in Mexico*, ed. Riodan Roett (Boulder, Colo.: Lynne Rienner, 1993), 19–20.

34. For an extended discussion, see John Booth and Mitchell Seligson, "The Political Culture of Authoritarianism in Mexico," *Latin American Research Review* 19 (1984): 106–24.

35. For comparisons with Costa Rica, a Latin American country that most Latin Americans consider "democratic," see Mitchell Seligson, "Political Culture and Democratization in Latin America," in *Latin America and Caribbean Contemporary Record*, ed. James Malloy and Eduardo A. Gamarra (New York: Holmes & Meier, 1990), A49–65.

36. Herbert McClosky and John Zaller, *The American Ethos: Public Attitudes Toward Capitalism and Democracy* (Cambridge, Mass.: Harvard University Press, 1984), 74.

37. Stanley and Niemi, *Vital Statistics on American Politics*, 28.

38. Alvarez Gutiérrez, "Cómo se sienten los mexicanos," 86.

39. *Dallas Morning News*, September 8, 1996, 1A.

40. Inglehart, Nevitte, and Basáñez, *Convergencia en Norte América*, chap. 7, 3.

4

Political Values and Their Origins: Partisanship, Alienation, and Tolerance

Public support of the Mexican government is substantial. The few national interview studies that have been conducted show that the overwhelming majority of politically conscious Mexicans are positively allegiant to the nation, whatever criticisms and complaints they may have about specific institutions, practices, and men. However, it has also been argued—sometimes on the basis of the same data—that what the masses "give" to the system is not their support in any positive sense but rather their acquiescence, often expressed in noninvolvement and apathy. These two perspectives are not at all incompatible; both provide important, albeit partial, views of popular orientations to politics.

RICHARD FAGEN AND WILLIAM TUOHY,
Politics and Privilege in a Mexican City

Many experiences have a bearing on the formation of values in general, and political values specifically. Values are general orientations toward basic aspects of life: abstract principles that guide behavior.[1] Children, for example, are affected by the attitudes of their parents, and most children

---

Values: general orientations toward basic aspects of life, abstract principles that guide behavior.

---

carry the consequences with them for years.[2] Other persons have reported the influence of education and the specific role of teachers and professors.[3] Experiences other than those within the family and in school contribute to the formative years of many citizens, especially when the experiences are

77

broad and deep, permeating the environment of an entire nation. The Great
Depression, for example, tremendously affected Americans, their political
and social values, and their voting behavior.[4] Undoubtedly, although we
have no surveys to prove it empirically, the revolution exerted a like influence in Mexico.[5] In the mid-1990s, Mexicans identified liberty and justice most strongly with the Revolution.[6] A small exploratory study of workers in three cities in 1978 revealed surprisingly strong memories of the
revolution among third-generation Mexicans. Although the size of the sample makes it impossible to generalize about the data, 45 percent reported
family participation in the event, and 25 percent reported lost property or
injury of a family member. Family involvement was associated with fears
of renewed violence and has helped discourage political protests in the present period.[7] Some individuals, generally as young adults, consciously or
unconsciously take on the values of their peers or of their working environment.

   Although there are few studies of formative phenomena in Mexico,
we know from studies of other countries that these are among the primary
sources. We also know that certain variables impinge most on political attitudes and values and typically include race, ethnicity, socioeconomic
background, level of education, occupation, region, and religion. Although
Mexico has an Indian population, Indians account for only approximately
8 percent of the population, depending on the definition of *Indian*. Indians,
however, are a minor political and economic presence and hence have not
been treated as a separate group in national political surveys. The typical
Mexican thinks of himself or herself as, and is, mestizo, thereby minimiz-
ing race or ethnicity as a significant variable in voting behavior. That circumstance could change if elections became more competitive and, more
important, if Indians in certain states or regions were to organize themselves politically. The consequences of this on a national level can be seen
as a result of the Zapatista National Liberation Army's (EZLN) uprising
in Chiapas in January 1994, which affected the larger political context
through 1995. This is particularly the case because the EZLN has demanded
indigenous autonomy in its negotiations with the Mexican government.

   Because of sharp social-class divisions, Mexican values are likely to
be influenced by income level. Furthermore, the origins of Mexico's leaders, particularly political and economic, set them apart from the ordinary
citizen. Consequently, it is important to ascertain differences between mass
and elite political opinion. And because political knowledge has much to
do with education, and disparities in schooling are substantial in Mexico,
education is a way of distinguishing one Mexican from another and is
strongly related to social class and occupation.[8] Historically, as suggested

in Chapter 2, regionalism played an important role in national politics. Although it had declined in prominence by the 1960s, it continues to exert an influence over some values, in the same way that it does in the United States. As opposition political movements strengthen their representation at the local and state levels, as indicated by the National Action Party's gubernatorial victories in 1995 and 1997 (Baja California, Guanajuato, Jalisco, Nueuo León, and Querétaro), and as regional–ethnic groups such as the Zapatistas focus on local social and economic issues, geography will become more important. Religion is often still another determinant of political behavior and in many societies, plays a role in the formation of social and political values, especially when religious diversity is present. In Mexico, however, the predominance of Catholicism has obviated sharp religious differences. Most of the disharmony historically related to religion can be described as a battle between secularism and religion, not among religions. Nonetheless, the rise of evangelical Protestantism throughout Latin America since the 1960s, although not yet as greatly felt in Mexico, and the presence of a small proportion of nonbelievers and atheists, render religious beliefs deserving of consideration, too.

INCOME AND POLITICS

The confidence people have in a political system and in their ability to influence the outcome of political decisions—level of political efficacy—depends on many things. One is income level. People who have achieved economic success not only perceive the system as fairer and more beneficial to their own interests but also believe they can change aspects of it that they dislike. When Gabriel Almond and Sidney Verba published the first results of their multicountry study in the 1960s, they declared that Mexicans had a much lower sense of political efficacy than did Americans or the English but was equivalent to that of the Germans.[9] In the late 1960s Rafael Segovia replicated the research on political efficacy among schoolchildren and found that Mexican children were characterized by low levels of political efficacy. He also found that the parents' socioeconomic background had something to do with those levels; as the parents' income increased, so did the children's political efficacy and confidence in the system.[10]

Table 4-1 illustrates the 1989 levels of political efficacy nationally by income. Half the respondents with high incomes believed they could do something about electoral fraud. By contrast, only one in four low-income

Table 4-1 Mexicans' Political Efficacy, by Socioeconomic Status

Response to the Statement "Can do nothing about electoral fraud"	Income Level			All Respondents (%)
	Low (%)	Medium (%)	High (%)	
Definitely true	11	6	7	8.9
True	50	47	32	47.3
False	27	38	47	31.5
Definitely false	3	5	8	4.0
Not sure	7	3	5	5.6
No answer	2	2	1	2.7

Source: Los Angeles Times poll, August 1989.

respondents so believed. In a study of residents of a state capital in the 1970s, Richard Fagen and William Tuohy also found very low levels of political efficacy; in fact, only 9 percent of the respondents thought they could do anything about a problem in their community.[11] Even so, the two researchers also discerned major differences based on income, with a sharp difference between upper-income and lower-income groups. The level of national political efficacy in the 1960s, when 38 percent of Mexicans thought they could change conditions, still holds in the 1990s, when 35 percent believe they can alter conditions. In the United States the feeling of political efficacy is higher: in 1988, 54 percent believed they could affect government, a figure that has been more or less consistent since 1974.[12] Although income is more evenly distributed in the United States than in Mexico, lower-income Americans also indicate less political efficacy, but not as little as do similarly situated Mexicans.

These findings do not signify that Mexicans cannot overcome a low sense of political efficacy. As Ann Craig and Wayne Cornelius argue, low-income people who become active in nongovernmental organizations and make demands on the system collectively develop a stronger sense of efficacy.[13] The growing numbers of such groups and their greater involvement ultimately will increase participation and enhance political efficacy.[14] Finally, economic growth itself, if it increases the proportion of Mexicans receiving higher incomes, likewise will enhance political efficacy.

The presence of some authoritarian values in Mexican culture was discussed earlier. In his survey of children in the 1960s Segovia found that authoritarianism was very much embedded in their value system. It is logical that those persons who have benefited least from the political system would turn toward opposition and alternative political choices. In fact, however, the reverse is true. Lower-income groups are slightly more *intolerant* of opposition growth and are least likely to encourage political alter-

Table 4-2 Mexicans' Political Tolerance, by Socioeconomic Status

Response to Statement "Other parties should increase strength"	Income Level			All Respondents (%)
	High (%)	Medium (%)	Low (%)	
Favor	62	62	54	56.3
Only the Institutional Revolutionary Party (PRI)	27	26	24	25.0
Not sure	7	10	16	13.5
No answer	4	2	6	5.2

Source: Los Angeles Times poll, August 1989.

natives. Regarding opposition parties, differences among income groups are slight, except when it comes to answering a question about whether they should be stronger (see Table 4-2).

Analysts of Americans' voting behavior have always been attentive to variables affecting political sympathies for the Republicans and Democrats. Their studies suggest that among the most important is personal income. This was also true in the case of Mexicans. The government party, the PRI, obtained its strongest support from upper-income voters; its weakest from low-income voters (see Table 4-3). Although low-income voters did not sympathize in large numbers with the populist, left-of-center opposition represented by the PRD, they proportionately represented its biggest constituency, although in percentages roughly equivalent to middle-income Mexicans. Sixteen percent of middle-income Mexicans sympathized with the PRD, compared with only 5 percent of higher-income Mexicans. By 1991, however, lower-income support for the PRD dropped to only 7 percent.[15] The PAN, considered by analysts to be a right-of-center party ideologically, not surprisingly attracts a disproportionate

Table 4-3 Mexicans' Partisan Sympathies, by Socioeconomic Status

Sympathy for Party	Income Level			All Respondents (%)
	High (%)	Middle (%)	Low (%)	
Institutional Revolutionary Party (PRI)	44	38	26	31.4
National Action Party (PAN)	21	13	12	13.1
Democratic Revolutionary Party (PRD)	5	16	17	15.5
Other	3	3	3	3.2
None	21	23	32	28.1
Don't know	4	5	7	6.4
No answer	1	1	2	2.2

Source: Los Angeles Times poll, August 1989.

percentage of high-income sympathy. The August 1989 *Los Angeles Times* poll is also important for what it tells us about voter values. These people who receive higher incomes and are more highly educated and therefore are characterized by higher levels of political sophistication are more decisive about their political choices and sympathies. They are the least likely to have no party sympathies. On the other hand, low-income Mexicans are more likely to be independent.

EDUCATION AND POLITICS

A variable closely related to income in determining political preference is education. Access to education, especially in a country like Mexico where opportunities are fewer than in the United States, is strongly related to parental income; the higher the income, the more likely a person will attend and *complete* higher education. For example, of the students at the National University in the early 1990s, more than 90 percent were from families with incomes in the upper 15 percent.[16] Many Mexicans attend the public universities, the fees of which are minimal, but most low-income students do not complete the degree requirements. Students with higher education obtain the necessary credentials to pursue the most prestigious professions, just as they do elsewhere, and thus on the whole earn more.

With education come knowledge, social prestige, economic success, and greater self-confidence. Consequently, when Mexicans were asked whether they could do something about political fraud, that is, effect political change, nearly 60 percent of those with higher education believed they could (Table 4-4). In contrast, a nearly equal percentage who had received only a primary education believed they could not change political

Table 4-4 Mexicans' Political Efficacy, by Level of Education

Response to Statement "Can do nothing about electoral fraud"	Education Level				All Respondents (%)
	Primary (%)	Secondary (%)	Preparatory (%)	University (%)	
Definitely true	11	8	6	9	8.9
True	48	52	51	31	47.6
False	26	32	33	49	31.7
Definitely false	2	4	6	8	4.0
Not sure	10	3	3	2	5.6
No answer	4	1	1	1	2.2

Source: Los Angeles Times poll, August 1989.

conditions. Expressed differently, only half as many of those with a primary education (28 percent) as with a college education or higher (57 percent) thought they could change political conditions. In the United States, education affects responses in the same direction and to the same degree.[17] More than twenty years ago, Richard Fagen and William Tuohy discovered an even more exaggerated sense of political inefficacy among poorly educated Mexicans: Only 9 percent thought they could change things.[18] If efficacy is taken to the next logical step, participation measured in terms of voting, a strong relationship exists between higher education and actual voter turnout. For example, 46 percent of the population has a primary education, but those with a primary education accounted for only 36 percent of the ballots cast in 1994. Mexicans with college degrees (only 8 percent of the population) accounted for twice as many (16 percent) of the actual voters.[19]

Education not only affects citizen confidence and knowledge about the political system but also determines to some extent citizens' acceptance of certain values. One of the values that education moderates is intolerance of other political ideas and views. Nearly one in three Mexicans who have completed college education favors expanding electoral competition (see Table 4-5), thereby reducing the potential for authoritarian politics. More than any other variable, including income, level of education reduces political intolerance and lessens support for authoritarian political behavior. Educated Mexicans are sure where they stand on political issues, and they are committed to greater acceptance of nonstandard political views. Increased availability of education in combination with higher incomes will chip away at the one party-dominant system, which does not mean, however, that voter support for the PRI will automatically diminish. This can be seen from survey data collected immediately before and during the highly competitive 1994 presidential elections. In May, two months before

Table 4-5 Mexicans' Political Tolerance, by Level of Education

Response to Statement "Other parties should increase strength"	Education Level				All Respondents (%)
	Primary (%)	Secondary (%)	Preparatory (%)	University (%)	
Favor	47	58	64	73	56.3
Only the Institutional Revolutionary Party (PRI)	28	24	23	18	25.0
Not sure	18	13	9	6	13.5
No answer	7	4	4	3	5.2

Source: Los Angeles Times poll, August 1989.

the election, only 32 percent of college-educated respondents said they would vote for the PRI, compared with 36 percent for the PAN. But on the day of the elections, when the PRI garnered approximately 50 percent of the ballots cast, 41 percent—compared with the 36 percent of college-educated Mexicans that voted for the PAN—actually voted for the PRI.[20] Although the PRI did receive the highest percentage of the college-educated vote, proportionately more Mexicans with a preparatory education or higher voted for both the PAN and the PRD, although more for the former, as would be expected. In any election, as in the case of 1994, other contextual political variables may be important, and such issues as continuity and stability override concerns about alternative choices.

In the United States, education as a single variable does not have a dramatic effect,[21] but because Mexico also is characterized by sharper class divisions, the relationship is stronger (see Table 4-6). If both the PRI and the PAN are thought of as center-right alternatives and the PRD as a center-left choice, the educational influence appears rather strong. Basically, as educational levels increase from primary to university, voters prefer the two traditional parties (the PRI and PAN). The inverse relationship is true for the PRD, which receives the least support from college-educated voters. However, the most exaggerated relationship is between college-educated voters and preference for the PAN, the party of the Right. Nearly twice as many college graduates as Mexicans in general prefer this party. Again, as with the issue of political efficacy, Mexicans with low educational levels are the least likely to have a definite choice, compared with only half as many college graduates who express no party preferences.

Table 4-6 Mexicans' Party Preference, by Level of Education

Preferred Party	Education Level				All Respondents (%)
	Primary (%)	Secondary (%)	Preparatory (%)	University (%)	
Institutional Revolutionary Party (PRI)	27	34	33	38	31.4
National Action Party (PAN)	10	13	14	24	13.1
Democratic Revolutionary Party	15	17	17	12	15.5
Other	3	4	3	2	3.2
None	35	24	24	18	28.1
Don't know	7	6	8	4	6.4
No answer	4	1	1	2	2.2

Source: Los Angeles Times poll, August 1989.

RELIGION AND POLITICS

Students of the Catholic heritage in Mexico identify it as an important contributor to authoritarian values within the family and within the culture generally. When ranking the role of God in their lives, Mexicans and Americans give it equal importance; only one in four Canadians consider God important.[22] Religion's potential for influencing the formation of societal norms is enhanced by the fact that most Mexicans consider themselves religious (see Table 4-7), and 85 percent declare they received a religious education in their homes.[23] Although it is true that the number of Mexicans who attend church services has fallen since the turn of the century, the number who attend regularly is higher than is typically believed. In 1991, 44 to 45 percent of all Catholics went to church weekly or more often, and 14 to 19 percent monthly.[24] In 1994, three-quarters of all Mexicans described themselves as practicing Catholics.

Given the overwhelming dominance of Catholicism, it would be useful to measure its effect on political values according to the intensity of belief. For example, when Gabriel Almond and Sidney Verba completed their classic study, which largely ignored religion, they discovered that the more religious a person was, regardless of faith, the more intolerant of others' political beliefs he or she would be.[25] I will offer some observations regarding the variable of intensity, but for comparative purposes, it is helpful to identify the potential influence of religion on some of the major political values discussed.

How does religion affect political efficacy? Table 4-8 presents responses according to religious belief. Because Catholics account for the overwhelming majority of Mexicans, their views and that of the average Mexican are likely to correspond closely, but Protestant Mexicans and those professing no religious beliefs, differ. First, Protestants' views of political efficacy are not nearly as definitive as those of Catholics; in other words,

Table 4-7 Mexicans' Religious Affiliations

Affiliation	Percentage of All Respondents
Catholic	92.2
Protestant	5.1
Other	.7
None	1.7
No answer	.3

Source: Los Angeles Times poll, August 1989.

Table 4-8 Political Efficacy of Mexicans by Religion

| Response to Statement "Can do nothing about fraud" | Religion | | | All Respondents (%) |
	Catholic (%)	Protestant (%)	None (%)	
Definitely true	9.1	2.6	12.8	8.9
True	47.4	46.8	46.2	47.3
False	31.3	35.1	30.8	31.5
Definitely false	4.1	0	5.1	4.0
Not sure	5.3	13.0	0	5.6
No answer	2.8	2.6	5.1	2.7

Source: Los Angeles Times poll, August 1989.

fewer thought they could definitely do something or nothing about fraud. They were more than twice as likely as Catholics to be unsure about their ability to affect political outcomes. Second, those professing no religion and those who were atheists had much stronger views. In fact, they were more likely to express views than religious Mexicans were about the political process and overall were more cynical about their ability to change conditions. Although there is no easy explanation for why Protestants are less sure of their political efficacy than Catholics are, the reason for stronger definitive responses among the nonreligious Mexicans can largely be attributed to education: The nonreligious are much better educated. Educated Mexicans are informed about the political process and consequently tend to have more definite ideas. Education may also explain differences between Protestants and Catholics; Protestants as a group are less educated, which contributes to their greater indecisiveness.

The contribution of religion to authoritarian political values is embedded in the Mexican culture. It would be difficult, if not impossible, to separate religion from cultural values in general. As Charles Davis pointed out, "The Catholic Church might function as an agent of indirect political socialization. . . . The authoritarian values and norms that the Church encourages for interactions with ecclesiastical authorities (deference, obedience, and respect for hierarchy) can also structure interactions with secular authorities."[26] The impact of different religions on political tolerance, however, can be measured. Among the three groups of Mexicans in 1989—Catholics, Protestants, and the nonreligious—Protestants supported the most liberal position, one favorable to the growth of opposition parties, although not to a significantly greater degree than did Catholics (see Table 4-9). Protestants' sympathies for the progressive political posture might be attributable in part to their self-perception as a fledgling minority in a dominant Catholic culture. Given their status in the religious realm, they may

Table 4-9 Mexicans' Political Tolerance by Religion

Response to Question "Do you believe parties other than the governing party should increase their strength?"	Religious Beliefs			All Respondents (%)
	Catholics (%)	Protestants (%)	None (%)	
Yes	55.1	59.7	43.6	55.1
Only the Institutional Revolutionary Party (PRI) should remain strong	25.1	15.6	20.5	24.5
Not sure	12.3	22.1	25.6	13.2
No answer	7.4	2.6	10.3	7.2

Source: Los Angeles Times poll, August 1989.

have a certain sympathy for minority political groups battling the PRI's hegemony. Again, although Protestants were less sure of their answers than were Catholics, they gave very low support to the PRI as the only party. Growth in Protestantism would provide fertile grounds for opposition parties. The probability is especially significant because Protestantism's greatest inroads have been in lower-income, rural areas, the very districts where the PRI reports its heaviest support. Interestingly, the nonreligious also were less supportive of a single party than Catholics were, but oddly, they did not favor a corresponding strengthening of other parties. A very high percentage were unsure, contradicting the unequivocal position of their answers on the issue of political efficacy and the rationale behind it.

What has most intrigued students of Mexican politics and religion is an assumed relationship between Catholicism and party affiliation. The reason for this assumption is that the National Action Party adopted many of the ideas of the European and Latin American Christian Democratic movements. Moreover, prominent early leaders of the party were known to be active Catholics.[27] Basically, the relationship between Catholicism and sympathy for the PAN is weak. In fact, as I pointed out in a more comprehensive examination of the issue, all the survey data from the 1980s and 1990s indicate that the only relationship between PAN and Catholicism is between the party and a tiny group of Catholics, 3.4 percent, who attend church daily (see Table 4-10). This group does differ from the rest of the population in its intensity of support for the PAN and the higher proportions of votes cast for the 1988 PAN presidential candidate, Manuel Clouthier.

As I have argued elsewhere, on the basis of church attendance, Mexicans indicate no significant difference in their party preferences, suggesting that contrary to a common belief, being Catholic has little or nothing

Table 4-10 Religious Partisanship in Mexico

| | Religious Beliefs | | |
Response to Question "Do you sympathize with any political party? Which one?"	Intense Catholic (%)	Moderate Catholic (%)	General Population (%)
National Action Party	18.2	9.5	11.4
Democratic Revolutionary Party	2.0	6.5	6.3
Institutional Revolutionary Party	9.2	25.1	24.8

Source: Miguel Basáñez, *Encuesta nacional de opinión pública, iglesia–estado*, 1990.

to do with party sympathy in Mexico. In fact, among those Mexicans attending church daily, only 12 percent supported the PAN, just half a percentage point above the national average.[28]

Religious and party preferences are revealing, even if a tie between the PAN and Catholicism does not exist. Indeed, it is the nonreligious and the Protestants who exhibit reformist political sympathies, not the Catholics. Using religion as a measurement, the strongest PAN supporters are Mexicans professing no religion (see Table 4-11). The nonreligious Mexican is also the weakest supporter of the PRI, the establishment party. Mexicans professing no religion have given stronger-than-average support for the PRD, suggesting their sympathy for the newest, most radical opposition movement. Again, their higher levels of education make them more receptive to political alternatives.

Protestants illustrate diverse political sympathies, indicating they may be a more heterogeneous group in terms of background characteristics. Protestants are much more diverse, however, in religious composition.

Table 4-11 Mexicans' Partisan Sympathies, by Religion

| | Religion | | | All |
Sympathy for Party	Catholic	Protestant	None	Respondents
None	27.5	35.1	28.2	27.9
Strong National Action Party (PAN)	5.2	5.2	7.7	5.2
National Action Party (PAN)	8.2	2.6	2.6	7.8
Strong Democratic Revolutionary Party (PRD)	6.6	10.4	12.8	7.0
Democratic Revolutionary Party (PRD)	8.4	9.1	7.7	8.5
Strong Institutional Revolutionary Party (PRI)	16.8	9.1	10.3	16.2
Instititional Revolutionary Party (PRI)	14.9	18.2	10.3	15.0
Other	3.2	1.3	5.1	3.2
No answer	8.9	9.1	15.4	9.1

Source: Los Angeles Times poll, August 1989.

From 1992 to 1994, the Secretariat of Government registered 2,010 religious associations in response to newly introduced constitutional reforms. Of those, only 21 percent were Catholic, and 77 percent were evangelical. The evangelicals could be subdivided as follows: independent groups, 48 percent; Baptists, 29 percent; Pentecostals, 21 percent; and traditional Protestants (such as Methodists), 2 percent.[29] This level of diversity is very important to differences in partisanship, because as recent research from the United States reveals, churches do have distinctive political orientations, and the extent of theological traditionalism prevailing in a congregation moves individual members toward more conservative positions on social issues and makes them more likely to identify themselves as political conservatives.[30] In short, substantial differences in religious–political orientations, if they exist, are most likely to occur within each individual religious community.

Protestant support for the National Action Party is about half that given by the average Mexican, regardless of religious belief. Protestants proportionately give their strongest preferences to the PRD, although not at the level of nonreligious Mexicans. They too, therefore, are more sympathetic to the newest party and to the underdog. They give somewhat less support than average to the PRI, but more important, they rank much lower among those Mexicans *strongly* supportive of the PRI.

The data in Table 4-11 suggest overall that non-Catholics, religious or otherwise, are more sympathetic to newer opposition parties and that they are therefore sources from which those parties can recruit successfully. The impact of religion on Mexican partisan politics, however, will continue to be moderated by the small numbers of non-Catholics. If Protestantism's growth were to mirror that found in Central America, where numbers have risen extraordinarily in the past two decades, religion could become a significant variable in Mexican voting behavior.[31] Recent research among Mexican evangelicals suggests that "a nascent Evangelical social and political movement is underway. . . . The evidence is fairly clear and seems to be mounting that a once reserved and almost invisible religious minority is now emerging and demanding a seat at the table."[32]

Still on the subject of religion, it is important to note that religious issues once again became prominent in the political arena at the behest of former President Salinas. Such major issues as the right of priests to vote, legal recognition of the church, and diplomatic relations with the Vatican were hotly debated in the 1990s.[33] Of all the issues involving the church and the state in Mexico, the political role of the church is the most controversial. Surveys from 1983 through 1990 make clear that between two-thirds to three-fourths of all Mexicans believe the church should not participate in politics. Even Catholics who regularly attend mass firmly reject political participation by the church. This is not to say that Catholicism and the church as an institution are not influential in Mexican life. Rather, Mexicans are a product of a liberal and Catholic heritage, and they distinguish between some liberal principles and other principles having to do with the church and the role of religion (Catholicism) in their society.

As I stated elsewhere, and recent survey data confirm, many Mexicans are interested in redefining the church's role in society. Their redefinition has serious, long-term implications for the role of the church as both an institution and a religion in Mexicans' political life. Fewer than half of all Mexicans define the church's task as religious, whereas more than half viewed its primary activities as political, social, moral, economic, or something else. This suggests that large numbers of Mexicans do not view church activities in a narrow and traditional sense, and this same group is most critical of the church's response to social and economic needs.[34] In 1994 large numbers of Mexicans believed that the Catholic Church should become involved in social work, health, and education, and more than two-thirds believed that the government should take the church into account on important social issues.[35]

GENDER AND POLITICS

One of the influences on values about which we have the least understanding is the role of gender in Mexico. A number of studies of Latin America examine political behavior from a female viewpoint. Research on the political behavior of women in the United States have rarely discovered sharp differences with men, but they typically note that women are not as interested in politics, have less knowledge of politics, and are somewhat more alienated from the political system than are men. In fact, one study concludes that a high level of alienation was associated with the rise of feminism and the recognition of their exclusionary treatment by the system.[36] Almond and Verba found the same pattern for Mexican women in the 1960s but with differences that were much more extreme.[37] For example, when asked if they discussed politics, 29 percent of Mexican women said yes, compared with 55 percent of Mexican men. In the United States, although fewer women than men discussed politics, the gap was relatively small: 70 versus 83 percent. Gender differences continue to remain marginally stronger.

Differences in political values and behavior attributable to gender can be explained by roles assigned to Mexican women.[38] Although many women today obtain an advanced education and a large percentage are in the workforce, opportunities for women are fewer than for men. In part this is due to education, since women over the age of fifteen accounted for 63 percent of illiterate Mexicans.[39] Moreover, the most detailed study of their values implies that most women are not yet committed to liberation and to a change in their traditional roles.[40] Given these and other conditions that have restricted women's roles in society and hence in politics, it is natural that they might feel more powerless to change the political system. A remarkable change in political efficacy seems to have occurred since the 1960s, however (see Table 4-12). When Fagen and Tuohy carried out a study of Jalapa, Veracruz, in the 1970s, they found extreme differences between men and women, regardless of social class. Typically, only half as many women as men reported high levels of political efficacy.[41] By 1989 almost no statistical difference existed between men and women on this issue. This finding is similar to recent U.S. data on women and men.[42] Only in agreeing with the statement that they "can do nothing about fraud" is definitely false do Mexican women differ significantly from men.

As Mexicans make the transition from a more authoritarian political culture to one characterized by democratic characteristics, it is desirable to understand women's potential role. Given their smaller percentage of definitive responses, women might be expected to be more accepting than men are of new political alternatives. In fact, however, women differ little from men on the issue of political tolerance; indeed, they tend to be slightly more in favor of the status quo and for a continuation of PRI dominance. Where women differ from men politically in Mexico is on political activism. Although few Mexicans have actually participated in some type of political protest, only half as many women as men have done so.[43]

These data could convey the false impression that women are not po-

Table 4-12 Mexicans' Political Efficacy, by Gender

Response to Statement "Can do nothing about electoral fraud"	Gender		All Respondents (%)
	Male (%)	Female (%)	
Definitely true	9	9	8.9
True	47	49	47.6
False	31	32	31.7
Definitely false	6	2	4.0
Not sure	5	6	5.6
No answer	2	3	2.2

Source: Los Angeles Times poll, August 1989.

litically active. In fact, recent research shows that women in urban areas are the backbone of the social and civic organizations that have flourished in Mexico in recent years. As one researcher commented, "Independent organizations are giving women a political experience which is profoundly affecting their lives, leading them to question the power relations which limit them at societal level, as well as within their personal, familial relations."[44]

This active feminist presence emerged in earnest in the 1970s, especially in Mexico City. By the 1980s, a network of women's organizations existed throughout Mexico, linking together NGOs, unions, and urban poor and middle-class organizations. As was true elsewhere in the region, socioeconomic differences among women created tensions in generating a common agenda.[45] The expansion of women into different employment opportunities, and the changing political landscape in the 1990s, encouraged the growth of women's organizations and increased the breadth and influence of a feminine political agenda. Sex crimes became the most important issue contributing to unification of a feminist agenda. More recently, as the democratic transition in electoral politics became a reality, women fought successfully for affirmative action quotas among party candidates for political office. Members of the PRD were the first to achieve this goal, persuading the party to require 20 percent of its candidates to be women in 1990. A year later they increased that level of representation to 30 percent of the party's candidates, and the same percentage among the party's national executive committee. Although PAN refused to pass such a mandate, the PRI accepted the same percentage levels among its national congressional candidates in 1996.[46] Some state legislatures have also begun replicating these patterns.

Studies of European countries have generally found women to be somewhat ideologically more conservative than men.[47] This does not hold for Mexican women today. However, more of them are uncommitted or support centrist views than men do, and fewer identify with leftist political ideologies.[48] Typically, women everywhere are less interested than men in politics and hence participate less; this also is true of Mexican women.[49] The ideological difference between men and women is translated into sympathy for political parties. Contrary to what some observers might allege, Mexican women express no more sympathy for the PAN, the conservative party, than do men. In fact, in a 1991 national survey, the PAN received stronger support from men than women. Women differ from men only slightly in support for the populist leftist party, the PRD, showing less sympathy.

REGION AND POLITICS

Many years ago Lesley Byrd Simpson wrote the classic *Many Mexicos.* *Many* in the title referred in large part to regionalism's influence on Mexican values. As Mexico developed and communications improved, regional differences declined, but they did not disappear. Economically speaking, the north is highly developed. It is characterized by heavy in-migration, dynamic change, industrialization, and of course, its proximity to and economic and cultural linkages with the United States. The south, on the other hand, is the least developed economically. It is rural; has a large Indian population, mainly in Oaxaca and Chiapas; and is the most isolated from the cultural mainstream. The center, which includes the Federal District, has been the traditional source of political leadership, religious infrastructure, industrialization, and intellectual activity.[50]

Regional differences can be translated into political behavior. In the first place, interest in politics varies among individual citizens on the basis of many variables, and region may be prominent among them. Northern and Mexico City residents are most interested in politics, measured by its importance to their daily lives. Furthermore, their level of sophistication produces an interest in politics that leads to greater political competition. As the data in Table 4-13 show, a majority of Mexicans, typically three out of four, discuss politics. But among those who *discuss it frequently*, nearly twice as many do so in the north and in Mexico City as in the south. It is impossible to determine whether Mexicans' interest in politics has increased electoral competitiveness in both regions or whether electoral competitiveness has exaggerated their interest. It is fair to conclude, however, that interest and activity are interrelated.[51]

Politically, regional differences have translated into electoral behav-

Table 4-13 Mexicans' Interest in Politics, by Region

Response to Statement "How often politics are discussed"	Region			
	North (%)	Center (%)	South (%)	Mexico City (%)
Frequently	19	13	11	18
Occasionally	53	58	63	54
Never	25	26	24	27
Don't know	3	3	2	1

Source: World Values Survey, 1990, courtesy of Miguel Basáñez.

ior. The National Action Party finds considerable strength in the north, where its more conservative economic platform has appeal. Baja California, located in this region, in 1989 elected the first PAN governor in this century, followed by Chihuahua in 1992. In 1995 Baja California became the only state to reelect an opposition governor. A Mexican expert on the region concluded that regional qualities contributed to what he labeled the early "citizenization" of the region, signifying civic activism.[52] Many Mexicans believe that its industrialized sector, concentrated in the Nuevo León capital city of Monterrey, produces people of a capitalist culture who hold attitudes different from those of Mexicans generally. The mythology is borne out by survey data. Repeated questions whose specific responses might connote stronger support for existing institutions suggest that northerners are much more likely to share that perspective than persons in other regions. For example, they have much more confidence in the legal system; they give much more positive marks to the armed forces; and they express a more favorable impression of police, who have the confidence of few Mexicans.[53]

In contrast, the south has been a bedrock of support for the PRI; indeed, without it the PRI would not have been able to sustain its victory, real or fraudulent, in the 1988 elections.[54] Because of the region's high percentage of agricultural workers with lower levels of income and education, one could expect that southerners would express lower levels of political efficacy than northerners. The data in Table 4-14 show a sharp contrast between the two cohorts in terms of self-perceived ability to alter political conditions, especially if we consider only the true and false responses to the statement that one can do nothing about electoral fraud. About the same percentage from each region says they can do nothing. But northerners, more than any other cohort, believe they can do something. Nearly half again as many northerners as southerners are of this opinion. Southerners have the least confidence in their political effectiveness.

Table 4-14 Mexicans' Political Efficacy, by Region

Response to Statement "Can do nothing about electoral fraud"	Region				All Respondents (%)
	North (%)	Center (%)	Mexico City (%)	South (%)	
True	54	58	60	55	56.5
False	41	37	31	28	35.7
Not Sure	4	3	6	11	5.6
No answer	1	2	3	5	2.2

Source: Los Angeles Times poll, August 1989.

Place of residence can also affect other values, including religion, which in turn, as was shown earlier, may have some effect on partisan political preferences. In terms of authoritarian values, the south, center, and north are indistinguishable (see Table 4-15). Only when respondents were asked about their sympathies for the major parties did region produce important differences. In Mexico's most dynamic regions—those showing the highest levels of economic growth—the opposition, primarily the PAN, gained a stronghold. The PAN's primary source of sympathizers is the north and the Federal District, including the Mexico City metropolitan area. The south and the center, with some exceptions, provide fewer sympathizers for this party. It also remains strong in the west, and performed well in several central states in 1997. Contrary to what might be expected, the PRI has the greatest appeal in the north and the center. How does this square with election results, in which the PRI obtains most of the south's vote? The answer can be found among voters who sympathized with no party. Nearly half of all Mexicans residing in the south are independents without strong party sympathies; independents nationally account for a little more than one-quarter of all citizens. The PRD, at its apex nationally in 1989, counted numerous adherents in Mexico City and in several central states, notably Morelos and Michoacán. It demonstrated its strength again in these states in 1997, and decisively won control of Mexico City in the capital's first mayoralty race in seventy years. Again, residents of the north proved most decisive in their political views and were willing to express an opinion, followed by capital city residents. The data reveal that the south is a

Table 4-15 Mexicans' Partisan Sympathies, by Region

Sympathy for Party	Region				All Respondents (%)	
	North (%)	Central (%)	Mexico City (%)	South (%)	1989	1994
Institutional Revolutionary Party (PRI)	41	35	24	18	31.4	38.8
National Action Party (PAN)	17	8	16	9	13.1	20.6
Democratic Revolutionary Party (PRD)	10	18	25	11	15.5	13.2
Other	5	2	4	1	3.2	4.6
None	21	30	19	48	28.1	22.8
Don't know	5	3	11	9	6.4	—
No answer	3	2	2	3	2.2	—

Source: Los Angeles Times poll, August 1989; Miguel Basáñez, "Problems in Interpreting Electoral Polls in Authoritarian Countries: Lessons from the 1994 Mexican Election," *International Social Science Journal*, No. 146 (December 1995): 643–50.

fertile region for opposition-party growth if opposition parties can offer something the southerners seek. The opposition successfully exploited this opportunity in 1994 and in 1997. Together, PAN and PRD won 134 of 300 federal congressional seats.[55]

The PRD was able to exploit the peculiarities of indigenous, rural dissent in Chiapas during the gubernatorial elections of 1994. Although the PRI claimed to have won that race fairly and its candidate, Eduardo Robledo, took office, the PRD made its largest gains ever in a southern state, demonstrating the PRI's potential weaknesses, and also that under certain conditions and a well-organized leadership, the PRD can generate high levels of interest and participation. It should not be concluded, however, that just because of the rebellion led by the Zapatista Army of National Liberation and the conflict in the state in 1994, all regions with similar general conditions would respond in the same way. The PRD provided strong competition in the south in 1997.

Regardless of the variables, Mexicans residing in the north are generally more interested in politics, discuss politics more frequently, and participate at higher levels in various forms of political behavior. Higher levels of political interest, activism, and sophistication are associated with higher levels of economic development, education, and urbanization. In turn, these qualities are most likely to promote the development of alternative political views, sympathy for political parties not in power, and opposition to the PRI and its decision-making style. One of the most strongly held beliefs among all Mexicans is that decision making is inaccessible and that local and state policymaking should be more autonomous and less under the thumb of the national authorities. Increasing political and economic difficulties at the beginning of the Zedillo administration suggest a growing pattern of resistance by state and local governments to unpopular, national executive decisions. Although these patterns are more likely to take hold in states or regions sharing qualities similar to those prevailing in the north—such as in the western state of Jalisco and the city of Guadalajara, where the PAN won an overwhelming victory in early 1995—victories in traditional opposition strongholds will have a ripple effect throughout other regions, as they demonstrated clearly in 1997 and 1998.

AGE AND POLITICS

Age often determines important variations in values and, more important, indicates changes in the offing as generations reach political maturity.[56] In their significant comprehensive study, Inglehart, Nevitte, and Basáñez found that thirty-four issues had been characterized by intergenerational change in the past decade.[57] Inglehart and others had discovered in earlier studies that economic conditions during a person's preadult years were the most significant determinant of adult values. Changing economic conditions, then, are likely to alter values from one generation to the next. For example, in the first *World Values Survey*, Inglehart learned that attitudes toward authoritarian values changed for each age cohort, moving in the direction of greater freedom and autonomy. The pattern peaked in all countries in the cohort aged twenty-five to thirty-four years old and began to reverse among the next generation.

Changing values in terms of obedience versus autonomy have been translated into political behavior, both in Mexico and elsewhere in the Western world. In an earlier chapter I remarked on the surge in unorthodox political activity in Mexico, with conventional political participation more than doubling from 1981 to 1990.[58] The rise is attributable, in large part, to changing attitudes among *younger* age groups toward participation rather than among all age groups. This is particularly significant in a country where more than half the population is younger than twenty.

Another consequence of generational change appears in party identification. As Inglehart reports, studies of Western Europe and in the United States demonstrate that older citizens identified more strongly with political parties but that in recent decades younger voters are less likely to identify with a specific party. Although better educated than their elders and more interested in politics, younger Mexicans, like people elsewhere, no longer exhibit strong party loyalty. This phenomenon makes it difficult to predict future partisan sympathies and gives the independent or uncommitted voter considerable power to determine electoral outcomes, barring widespread fraud.

Younger Mexicans are much more likely to be attracted to opposition parties. Specifically, in the 1990s, voters under age twenty-four show a marked preference for the National Action Party. Before the 1994 presidential election, 19 percent of the potential voters said they would cast their ballots for the PAN, but 29 percent of the eighteen-to-twenty-four age group, a difference of 65 percent, claimed they would vote for the PAN. When the elections were held in August, 32 percent of this age group supported the PAN, and among all occupational groups, the PAN did better among students (5 percent of the voting population) than any other group, with 41 percent voting for their candidate. If larger numbers of younger voters participate in the electoral process in the future, they will increase the potential for political pluralism.

CONCLUSION

The foregoing brief analysis of just a few variables in the making of political values demonstrates the complexities of the research enterprise. Although many Mexicans have gained confidence in their ability to change the political system, large numbers believe themselves powerless. Those expressing the least confidence in their ability are women, the uneducated, and the poor. Nevertheless, the civic attention focused on the 1994 presidential elections and the unprecedented turnout of nearly four-fifths of Mexican voters indicate that numerous citizens took their responsibilities seriously and that even many first-time voters believed that they might make a difference. Although turnout was lower in the 1997 congressional elections, voters further strengthened opposition representation nationally and among governors. The opposition's victories may lead to a growing sense of confidence.

Mexican values are undergoing change, and support for authoritarian structures is among those being recast. Younger people are contributing most to this alteration, as are those who are more highly educated, who come from affluent backgrounds, and who live in the most dynamic regions. Although many of these Mexicans are desirous of increasing political alternatives, including parties, it does not mean they necessarily would vote for any party other than the PRI.

The PRI continues to be viewed sympathetically by various segments of Mexican society. It has national strength and by 1991 had recovered from a historic low in the 1988 elections. It retained about the same support nationally in 1994 as in 1988, receiving half the votes, but its support was more balanced regionally. The appeal of the PAN was historically, and is in the 1990s, to people in the north, the Federal District, and selected states in the center, the west, and the Gulf. Mexicans are religious, but their Catholicism does not impinge on their political behavior, their support of authoritarianism, or their partisanship. Many of the trends in political values as well as values in general that are apparent in Mexico appear in other countries as well, including the United States.

NOTES

1. Joseph A. Kahl, *The Measurement of Modernism: A Study of Values in Brazil and Mexico* (Austin: University of Texas Press, 1974), 8.

2. K. L. Tedin, "The Influence of Parents on the Political Attitudes of Adolescents," *American Political Science Review* 68 (December 1974): 1592.

3. Alex Edelstein, "Since Bennington: Evidence of Change in Student Political Behavior," in *Learning about Politics*, ed. Roberta Sigel (New York: Random House, 1970), 397.

4. Richard Centers, "Children of the New Deal: Social Stratification and Adolescent Attitudes," in *Class, Status and Power*, ed. Richard Bendix and Seymour Martin Lipset (New York: Free Press, 1953), 361.

5. For example, see such memoirs as Ramón Beteta, *Jarano* (Austin: University of Texas Press, 1970); and Andrés Iduarte, *Niño, Child of the Mexican Revolution* (New York: Praeger, 1971).

6. Ulises Beltrán, *Los mexicanos de los noventa* (Mexico: UNAM, 1996), 137.

7. See Linda Stevenson and Mitchell Seligson, "Fading Memories of the Revolution: Is Stability Eroding in Mexico?" in *Polling for Democracy: Public Opinion and Political Liberalization in Mexico*, ed. Roderic Ai Camp (Wilmington, Del.: Scholarly Resources, 1996), 61–80.

8. The most important variable determining the level of education that a child obtains in Mexico is the socioeconomic status of the father, according to Kahl, *The Measurement of Modernism*, 71.

9. Gabriel Almond and Sidney Verba, *The Civic Culture: Political Attitudes and Democracy in Five Nations* (Boston: Little, Brown, 1965), 142.

10. Rafael Segovia, *La politización del niño mexicano* (Mexico City: El Colegio de Mexico, 1975), 130.

11. Richard Fagen and William Tuohy, *Politics and Privilege in a Mexican City* (Stanford, Calif.: Stanford University Press, 1972), 117.

12. Michael M. Gant and Norman R. Luttbeg, *American Electoral Behavior, 1952–1988* (Itasca, N.Y.: Peacock Publishers, 1991), 140.

13. Ann Craig and Wayne Cornelius, "Political Culture in Mexico, Continuities and Revisionist Interpretations," in *The Civic Culture Revisited*, ed. Gabriel Almond and Sidney Verba (Boston: Little, Brown, 1980), 369.

14. For evidence of these ongoing changes and their linkage to politics, see Joe Foweraker and Ann L. Craig, eds., *Popular Movements and Political Change in Mexico* (Boulder, Colo.: Lynne Rienner, 1990).

15. *Los Angeles Times* poll, September 1991, courtesy of Miguel Basáñez.

16. Ramon Eduardo Ruiz, *Triumphs and Tragedy: A History of the Mexican People* (New York: Norton, 1992), 469.

17. Gant and Luttbeg, *American Electoral Behavior*, 141, indicates that in 1988, only 25 percent of college-educated Americans reported little political efficacy, compared with 57 percent of those with less than a high school diploma.

18. Fagen and Tuohy, *Politics and Privilege in a Mexican City*, 117.

19. Rafael Giménez-Valdés, "Las encuestas en México durante el proceso electoral federal de 1994," Paper presented at The National Latin American Studies Association, Washington, D.C., 1995.

20. *New York Times* exit poll, August 24, 1994; Belden and Russonello, "Mex-

ico 1994, A National Poll of the Mexican Electorate" Belden and Russonello (Washington, D.C., August 10, 1994).

21. William Flanigan and Nancy Zingale, *Political Behavior of the American Electorate*, 7th ed. (Washington, D.C.: Congressional Quarterly Press, 1991), 68.

22. Ronald Inglehart, Neil Nevitte, and Miguel Basáñez, *Convergencia en Norte América, comercio, política y cultura* (Mexico City: Siglo XXI, 1994). Figure 3-20. Forty-six percent of citizens in the United States and 40 percent in Mexico consider God important in their lives.

23. *World Values Survey*, 1990.

24. Miguel Basáñez, *Encuesta nacional de opinión pública, iglesia y estado* (1990), 14.

25. Almond and Verba, *Civic Culture*, 101.

26. Charles L. Davis, "Religion and Partisan Loyalty: The Case of Catholic Workers in Mexico," *Western Political Quarterly* 45 (March 1992): 227.

27. See Donald Mabry, *Mexico's Acción Nacional: A Catholic Alternative to Revolution* (Syracuse, N.Y.: Syracuse University Press, 1973), for the well-documented ideological influence. For the stereotypical allegation, without foundation, see Carlos Martinez Assad, "State Elections in Mexico," in *Electoral Patterns and Perspectives in Mexico*, ed. Arturo Alvarado (La Jolla, Calif.: Center for U.S.–Mexican Studies, UCSD, 1987), 36.

28. See Roderic A. Camp, "The Cross in the Polling Booth: Religion, Politics, and the Laity in Mexico," *Latin American Research Review* 29 (1994): 89–90. Charles Davis, in an analysis of survey data of Catholic workers in 1979/80, had similar findings. See his "Religion and Partisan Loyalty," 279.

29. Rubén Ruíz Guerra, "Las verdades de las cifras," *Este País*, May 1994, 17.

30. Kenneth D. Wald, Dennis E. Owen, and Samuel D. Hill Jr., "Churches as Political Communities," *American Political Science Review* 82 (June 1988): 543–44.

31. For figures on this phenomenal growth, see David Stoll, *Is Latin America Turning Protestant? The Politics of Evangelical Growth* (Berkeley and Los Angeles: University of California Press, 1990).

32. Paul J. Bonicelli, "Testing the Waters or Opening the Floodgates? Evangelicals, Politics and the 'New' Mexico," *Journal of Church and State* 39 (Winter 1997); 107–30.

33. The president announced in his 1991 state of the union address that new legislation governing the relationship would be forthcoming. *El Nacional*, November 2, 1991, 1. This legislation, reversing constitutional restrictions on the church, was passed in early 1992.

34. Camp, "The Cross in the Polling Booth," 92–93.

35. "Estado, élites y clerecía," a survey of 458 public, private, and social leaders, October-November 1993, 4.2 percent margin of error, reported in *Este País*, May 1994, 23–29.

36. Robert S. Gilmour and Robert B. Lamp, *Political Alienation in Contemporary America* (New York: St. Martin's Press, 1975), 55.

37. The best study using these data for Mexico is William J. Blough, "Political Attitudes of Mexican Women: Support for the Political System Among a Newly Enfranchised Group," *Journal of Inter-American Studies and World Affairs* 14 (May 1972): 201–24.

38. Almond and Verba, *Civic Culture*, 327.

39. Alicia Inés Martínez, "Políticas hacia la mujer en el México moderno," paper presented at the Latin American Studies Association, Atlanta, March 1994, 36.

40. Enrique Alducin, *Los valores de los mexicanos, México: Entre la tradición y la modernidad* (Mexico City: Banamex, 1986), 189.

41. Fagen and Tuohy, *Politics and Privileges in a Mexican City*, 117.

42. Forty percent of men and 43 percent of women asserted a lack of political efficacy in 1988. Gant and Luttberg, *American Electoral Behavior*, 141.

43. *World Values Survey*, 1990, courtesy of Miguel Basáñez.

44. Nikki Craske, "Women's Political Participation in *Cononias Populares* in Guadalajara, Mexico," in *Viva: Women and Popular Protest in Latin America*, ed. Sarah A. Radcliffe and Sallie Westwood (London: Routledge, 1993), 112.

45. Marta Lamas et al., "Building Bridges: The Growth of Popular Feminism in Mexico," in *The Challenge of Local Feminisms: Women's Movements in Global Perspective*, eds. Amrita Basu and Elizabeth McGrovy (Boulder: Westview, 1995), 340–41.

46. Linda Stevenson, "Gender Politics in the Mexican Democratization Process: Sex Crimes, Affirmative Action for Women, and the 1997 Elections," Paper presented at the David Rockefeller Center for Latin American Studies, Harvard University, Cambridge, 1997.

47. For perceptions of this during the revolutionary era, see Sandra McGee Deutsch, "Gender and Sociopolitical Change in Twentieth-Century Latin America," *Hispanic American Historical Review* 71 (May 1991): 270–71.

48. *World Values Survey*, 1990, courtesy of Miguel Basáñez.

49. Ivan Zavala, "Valores políticos," in *Cómo somos los mexicanos*, ed. Alberto Hernández Medina and Luis Narro Rodríguez (Mexico City: CREA, 1987), 97.

50. The most comprehensive historical and theoretical exploration of this issue in Mexico can be found in Eric Van Young, ed., *Mexico's Regions, Comparative History and Development* (La Jolla, Calif.: Center for U.S.–Mexican Studies, UCSD, 1992).

51. See Roderic Ai Camp, "Province Versus the Center, Democratizing Mexico's Political Culture," in *Assessing Democracy in Latin America: A Tribute to Russell H. Fitzgibbon*, ed. Philip Kelly (Boulder: Westview Press, 1998), 76–92.

52. Tonatiuh Guillén López, "La cultura política desde la frontera norte de México," *Estudios Fronterizos*, Vol. 34 (July/December 1994): 85–116.

53. *World Values Survey*, 1990.

54. For an analysis of its importance and regional support, see Joseph Klesner's discussion in "Changing Patterns of Electoral Participation and Official Party Support in Mexico," in *Mexican Politics in Transition*, ed. Judith Gentleman

(Boulder, Colo.: Westview Press, 1987), 113ff. For the 1988 election results, see Edgar W. Butler et al., "An Examination of the Official Results of the 1988 Mexican Presidential Election," in *Sucesión Presidencial: The 1988 Mexican Presidential Election*, ed. Edgar W. Butler and Jorge A. Bustamante (Boulder, Colo.: Westview Press, 1991), 20.

55. For some analysis of regional trends in the 1997 elections, see Joseph Klesner, who has long argued the importance of regionalism, in "Democratic Transition? The 1997 Mexican Elections," *PS* 30 (December 1997): 703–11.

56. Russell J. Dalton, *Citizen Politics in Western Democracies: Public Opinion and Political Parties in the United States, Great Britain, West Germany, and France* (Chatham, N.J.: Chatham House, 1988), 85ff.

57. Inglehart, Nevitte, and Basáñez, *Convergencia en Norte América*, chap. 1, 12.

58. Ibid., chap. 4, 13.

5

Rising to the Top: The Recruitment of Political Leadership

> One of the most critical sets of questions about any political system concerns the composition of its leadership: Who governs? Who has access to power, and what are the social conditions of rule? Such issues have direct bearing on the representativeness of political leadership, a continuing concern of democratic theorists, and on the extent to which those in power emerge from the ranks of "the people"—or from an exclusive oligarchy. These themes also relate to the role of the political system within society at large, and to the ways in which careers in public life offer meaningful opportunities for vertical (usually upward) social mobility.
>
> PETER H. SMITH, *Labyrinths of Power*

Most citizens in a society where elections are typical participate by voting. A small number become involved in a political demonstration or join a party or organization to influence public policy actively. An even smaller number seek political office and the power to make decisions.

The structure of a political system, the relationships between institutions and citizens, and the relationships among various political institutions affect how a person arrives at a leadership post. The collective process by which people reach such posts is known as political recruitment.[1]

Political recruitment: the collective process by which persons reach political offices.

An examination of political recruitment from a comparative perspective is revealing for what it tells us about leadership characteristics and, equally important, what it illustrates about a society's political process.

103

All political systems and all organizations are governed by rules that prescribe acceptable behavior. The rules of political behavior are both formal and informal. The formal rules are set forth in law and in a constitution. The informal rules often explain more completely the realities of the process, or how the system functions in practice as distinct from theory. The political process melds the two sets of rules, and over time each influences the other to the extent that they often become inextricably intertwined.

THE FORMAL RULES

Formally, the Mexican political system has some of the same characteristics of the U.S. system. It is republican, having three branches of government—executive, legislative, judicial—and federal, allocating certain powers and responsibilities to state and local governments and others to the national government. In practice, the Mexican system has been dominated by the executive branch, which has not shared power with another branch from the 1920s until the 1990s, and allocates few powers to state and local governments. While this pattern was the norm for nearly seventy years, political transformations are changing the structural balance of power nationally and between the federal and state governments, altering well-established recruitment patterns.

In a competitive, parliamentary system, such as that found in Britain, the legislative branch is the essential channel for a successful, national political career. The legislative branch is the seat of decision-making power and the most important institutional source of political recruitment. In the United States, decision-making power is divided among three branches of government, although in the legislative policy process both the executive branch and Congress play equally decisive roles. Not only is the structure in the United States different, measured by the actual exercise of political authority, but two parties have alternated in power.

The significance of these characteristics for recruitment is that they affect how candidates for office are chosen. The degree to which the average citizen participates effectively in the political process determines, to some extent, his or her voice in leadership selection. Of course, it is not just a choice between candidates representing one political organization or party versus another, but how specific persons initially become candidates. The narrowness of the possible paths followed by potential political leaders in Mexico contrasts, although undergoing significant change the last few years, with the great breadth of approaches possible in the United States. The reason for the discrepancy was the dominance of a single political organization, the PRI and its antecedents, and a single leadership group within Mexico's political system.

In the formal structure, given the monopoly exercised by the PRI historically, one would expect the party itself to be crucial to the identification and recruitment of future political leaders. Until 1994, its role has been minimal. The reason is that the PRI was not created nor has it functioned as an orthodox political party, that is, to control governance. The PRI, as suggested earlier, was formed to help *keep* a leadership group in power. Yet even a tight leadership group that exercises power in an authoritarian fashion must devise channels for political recruitment. Not to do so would eventually deprive it of the fresh replacements necessary to its continued existence.

When individual people in a small group exercise power over a long period of time, they tend to develop their own criteria for selecting their successors.[2] Moreover, they personally exercise the greatest influence over

---

Sponsored selection: political recruitment dominated by incumbent officeholders.

---

the selection process. Students of political recruitment call this *incumbent*, or *sponsored, selection.*[3] In other words, other groups in the society, such as voters, do not really have a decisive voice concerning future leaders.[4]

Sponsored selection is well illustrated by the Mexican candidate-selection process for the presidency. Presidential candidates of the government party (the PRI) are formally chosen by party delegates in what appears to be an internal, democratic procedure. In reality, party rank and file, and even party leadership have little, if anything, to do with it. The incumbent president actually designates his successor, who then becomes the PRI nominee. Although characteristics of presidential selection varied slightly in the past decade, the essential qualities persist.[5] Basically, one way or another, in the last third of an administration, the names of possible nominees emerge. For many years, they have always been members of the cabinet, implying, of course, that membership in it is essential to the career of a supremely ambitious politician. In contrast, rarely has a U.S. president held a cabinet post. For example, Jimmy Carter and Bill Clinton won the Democratic nomination after serving as a state governor. Ronald Reagan also had been a governor. None of them had ever held a national appointive political office. George Bush's career most closely matches a

Mexican president's political career—largely appointive and in the executive branch. Even Bush, however, reached the presidency from *elective*, not appointive, office.

In the past, once several cabinet members were openly talked about as potential presidential candidates, politicians in the government and PRI supporters identified with the one who they hoped would become the incumbent president's choice. Under President Miguel de la Madrid (1982–1988), each of several contenders gave a formal presentation to Congress, and each organized separate conferences to express their policy views publicly. The strongest potential candidates were Manuel Bartlett, secretary of government; Alfredo del Mazo, secretary of energy; and Carlos Salinas, secretary of programming and budgeting. De la Madrid chose Salinas as the PRI candidate, amidst considerable controversy within the political leadership, and Salinas organized his own campaign. When faced with choosing his successor—despite changes reflecting some liberalization in the process—President Salinas proceeded almost precisely in the same manner as his predecessors had, selecting Luis Donaldo Colosio, his secretary of social development, from among three leading contenders, including Manuel Camacho, head of the Federal District Department, and Pedro Aspe, the treasury secretary. When Colosio was assassinated in mid-campaign and pressures increased for party delegates to choose a replacement candidate, the president imposed his own choice on the party, Ernesto Zedillo, the former programming and budgeting, and public education secretary.

Both during his campaign and as president, President Zedillo has promised to remove himself from the selection process and to introduce an internal delegate system for local, state, and national party candidates, including those for the presidency. Such a system was used on local and state levels in several states in late 1994 and early 1995, including the PRI's gubernatorial candidate in Jalisco. In 1998, for the first time, PRI began experimenting with a primary system in the selection of gubernatorial candidates in the states of Chihuahua, Tlaxcala, Puebla, Sinaloa, and Tamaulipas. The other parties are watching this process with considerable interest. As the internal competition for presidential candidates begins for the 2000 race, Zedillo has remained aloof.

Among the opposition parties, internal competition is much more common, especially in the National Action Party, whose delegates select their national presidential candidates in open conventions similar to those of the U.S. Democratic and Republican parties. The newness of the PRD (1989) makes it impossible to identify long-term recruitment trends, especially since many of its initial national leaders were former PRIistas. But PAN politicians, who are concentrated in state and local offices and hold numerous posts in the national legislature, do provide an alternative set of recruitment characteristics, which include, given the party's lack of executive branch control, much greater emphasis on local party careers and peer selection processes.[6] Since the mid 1990s, this same pattern has become more important within PRI.

A shift in recruitment practices has begun to take place for two reasons. First, within the government leadership, given President Zedillo's posture on designating his own choice as the PRI contender, the party, and national party and governmental leaders, have increased their influence over the process. Moreover, in 1996 PRI leadership passed a series of resolutions restricting the party's candidates to individuals with certain party and electoral credentials, the most important of which is that a presidential candidate must have held elective office *prior* to his nomination, a requirement no president since Luis Echeverría (1970–1976) has met. Second, the major electoral success of the PAN and the PRD in taking control of congress, and in winning an increasing number of gubernatorial races, has shifted greater political power into the legislative branch of government nationally, and into the hands of state and local governments regionally. This shift makes the congress and the state executives much more important to the recruitment process. The importance of this shift can be seen among some of the strongest early contenders for the three major parties' presidential candidates: Vicente Fox Quesada, governor of Guanajuato, for PAN; Cuauhtémoc Cárdenas, governor of the Federal District, for PRD; and PRI contenders Manuel Bartlett and Francisco Labastida, former governors of Puebla and Sinaloa, respectively.

THE INFORMAL RULES: WHAT IS NECESSARY TO RISE TO THE TOP

If neither the governing party nor the electorate is significant in Mexican/national political recruitment on the executive level, which institutions are? Even when individual persons determine the outcome of the process, from the president on down, institutions facilitate the initial stages of a prospective leader's career. Strangely, the most important institution in the initial recruitment of national political leaders is the university.

Mexico's postrevolutionary leadership, building on the concept of the National Preparatory School introduced by the liberals in the midnineteenth century, used public education as a means of preparing and identifying future politicians. In the nineteenth century, many of the prerevolutionary leaders were educated at the National Preparatory School, and it continued to function in this way after 1920. Some politicians who served in national posts in the 1920s and 1930s never obtained higher education; they were self-made, largely on revolutionary battlefields from 1910 to 1920. Many continued as career military officers in the new postrevolutionary army.

A rapid shift occurred in credentials between the revolutionary generation of political leaders (holding office from 1920 to 1946) and the postrevolutionary generation (holding office from 1946 through the 1960s). The importance of higher education in political recruitment and the rapid decline of battlefield experiences are clearly illustrated by the personal experiences of presidents Lázaro Cárdenas (1934–1940) and Miguel Alemán (1946–1952) and the persons they recruited to political office. More than half of all national officeholders from 1920 to 1934 had fought in the revolution. Cárdenas joined the revolution as a young man and rose through the ranks to become a division general, Mexico's highest-ranking officer. He had no formal education beyond primary school in his hometown. Although he pursued a political career in the 1920s, he remained in the army, eventually serving as secretary of defense. On the other hand, Miguel Alemán, son of a prominent general, was too young to have fought in the revolution. Encouraged by his father to get a good education, he was sent to Mexico City where he studied at the National Preparatory School and then the National School of Law, graduating in 1929.

The personal experiences of a president influences his sources of initial political recruitment (see Table 5-1). In the case of Cárdenas, the revolution was central. After all, men under battle conditions develop trust in one another and respect for survival skills. A third of Cárdenas's collaborators had come in contact with him through shared service in the revolution. Once Cárdenas began his political career, he met other men in the bureaucracy who accompanied him up the political ladder. Although relatively unschooled, when he was governor of his home state, he held weekly sem-

Table 5-1 Political Recruitment Sources for Presidents Cárdenas and Alemán

| President | Sources of Initial Recruitment | | | | | |
	Revolution (%)	State (%)	Bureaucracy (%)	Party (%)	School (%)	Relatives (%)
Cárdenas	34	18	26	0	18	3
Alemán	0	10	3	3	85	0

Source: Roderic Ai Camp, *Mexico's Leaders, Their Education and Recruitment* (Tucson: University of Arizona Press, 1980), 22.

inars for students and professors from the local university, forming close ties with people whom he brought into political life later on. Cárdenas served as president of the National Revolutionary Party (PNR), an antecedent of the PRI, but did not recruit from this source. The contrast between him and Alemán could not be more remarkable. Over four-fifths of Alemán's chosen political associates had been classmates or professors at the two schools he had attended in Mexico City.

Alemán established the overwhelming value of preparatory and university education as the institutional locus of Mexican political recruitment. Its importance increased as greater numbers of future politicians began to attend the National Preparatory School and, more significant, the National University. Having attended the former reached an all-time high during the 1958–1964 administration, in which 58 percent of the appointees were graduates. Graduates of the National University reached their highest level under President de la Madrid (1982–1988), when they accounted for 56 percent of his college-educated officeholders. Midway through the Salinas administration, National University graduates accounted for half of all national politicians.

The university and preparatory school became important sources of political recruitment for two reasons (see Table 5-2). Many future politicians teach at these two institutions, generally a single course. Three-quarters of national political figures have taught at the college level. Sali-

Table 5-2 University Graduates by Presidential Administration, 1920–1991

| President | Institution | | | |
	Universidad Nacional Autónomo de Mexico (%)	Military (%)	Private (%)	Other (%)
Obregón, 1920–1924	50	9	0	41
Calles, 1924–1928	37	0	5	58
Portes Gil, 1929–1930	33	0	0	67
Ortiz Rubio, 1930–1932	43	21	0	26
Rodríguez, 1932–1934	50	0	0	50
Cárdenas, 1934–1930	27	7	3	74
Avila Camacho 1940–1946	36	7	4	53
Alemán, 1946–1952	50	5	4	41
Ruiz Cortines, 1952–1958	36	8	1	55
López Mateos, 1958–1964	47	7	1	45
Díaz Ordaz, 1964–1970	51	7	1	41
Echeverría, 1970–1976	54	7	2	37
López Portillo, 1976–1982	52	7	2	39
De la Madrid, 1982–1988	56	5	6	33
Salinas, 1988–1991	51	9	13	27

Source: Roderic Ai Camp, *Mexican Political Biography Project*, 1995.

nas was an adjunct professor at his alma mater, the National University, and President Zedillo taught at two of Mexico's leading institutions. They use the school in part as a means to teach students intellectual and political skills, helping them get started in a public career. Typically, they place a student in a government internship or part-time job, followed by a full-time position after graduation. De la Madrid is an excellent illustration of this, having started his career in the Bank of Mexico (Mexico's "federal reserve bank") on the recommendation of an economics professor.[7] These same teaching experiences are not true of some of the major party leaders. Although Cuauhtémoc Cárdenas graduated from the National University, and made several important contacts there, he never taught at his alma mater. Vicente Fox, a graduate of a regional branch campus of the influential Ibero-American University in his home sale, was a successful businessman and did not even become politically active until 1987.

Some Mexicans with political interests start out in federal agencies, in technical posts or as advisers. As their interest in politics grows, they develop contacts with other ambitious figures, including an agency superior. That person, like the politician-teacher, initiates their rise within the national bureaucracy. Today the federal bureaucracy ranks second only to the university as a source of political recruitment and grows in usefulness once the protégé is launched in politics.

In the United States, Democratic and Republican party organizations are often the source of nationally prominent politicians. The parties carry much more weight in the recruitment of politicians because of their role in the candidate-selection process and in the competition for offices that influences policymaking a great deal. In other words, the American politician must impress not only the electorate but also local, state, or national party leadership in order to obtain the party's nomination.

In Mexico few *national* politicians have been recruited through party channels, especially at the local and state levels, with the exception of opposition-party leaders, although many prominent figures at the state and local levels are recruited in such fashion. Because executive-branch leadership has controlled the party and decision making was centralized in the executive branch rather than in the legislative bodies, a career in the national bureaucracy was the foremost means of ascent. Among national officeholders in the Salinas administration, only a minuscule 2 percent served in a local government post. In recognition of this fact of life, budding politicians sympathetic to PRI descended on Mexico City, there to carve out careers in the federal government.

The salience of the federal bureaucracy in the recruitment process contributes to another informal characteristic of upward political mobility in

Mexico: the significance of Mexico City. Politicians who come from Mexico City, in spite of its tremendous size, are overrepresented in the national political leadership. This was true before the revolution of 1910, but those violent events introduced a leadership whose birthplaces deemphasized the importance of the capital (see Table 5-3). That remained true until the 1940s, when the presence of Mexico City in the backgrounds of national politicians increased substantially. By the presidency of Luis Echeverría (1970–1976), when fewer than one in ten citizens was born in Mexico City, one in four national political figures named it as a place of birth. In the

Table 5-3 Region of Birth of First-Time National Officeholders by Presidential Administration, 1884–1991

Presidential Administration	Region of Birth (%)							
	Federal District	East Central	West	North	South	Gulf	West Central	Foreign
Díaz	15	13	15	15	12	18	11	1
1889–	7	10	19	16	19	19	10	0
1893–	12	24	6	15	15	9	18	0
1897–	13	11	11	16	4	31	13	0
1901–	22	5	5	24	8	22	11	3
1905–	14	9	11	29	11	17	9	0
1910–	23	6	0	35	0	24	6	6
De la Barra	6	22	28	28	6	0	11	0
Madero	13	13	20	18	6	20	9	0
Huerta	16	10	16	24	8	12	16	0
Convention	5	11	19	32	5	5	22	0
Carranza	4	17	16	26	10	13	12	1
Obregón	6	14	19	19	13	21	8	0
Calles	3	15	18	20	13	12	18	0
Portes Gil	0	21	14	29	0	29	7	0
Ortiz Rubio	8	8	12	28	4	12	28	0
Rodríguez	0	15	0	46	17	0	8	0
Cárdenas	6	20	15	13	13	13	20	1
Avila Camacho	10	20	15	16	10	11	25	1
Alemán	11	15	12	20	9	16	15	1
Ruiz Cortines	3	18	20	16	12	17	17	1
López Mateos	9	19	16	17	10	11	15	0
Díaz Ordaz	8	11	23	15	7	15	12	0
Echeverría	24	15	14	13	9	12	13	1
López Portillo	26	12	13	13	8	13	12	3
De la Madrid	39	13	11	11	8	6	10	1
Salinas	45	6	11	15	2	13	4	4
Total	16	14	15	15	9	14	13	1
1910 Census[a]	5	22	16	11	14	12	21	
1950 Census[a]	12	18	14	15	13	12	17	

Source: Roderic A. Camp, *Mexican Political Biography Project*, 1995.
[a]Percentage of general population from each region.

past twenty years, that figure increased dramatically: Mexico City was the birthplace of nearly half of President Salinas's appointees who held national office for the first time, nearly four times that of the general population of the same age. These figures show that for a variety of reasons, growing up in Mexico City is a tremendous advantage to the politically ambitious.

In all political systems, whom one knows has much to do with political recruitment and with appointment to an important political office. U.S. politics is replete with examples of prominent figures who sought out old friends to fill responsible political offices. In fact, knowing someone is often a means for obtaining employment in the private sector as well. In Mexico, whom one knows in public life is even more telling, given the fact that incumbent officeholders often decide who obtains influential posts. Mexicans with political ambitions can enhance personal contacts at school, in the university, or during their professional and public careers through family ties.

Americans have produced a few notable political families, say, the Adamses and Kennedys, and George Bush is the son of a U.S. senator, but such families are numerous in Mexico. One reason, as studies of British and U.S. politicians have shown, is that children of political activists are more likely to see politics as a potential career than are children reared in a nonpolitical environment.[8] It is natural that a youngster growing up in a political family would come in contact with many political figures. More than one in eight Mexican national politicians from 1970 through 1988, including President Salinas, were the children of nationally prominent political figures. Salinas's father, who served in the cabinet in the 1960s, helped his son's early career. Cuauhtémoc Cárdenas, PRD's leading figure, is the son of President Lázaro Cárdenas. If extended family ties are considered, between one-fifth and one-third of all politicians were related to national political figures during the same period. The same is true on the state level and has been documented in detail by Javier Hurtado in his examination of Jalisco, an important western state.[9]

Politically active families are not the only factor that makes family background important. Social and economic status is another. Studies of politicians worldwide, in both socialist and nonsocialist societies, reveal the importance of middle- and upper-middle-class backgrounds.[10] In Third World countries without competitive political structures, family origins become even more significant to career success.

Higher socioeconomic backgrounds are helpful in political life because well-off parents provide opportunities for their children. Education, as we have seen is such a significant means of political recruitment, hence *access* to it enables making the right contacts and obtaining the necessary informal credentials. Some Mexicans from working-class backgrounds manage to attend preparatory school and even a university, but few actually complete degree programs. Financial ease contributes to the acquisition of a degree if desire and intellectual capacity are present. This explains why Mexico's youngest generation of national politicians, those born since 1940 (Presidents Salinas's and Zedillo's generation), are almost exclusively from middle- and upper-middle-class backgrounds. President Zedillo, however, is an exception, the first chief executive in decades to come from a working-class family of modest means.

THE RISE OF WOMEN

Another informal credential universal to political leadership in all countries is gender. Politics has been, and remains, dominated by men. Nevertheless, women have made substantial inroads in national political office. On the whole, women have been far more successful politically in Mexico than in many other countries, including the United States. For example, several women served on the supreme court in Mexico, long before Sandra Day O'Connor was appointed by President Reagan. Numerous women have held senate positions. Cabinet posts have occasionally been filled by women, but men have a virtual lock on that domain, especially in the major agencies. President Zedillo increased the number of women in his cabinet to three, the highest ever, and a woman became president of PRI. Most important, in 1998, Rosario Green became secretary of foreign relations, the first woman to hold a significant cabinet post.

Slightly different recruitment patterns have traditionally been followed by women interested in politics. This fact worked against their obtaining the higher positions because they do not come in contact with current and future political figures who could assist them up the bureaucratic ladder.[11] Typically, women politicians have been found far more frequently in party posts and in the legislative branch, and they have not had the same type or level of education (see Table 5-4). Younger women who are politically ambitious are now taking on many of the characteristics of their male peers. Among younger political figures (born after 1950) at the national level, women now account for one in four. The representation of women in national political offices (cabinet, subcabinet, and top judicial and legislative posts) increased substantially after 1976, during the administration of José López Portillo (see Table 5-5). The lower figure for Salinas does not nec-

Table 5-4 Credentials of First-Time Officeholders by Gender, 1934–1991

Credential	Women (%)	Men (%)
Education		
Primary, secondary, preparatory only	22	19
Normal only	22	5
University	32	51
Graduate	26	25
Degree earned		
None	43	27
Law	38	51
Economics	19	12
Medicine	6	9
Engineering	5	14
Other	32	15
Political office		
Private secretary	3	9
Union leader	13	13
Kinship ties		
Relative in public office	15	28
Father in politics	8	9
Party office		
President of PRI	0	1
Secretary of PRI	6	8
Federal District director	0	1
State director	8	4
Other post	43	17
All PRI posts combined	50	22

Source: Roderic A. Camp, *Mexican Political Biography Project,* 1995.

essarily represent a decline in the representation of women, as the data are for only the first half of his administration. For example, in the Salinas administration, 12 percent of the legislative branch, 12 percent of the judicial branch, and 6 percent of the executive branch were women.[12] In the first legislative session of the Zedillo administration (1994–1997), women accounted for 14 percent of the deputies and 12 percent of the senators. (See Table 5-6.) Among the major political parties, in the National Executive Committee, women controlled 24, 13, and 11 percent, respectively, of the PRD, PRI, and PAN posts. The PRD, similar to some Scandinavian parties, began experimenting with a quota system. In 1993, they instituted a 30 percent rule, guaranteeing women that level of representation among the party's candidates for office. After the implementation of this rule, women deputies from the PRD increased from 8 to 23 percent.

Women in the 1980s and 1990s began to acquire the credentials that men had, thus increasing their opportunities for closer contact with potential future politicians. Although women traditionally have not been as well educated as men, younger women have received much more university train-

Table 5-5 Women's Recruitment to National Political Office by Administration, 1935–1991

President	Percentage of Women in Administration
Cárdenas, 1934–1940	0
Avila Camacho, 1940–1946	1
Alemán, 1946–1952	2
Ruiz Cortines, 1952–1958	4
López Mateos, 1958–1964	4
Díaz Ordaz, 1964–1970	6
Echeverría, 1970–1976	8
López Portillo, 1976–1982	19
De la Madrid, 1982–1988	17
Salinas, 1988–1991	11

Source: Roderic A. Camp, *Mexican Political Biography Project*, 1995.

ing, putting them on par with men holding influential posts in the 1970s and 1980s. In 1995, women were only two-tenths of a year behind men in their average number of years of schooling.[13] The major difference in recruitment qualities among female and male politicians today is that women are not receiving the same level of graduate education and, more important, are attending graduate schools that are no longer considered prestigious by men. But women continue to have much broader and deeper experiences in their parties and in civic and nongovernmental organizations. These career differences, though working against female political recruitment in the short run, may very well give women stronger skills in a changing, plural political context and thus an advantage in an increasingly democratic Mexico.

Table 5-6 Women's Recruitment to National Legislative Office by Administration, 1952–1997

Administration	Percentage of Women in Office	
	Chamber of Deputies	Senate
1952–1958	2	0
1958–1964	5	0
1964–1970	6	3
1970–1976	7	3
1976–1982	9	6
1982–1988	12	9
1988–1994	10	11
1994–1997	14	12

Source: Adapted from Anna M. Fernández Poncela, "The Political Participation of Women in Mexico Today," in *Changing Structure of Mexico: Political, Social and Economic Prospects* (Armonk, N.Y.: Sharpe, 1996), 307–14.

Successful political recruitment in Mexico thus requires certain informal credentials. Higher education is an essential; higher education in Mexico City, and at the National University, is extremely advantageous. For younger politicians, graduates of the Autonomous Technological Institute of Mexico and Ibero-American University have taken on increased importance. Second, it has been very helpful to a political career to have been born in the capital, which strengthens the potential for attending the universities from which most establishment politicians graduated. Third, young professionals who join the federal bureaucracy rather than the party bureaucracy or state and local agencies have been much more likely to reach the top. Fourth, a middle-class background is almost essential to achievement of the education necessary for a public career. Finally, family ties to successful politicians have enhanced the career opportunities of many of Mexico's leading public figures; all the presidents between 1970 and 1994 have been related to prominent political figures.

Many women, however, may be well positioned in the future for successful political careers. As electoral competition increases and party bureaucracies increase their importance, women will benefit. The same is true of women's local and regional career patterns, as local politics takes on much greater significance regionally and nationally.

THE CAMARILLA: GROUP POLITICS IN MEXICO

Perhaps the most distinctive characteristic of Mexican politics, knowledge of which is essential to understanding the recruitment process, is the political clique, the *camarilla*. It has determined, more than any other variable discussed, who goes to the top of the political ladder, what paths are taken, and the specific posts they are assigned. Many of the features of Mexican political culture predispose the political system to rely on camarillas. A camarilla is a group of people who have political interests in common and rely on one another to improve their chances within the political leadership (see Table 5-7).

A camarilla is often formed early, even while the members are still in college. The members place considerable trust in one another. Using a group of friends to accomplish professional objectives is a feature found in other sectors of Mexican society, including academia and the business community. A camarilla has a leader who acts as a political mentor to other mem-

---

Camarilla: a group of persons who share political interests, and rely on one another to improve their chances in the political leadership.

Table 5-7 Fifteen Characteristics of Mexican Camarillas

1. The structural basis of the camarilla system is a mentor-disciple relationship that has many similarities to the patron-client culture throughout Latin America.

2. The camarilla system is extremely fluid, and camarillas are not exclusive but overlapping.

3. Most successful politicians are the products of multiple camarillas, that is, rarely does a politician remain within a single camarilla from the beginning to the end of his or her career.

4. Mexicans who successfully pursue politics as a profession initiate their own camarillas simultaneously with membership in mentors' camarillas.

5. Every major national figure is the "political child," "grandchild," or "great grandchild" of an earlier, nationally known figure.

6. The larger the camarilla, the more influential its leader and, likewise, his disciples.

7. Most significant camarillas today can be traced back to two major political figures: Lázaro Cárdenas and Miguel Alemán.

8. Some camarillas are characterized by an ideological flavor, but other personal qualities generally determine disciple ties to a mentor.

9. Disciples often surpass the political careers of their mentors, thus reversing the benefits of the camarilla's relationship and the logical order of camarilla influence.

10. Camarillas formed largely within an institutional environment have become increasingly significant as decision making, especially in the economic realm, has become more complex. The single-most-important public institution representative of this trend, especially relative to its size, is the Bank of Mexico.

11. Kinship and educational companionship are the major sources of camarilla loyalties today, but professional merit, contrary to popular assumptions, has become increasingly important.

12. All politicians automatically carry with them membership in an educational camarilla, represented by their preparatory, professional, and graduate school generation.

13. Politicians with kinship camarillas have advantages over peers without such ties.

14. Politicians who are not adept at building camarillas on the basis of professional merit have the largest and most successful groups over time but are not necessarily the most likely to achieve the presidency.

15. Because of the overlapping quality of camarillas, some politicians have shared loyalties. Normally, most politicians, at a given time, can be identified with a specific camarilla. It is acceptable to shift loyalties when the upward ascendancy of the political mentor is frozen.

Source: Roderic Ai Camp, "Camarillas in Mexican Politics: The Case of the Salinas Cabinet," *Mexican Studies* 6 (Winter 1990): 106–7.

bers of the group. He typically is more successful than his peers and uses his own career as a means of furthering the careers of other group members. As the leader of a camarilla ascends in the bureaucracy, he places members of his group, when possible, in other influential positions either within his agency or outside it. The higher he rises, the more positions he can fill.[14]

Because it has retained a monopoly for more than seventy years, Mexico's political leadership can be viewed as overlapping and hierarchical camarillas, all linked. They are fluid groups, and if a mentor's career does not advance, it is acceptable to shift loyalties to another camarilla. It is also permissible to have ties to more than one camarilla, although at a given time, one is identified specifically with only a single group.

Mexican politics, from the postrevolutionary generation onward, has been built on the interrelationships of the camarillas. Indeed, all contemporary camarillas have their origins in two major forebears: the camarillas of Cárdenas and Alemán. Cárdenas's personal camarilla spawned four successive generations of camarillas, accounting for at least 144 national officeholders. Cárdenas's most important disciple today is his own son, Cuauhtémoc, who took the unusual step of leaving the establishment leadership in 1987 to form his own party. He ran for the presidency in 1988, winning the largest percentage of presidential votes ever recorded for an opposition party in modern Mexican history and coming in third in the 1994 race.

The interrelatedness of the camarillas is reflected by the fact Alemán was a disciple of Cárdenas's. Nevertheless, it was Alemán who altered the nature of political recruitment as exercised by his mentor, emphasizing the importance of educational and bureaucratic contacts over Cárdenas's relationships derived from the Revolution.

All of the qualities described in Table 5-7 remain true for national government officeholders and PRI careerists. But the universality of these qualities will break down as PAN and PRD members acquire more posts, and especially if their candidate wins the presidency. Camarillas will not disappear, but other characteristics will increase in importance and other variables will moderate camarillas' influence.[15]

The camarilla takes on added importance in politics because the mentor establishes the criteria by which he chooses his disciples. The most successful camarilla reaches the presidency, thus influencing the entire system. The implications for political recruitment are crucial. It has been shown that politicians, like most people, tend to recruit those with similar credentials or experience, who in many ways mirror themselves.[16] Over time, incumbents can structure the recruitment process to favor certain credentials. Generally, however, presidents, because they exercise the most comprehensive influence over political appointments, have the greatest impact on the recruitment process.

It has been pointed out that Alemán introduced some new credentials because of the persons he chose for high political office, giving his peers the opportunity to reinforce those same credentials. From the 1940s through the 1970s, as the camarillas introduced by Alemán and his generation rose to the top, certain credentials became increasingly important: a college education, preferably from the National University; an urban birthplace, preferably Mexico City; a career in national politics, preferably the federal bureaucracy; pursuit of a law degree and legal career; and entrance into public service at a young age, often while still in college.

In the 1980s, and in some instances earlier, a change began to occur in the informal credentials required of the most successful politicians. A policy setting forth these changing requirements was not established; rather, they emerged naturally as the politicians themselves changed their credentials. These recent trends have become sharper and more easily recognized under Salinas and Zedillo.

The three most important sources of contemporary political camarillas in Mexico are family, education, and career. Family has remained consistently at the fore and has changed only in the sense that today's politicians are increasingly the children of national political figures. In the past, family relationships were common but not as direct.

Politicians' educational and career characteristics have changed markedly in the past two decades. The most persistent change has been the constant increase in *level* of education. Not only are all national political leaders, with a few exceptions in the legislative branch, college educated, but graduate education has reached new highs. De la Madrid, Salinas, and Zedillo obtained graduate degrees. De la Madrid has an M.A. degree in public administration from Harvard; his disciple and successor, Salinas, has two M.A. degrees as well as a Ph.D. degree from Harvard; and Salinas' successor, Zedillo, received his M.A. and Ph.D. from Yale. They reflect the importance given to advanced education in Mexican politics. Of the *new* national officeholders under de la Madrid, nearly half, like the president, had graduate degrees. Only six years later, beginning with the Salinas administration in 1988, 70 percent had received graduate training; many of them are Ph.D. degree holders. Of Zedillo's cabinet members, 66 percent claim such educational credentials. Graduate education has become such a preferred credential that top political figures have been known to lie about having it. For example, there was a scandal involving Zedillo's first education secretary, who never completed his B.A. or his Ph.D.[17]

De la Madrid and Salinas introduced another informal credential into the recruitment process. Their camarilla selections emphasized politicians who had been educated outside Mexico, particularly at the graduate level. Zedillo did likewise. It can be said that Salinas was following in the footsteps of his father, who also graduated from Harvard with an advanced degree. Zedillo followed in the footsteps of his mentor, economist Leopoldo Solís, a Yale graduate. The point is that numerous political figures began to study abroad, generally at the most prestigious universities in the United States. In Salinas's administration Harvard and Yale graduates were the most common. These patterns have been carefully traced since the 1970s. In 1972, 58 percent of Mexico's national political figures with Ph.D.s received them from the National University, and only 13 percent from U.S.

universities. By 1989, only 29 percent had graduated from an institution in their native country, compared with 48 percent from U.S. institutions.[18]

A third change in the educational background of contemporary politicians, and perhaps the most significant, is the discipline studied. Law, as in the United States, has always been the field of study of most future politicians, with engineering and medicine coming in second. This means that law school is the most likely place to meet future politicians and political mentors. The most remarkable change is from the primacy of law to economics. Salinas is the first president with that specialty, and his political generation is the first to count as many economists as lawyers among its members. Zedillo duplicated this pattern personally and among his collaborators.

The new discipline emphasis has led to another significant change in recruitment characteristics: the elevation of private over public education. This characteristic is less pervasive than the others but even more remarkable. Between the administration of de la Madrid and Salinas, a sixfold increase in the percentage of private-school graduates took place. Instead of the National University and public universities maintaining their level of dominance, private institutions have begun to make serious inroads. This trend is enhanced by the fact many PAN politicians are private school graduates, and as more businesspeople choose political careers, private university graduates will increase. Vicente Fox Quesada, the leading PAN presidential contender, is a case in point. This is significant for political recruitment because it will change not only informal credentials but also the locations where recruitment takes place. In fact, it contributes to the diversity of the recruitment process, a process that traditionally has relied on fewer educational sources.

THE RISE AND DECLINE OF THE TECHNOCRAT?

As the recruitment process changed and the credentials of future politicians were modified, some scholars labeled the younger generation of politicians in Mexico as technocrats, *técnicos*. The rise of technocratic leadership took place throughout Latin America. A number of attributes have been associated with this class of leaders in Brazil and Chile, and many have been mistakenly applied to Mexico's leaders. This has generated some confusion about technocrats.[19]

Mexico's technocratic leadership is characterized by new developments in their informal credentials. In particular, they are seen as well educated in technologically sophisticated fields; as spending most of their careers in the national bureaucracy; as having come from large urban centers, notably Mexico City; as having middle- and upper-middle-class backgrounds; and as having studied abroad (see Table 5-8). By implication, in contrast to the more traditional Mexican politician, they have few direct ties to the masses and, in terms of career experience, lack elective office-holding and grassroots party experience.

For some years the typical Mexican politician has been a hybrid, exhibiting characteristics found among *técnicos* and traditional politicians. The assertion by some scholars that technocrats lack political skills is incorrect and misleading. Technocrats as a group do not have an identifiable ideology. The political-technocrat, a more apt label, is primarily distinguished from the politician of the 1960s or 1970s by lack of party experience, by the fact that he or she has never held elective office, and by specialized education abroad. These characteristics, for example, are found in President Zedillo's own career (see Table 5-9). The implication of these three characteristics is that the politician-technocrat, although highly skilled, does not possess the same political bargaining skills as does the peer who has had a different career track and that such a person *may* be more receptive to political and economic strategies used in other cultures as a consequence of foreign education. For example, some critics suggest that Salinas's economic cabinet, including Zedillo, whose members share these technocratic characteristics, welcomed the economic liberalization

Table 5-8 Characteristics of Mexico's Politician-Technocrats in the 1990s

Characteristic	Percentage Having
Urban birthplace	94
Male	87
Middle-class parents	85
College educated	83
Graduate of the National University	58
Taught	57
Prior national political post	56
Born between 1920 and 1939	52
Graduate education	46
Lawyer	37
Taught at the National University	37
Graduate of the National Preparatory School	29
Ph.D. degree	20
Graduate work in the United States	19
Economist	16

Source: Roderic A. Camp, *Mexican Political Biography Project*, 1995.

Table 5-9 Career Progression of Ernesto Zedillo Ponce de León, Technocrat President

1992–1993	Secretary of Public Education[a]
1988–1992	Secretary of Programming and Budgeting[b]
1987–1988	Subsecretary of Programming and Budgeting
1983–1987	Director, Exchange Risks Trust Fund, Bank of Mexico
1982–1983	Assistant Manager, Treasury Research, Bank of Mexico
1981–1983	Professor, economics, El Colegio de México
1978–1982	Economist, Bank of Mexico
1978–1980	Professor, economics, National Polytechnic Institute (IPN)
1974–1978	M.A. and Ph.D., economics, Yale University
1973–1974	Professor, economics, National Polytechnic Institute (IPN)
1973	Studies, University of Bradford, England
1971–1974	Researcher, Economic and Social Planning Division, Secretariat of the Presidency
1969–1971	Accounting assistant, Bank of the Army and Navy
1969–1972	Economics studies, National Polytechnic Institute
1967–1969	Vocational School No. 5, National Polytechnic Institute (IPN), Mexico City
1964–1967	Public School No. 18, Mexicali
1958–1964	Leona Viario and Cuauhtémoc Schools, Mexicali, Baja California

[a]Zedillo became Luis Donaldo Colosio's campaign manager in 1993/1994, making him one of the few prominent figures eligible constitutionally in March 1994 to become the new PRI candidate.
[b]This secretariat was incorporated into the Treasury in 1992.

philosophy of western Europe and the United States because of their economic background and education abroad. Zedillo's critics charge that his economic cabinet lacks political skills, which explains their disastrous devaluation policy and subsequent economic solutions (see Figure 5-1).

Much of the dissension in the Mexican political leadership in the 1990s can be attributed to a division between the technocratic leadership and traditional political figures, popularly called *los dinos*, or dinosaurs. Essentially, the argument is that the *técnicos* have replaced the traditional politicians; have devalued their skills and experiences, primarily their electoral and party experiences; and have opposed their unprogressive authoritarian practices with modernizing political and economic alternatives. The crux of the divisions is the alleged ideological differences between the two groups. But this explanation for what is happening in Mexican politics places too much emphasis on artificial ideological divisions and insufficient attention to access to power. It is not so much a question of who advocates what but who governs. More important, as Miguel Centeno pointed out, the central issue introduced by this technocratic elite is not "an ideology of answers or issues but. . .an ideology of method. The ideological cohesion of the new elite was not necessarily based on philosophical agree-

Figure 5-1 General Characteristics of the Zedillo Cabinet

	Place of Origin	
Federal District		Province
68%		32%
	University Attended	
Private		Public[a]
18%		82%[a]
	Undergraduate Degree	
Economics	Law	Other
36%[b]	32%	32%
	Graduate Work Abroad	
United States		England/Europe
50%		32%
	Executive Experience Under Salinas	
Cabinet		Subcabinet
9%		36%
	Electoral Experience	
Elective Office		None
23%		77%

[a]Except for the two career officers, all cabinet members who graduated from a public university were National University alumni.
[b]Includes two degrees in business administration.

ments on policy but an agreement on how such a policy ought to be pursued."[19]

The presence of these technocratic leaders since 1989 suggests an additional characteristic, a belief that the institutions they lead are the undisputed arbiters of economic and political decision making. Even so, they have shown an inability to listen and an intolerance of their domestic opponents. This pattern increasingly isolates the technocratic leaders from other groups, both within and outside Mexico's leadership. This may explain to some extent the difficulties that Zedillo's economic cabinet is having. The selection of top decision makers from an increasingly younger group of Mexicans also means that they do not come with the range of experiences that their predecessors offered. Technocrats like Zedillo have smaller and smaller camarillas because their relative youth allows them less political experience, and this experience has covered a narrower range of institutions and agencies. It can be argued that it is much easier to teach well-experienced political generalists about economic policies than it is to instruct well-trained economists how to make political decisions.

This pattern of relative youth and inexperience also introduces another element contributing to instability *within* the political leadership. For many decades, Mexican presidential administrations have allocated twelve years of consecutive representation to the president's own generation. Echeverría and López Portillo did this from 1970 to 1982, but Salinas deprived President de la Madrid's generation (born in the 1930s) of six years when he introduced a younger generation, Salinas's own, which dominated both his and Zedillo's leadership.

As prominent politicians inside and outside PRI position themselves for the presidential race in 2000, the entrenched position of the technocrats appears more tenuous. Only one of the leading contenders for the PRI nomination by mid-1998, José Gurría, the Treasury Secretary, could be considered a technocrat. If PRI does not rescind its requirement for prior elective experience, almost all potential technocrats would be eliminated. Neither Cárdenas nor Fox fall into the technocratic category. A victory by a non-technocrat president would not eliminate their presence; rather it will reopen national bureaucratic leadership to candidates with other personal qualities.

No longer, however, is the central criticism of technocrats only that they lack electoral and political experience, compared with that of their predecessors. Actually, as pointed out earlier, Zedillo's cabinet is no less experienced than his immediate predecessors and is more experienced than that of Miguel de la Madrid's first cabinet. Rather, a new issue is that as the Mexican political system becomes increasingly plural and the rules of the political game change, no one among the experienced national leaders can claim to have been prepared in a democratic setting. Indeed, such a setting will require entirely new, untested political skills.

CONCLUSION

The formal structure of Mexico's political system sheds little light on how interested Mexicans pursue successful political careers. The political recruitment process is strongly affected by the centralization of political authority and the reality of incumbent selection. Because other variables and groups exercised little influence over the appointment and "election" of government officials, informal credentials have replaced more formal requirements as helpful or essential to political recruitment. The growth and victories of the PAN and PRD at the local and state levels in all branches and in the national legislative branches introduce different leadership characteristics and legitimize new recruitment practices. One of the most divergent qualities these groups bring with them is the lower socioeconomic origins of the PRD politicians, in sharp contrast to both the PRI and PAN figures. PAN is likely to introduce more politicians with business rather than government backgrounds.

The informal credentials have been associated with generations of political leaders since the 1920s. As incumbent leaders have changed their own credentials, they have passed on the changes to succeeding generations of politicians. Contrary to expectations, and different from the United States, educational institutions have very important roles in political recruitment. Many Mexican politicians teach at the university level and use their classes as a means of recruiting potential politicians. The most important governmental source of political recruitment is the national bureaucracy, not the legislative branch. Mexico's centralization of authority also contributes to the importance of national institutions and to the neglect of local and state institutions in the backgrounds and career experiences of politicians. But as decentralization of authority occurs, both the legislative structure and state and local institutions will increase their recruitment roles.

The political clique, the camarilla, has played the most important role in the recruitment process. It is an informal structure built on several characteristics of the general culture, a structure emphasizing the importance of placing career loyalties in the hands of close friends, and using a group of friends to enhance one another's career success. All prominent Mexican politicians, excluding the opposition, are members of camarillas and are tied to one another through fluid linkages among the many cliques. Contemporary politicians can trace their camarillas back to those originated by Cárdenas and Alemán.

The most salient characteristics of a successful contemporary politician—reflected in the background of President Ernesto Zedillo, except for his socioeconomic background—include high level of education; graduate training abroad; a degree in economics or a more technically specialized discipline; a middle-class social background; a career in the national bureaucracy, especially economics-oriented agencies like Treasury; residence in an urban center, especially Mexico City; and, increasingly, graduation from a private, not a public, institution in the capital.[20]

The changing features of the recruitment process and the changing characteristics of politicians themselves enabled the rise of a new politician in Mexico, commonly labeled a technocrat. Zedillo is a prototype. Politician-technocrats have increasingly dominated the government, especially the executive branch, and control Zedillo's economic cabinet. Several phenomena have been attributed, often incorrectly, to these people's personal qualities. If Zedillo's policies are deemed worthwhile, politician-technocrats are likely to dominate the government through the end of the century. But under Zedillo, both his policies and this type of leadership face severe challenges, and the chances are strong that a non-technocrat will replace Zedillo in the presidency.

NOTES

1. Lester G. Seligman, *Recruiting Political Elites* (New York: General Learning Press, 1971).

2. Kenneth Prewitt, *The Recruitment of Political Leaders: A Study of Citizen-Politicians* (Indianapolis: Bobbs-Merrill, 1970), 13.

3. See Ralph Turner, "Sponsored and Contest Mobility and the School System," *American Sociological Review* 25 (December 1960): 855–56.

4. See Robert D. Putnam, *The Comparative Study of Political Elites* (Englewood Cliffs, N.J.: Prentice-Hall, 1976), 45ff.

5. See Roderic A. Camp, "Mexican Presidential Candidates: Changes and Portents for the Future," *Polity* 16 (Summer 1984): 588–605.

6. For more detailed information about the recruitment characteristics of PAN and PRD members, see Roderic A. Camp, "The PAN's Social Bases: Implications for Leadership," in *Opposition Government in Mexico*, ed. Victoria Rodríguez and Peter M. Ward (Albuquerque: University of New Mexico Press, 1995), 65–80, and "The Opposition: An Alternative Path to Leadership?" in my *Political Recruitment Across Two Centuries, Mexico, 1884–1993* (Austin: University of Texas Press, 1995), 194–215.

7. Interview with Miguel de la Madrid, Mexico City, 1991.

8. See, for example, Richard Rose's statement that "the number of politicians from political families is disproportionately high in every Cabinet." *Politics in England: Change and Persistence*, 5th ed. (Boston: Little, Brown, 1989), 177. For the United States, see Alfred Clubok et al., "Family Relationships, Congressional Recruitment, and Political Modernization," *Journal of Politics* 31 (November 1969): 1036.

9. See his *Familias, política y parentesco, Jalisco 1919–1991* (Mexico City: Fondo de Cultura Económica, 1993).

10. Thomas R. Dye, *Who's Running America? Institutional Leadership in the United States* (Englewood Cliffs, N.J.: Prentice-Hall, 1976), 152; George K. Schueller, "The Politburo," in *World Revolutionary Elites*, ed. Harold D. Lasswell and Daniel Lerner (Cambridge, Mass.: MIT Press, 1966), 141.

11. For excellent background information on women in Mexican national politics, see María Emilia Farías, "La participación de la mujer en la política," *Méx-*

ico 75 años de revolución, desarrollo social (Mexico City: Fondo de Cultura Económica, 1960), 693–816; Alicia Inés Martínez, "Políticas hacia la mujer en el México moderno," paper presented at the Latin American Studies Association, Atlanta, 1994; Anna M. Fernández Poncela, "El reto de la política y la apuesta de las mujeres," *Este País*, January 1995, 2–4; "La mujer y el poder legislativo," *Foro Electoral* 1 (1991): 19–23; and "Participación social y política de la mujer en México," in *Participación política: Las mujeres en México al final del milenio* (Mexico City: El Colegio de México, 1995). The best example of female recruitment from personal experience is Griselda Alvarez, *Cuesta Arriba* (Mexico: Fondo de Cultura Económica, 1992), 49.

12. *Diccionario biográfica del gobierno mexicano* (Mexico City: Fondo de Cultura Económica, 1992), 1042, 1051, 1063.

13. Mexico is well behind other Latin American countries in total average years of schooling, ranking among the median group at 5.0 and 4.8 years, respectively, for men and women. In some countries, such as Argentina, women are better educated than men. See *Statistics for Latin America and the Caribbean* (UNICEF, 1997), 40.

14. For an excellent description of this process, see Merilee S. Grindle, "Patrons and Clients in the Bureaucracy: Career Networks in Mexico," *Latin American Research Review* 12 (1977): 37–66.

15. Joy Langston, who has provided the most detailed examination of a camarilla's influence, reached a similar conclusion. See her "Sobrevivir y prosperar: una búsqueda de las causas de las facciones políticas intrarrégimen en México," *Política y Gobierno* 2, 2 (1995): 243–77.

16. Kenneth Prewitt and Alan Stone, *The Ruling Elites: Elite Theory, Power, and American Democracy* (New York: Harper & Row, 1973), 142.

17. This person, Fausto Alzate, was forced to resign in disgrace. He claimed to have received a Ph.D. from Harvard, where he did study but did not graduate. The same happened to José Córdoba, Salinas's chief of staff. Two other Zedillo cabinet members admitted that their master's degrees were incomplete.

18. Alfonso Galindo, "Education of Mexican Government Officials," *Statistical Abstract of Latin America*, vol. 30, pt. 1 (Los Angeles: UCLA, 1992), 599. See my chapter and the editors' introduction: "Technocracy a la Mexicana, Antecedent to Democracy," in *The Politics of Expertise in Latin America*, ed. Miguel Angel Centeno and Patricio Silva (New York: St. Martin's Press, 1997), 196–213.

19. Miguel Angel Centeno, *Democracy Within Reason, Technocratic Revolution in Mexico* (University Park: Pennsylvania State University Press, 1994), 209; Juan D. Lindau, "Technocrats and Mexico's Political Elite," *Political Science Quarterly* 111, 2 (1996): 295–322, offers still another view.

20. Roderic Ai Camp, "The Zedillo Cabinet: Continuity, Change, or Revolution?" Western Hemisphere Election Studies Series (Washington, D.C.: CSIS, January 5, 1995). Zedillo was born in Mexico City but moved to Mexicali at age three. He returned to the capital for high school and college, during which time he lived with his grandmother.

6

Groups and the State:
What Is the Relationship?

> The growth of electoral competition in Mexico has had uneven
> and ambiguous consequences on the role and shape of clien-
> telistic interest-intermediation arrangements. As elsewhere in
> Latin America, democratization has clearly failed to destroy the
> political centrality of clientelistic structures. Rising electoral
> competition has not left, however, clientelism unchanged. The
> combination of more open political contestation, fiscal strin-
> gency and market reform has introduced major changes in the
> nature and scope of clientelistic arrangements.
>
> BLANCA HEREDIA, *"Clientelism in Flux"*

All political systems, regardless of whether the struggle for political power
is highly competitive or strongly monopolized by a small leadership group
or single party, must cope with political interests and groups. In the United
States various interest groups, as they are labeled, express their demands
to the executive and legislative branches and contribute significant sums
of money to parties and candidates. In Mexico, because the political system's structure is different from that of the United States, both the type of
groups and their means for influencing public policy are different from
what obtains north of the border.

THE FALTERING CORPORATIST STRUCTURE

The importance of corporatism to the Mexican political culture and model
was noted earlier.[1] Corporatism describes the more formal relationship between selected groups or institutions and the government or state. Since
the revolution—that is, for most of the twentieth century—Mexico has been

using an interesting structure to channel the most influential groups' demands that has enabled the government to monitor the demands and mediate among them. The government has sought to act as the ultimate arbiter and to see to it that no one group becomes predominant.

The corporatist structure was largely devised and put in place under President Lázaro Cárdenas (1934–1940). Although Cárdenas wanted to strengthen the state's hand in order to protect the interests of the ordinary worker and peasant, he ironically created a structure that for the most part has benefited the interests of the middle classes and the wealthy, not unlike that of many other political systems.[2] The reason for this outcome is that the commitment of Cárdenas to the social welfare of the less well off has not been shared by most of his successors, who have responded to other concerns and groups.

What is important, however, is that although the ideological orientation has changed and various economic strategies have been experimented with since the 1930s, the arrangement remained largely intact until the 1990s.[3] Only under President Salinas was there some interest in restructuring the corporatist relationship,[4] in response to Salinas's promises of political modernization and democracy. Observers argue that corporatism contradicts democracy and that the greatest stumbling block to a functioning Mexican democracy is the continuation of the corporatist structures of Cárdenas and his successors.[5] Some changes in the corporatist structure have been introduced by recent presidents. Others, however, are the result of larger economic and political changes. Not only does the government have fewer resources to offer various groups, but its electoral competitors have challenged PRI's monopoly regionally.[6]

The corporatist features of the political system allow two types of channels for making political demands, and consequently two types of institutional representatives have arisen. The institutional relationship with the government under this type of system is traditionally a formal one: The state establishes an organization, requiring those persons meeting the criteria of a special interest to belong to it. For example, the state created several business organizations to which businesses employing a certain number of employees must belong.[7] The state, however, has not always managed to control all institutions representing various groups. Those it controls are considered to be quasi-governmental interest organizations. As some interest groups' influence grew and they became more autonomous, they created their own organizations, considered to be independent or autonomous. For example, the business community established the Mexican Association of Employers (Coparmex), an influential private-sector voice, the most vociferous organization in this sector in its opposition to Zedillo's austerity plan.

The other kind of channel is the informal channel, which is charac-teristic of all government models. Certain groups in Mexico do not use for-mal institutions, independent or governmental, to exercise their consider-able influence but instead use informal channels. The informal channels may be incorporated in the governmental structure or remain independent of it. Although we cannot assert with complete certainty that the informal channels are more significant than the formal channels, given the lack of relevant studies, most observers of Mexican politics believe that to be the case.

INSTITUTIONAL VOICES

The range of interest groups in the United States is formidable because of the political system's openness and the ability of multitudes of like-minded citizens and institutions to organize. Such collectivities in Mexico are fewer and weak, and do not figure as significantly in decision making.[8] Remember that decision making remains centered in the executive branch, thus block-ing the ability of diverse interests to pressure the legislative branch despite its growing influence. Further, the prohibition against running consecu-tively for legislative seats limits the potential threat that interests can level against individual members of Congress.

The most important groups incorporated formally and informally in the corporatist structure are the military, the Catholic Church, business, or-ganized labor, intellectuals and the media, nongovernmental organizations, and guerrillas. Each has a somewhat different institutional relationship to the government.[9] Most have stood out historically in other Latin American countries, suggesting the significance of similar past experiences and the influence of the colonial heritage on contemporary politics in the region.

The Military

No group has played a more significant role in Latin American political life than the military. However, since the 1930s its pattern of influence in Mexico has been quite different from that found elsewhere in Latin Amer-ica. Most important, the military has found it necessary to intervene polit-ically in every Latin American country except Mexico since that decade, and in most countries the military seized power in the 1970s and 1980s.[10]

The military's relationship to the Mexican state or government is dif-ferent from that of most other groups. The reason is that the military does not function as a separate political actor; rather, it is part of the government apparatus and operates under civilian leadership. This does not mean that the military does not have institutional interests; rather, it publically subsumes its differences from those of the state.

Since the 1930s Mexico's civil-military relationship has been increasingly characterized by subordination of the military and of its interests to those of society as defined by the civilian leadership.[11] Aside from Costa Rica, which has operated without an army since the late 1940s, and Venezuela, which began subordinating the military to civilian rule in the late 1950s, Mexico is an exception. How did its unusual relationship come about?

When Cárdenas became president—and he was part of the generation that had participated in Mexico's civil war—he incorporated the military into the recently established government party, the National Revolutionary Party (PNR). He wanted to balance the military against the agrarian and labor sectors within the party and thus lessen its overall political influence.[12]

Cárdenas's successor in the presidency, General Manuel Avila Camacho, altered this major characteristic of the early corporatist structure by removing the military as a separate party sector.[13] Basically, he did not want to recognize the military as having a public political voice and did not want to give it equal standing with other notable interest groups. From the 1940s to the present, then, the military's relationship to the government has been determined by its formal structural ties to the executive branch and through informal channels.

The political leadership gradually reduced the military's political influence through a variety of techniques. In the first place, as James Wilkie showed, each successive government reduced the military's allocation as a percentage of the federal budget;[14] the amount increased slightly each year, but the *percentage* went down. The size of the military in relation to population, and the sum budgeted to the military per capita, was among the lowest worldwide, far below the figures for the United States,[15] but has risen significantly in the 1990s. Under Zedillo, military expenditures are averaging 5 percent instead of 2 to 3 percent, placing it midway among countries' per capita expenditures. The armed forces were 170,000 in 1986, and reached 229,000 in 1996. They now number approximately 240,000.[16]

As the political leadership gradually reduced the size and potential influence of the military, it strengthened the legitimacy of political institutions, including the official party. The leadership had the advantage of operating in a semiauthoritarian fashion within the electoral arena. Military intervention is generally facilitated by competing political groups in a society that are seeking allies in the military. In Mexico, however, the military had to be either for the establishment—that is, the civilian leadership—or against it, and it had no outside civilian allies after 1952. During the 1940s, 1950s, and 1960s, military officers who pursued political careers helped bridge the gap between the civilian and military leaderships. In other words, these political military officers provided a significant, *informal* channel of communication, allowing the civilian leadership to solidify its control and to establish its legitimacy.

Civilian leadership also cemented its control over the military through the professional socialization process. Civilian politicians established several military schools, most notably the Heroic Military College, the Superior War College, and in 1981 the National Defense College, to train officers. One of the most important themes in the curriculum of the schools is respect for authority, for one's superior officer, and for the commander in chief, the president. Although all military schools tend to drill in their cadets the concept of subordination to authority, Mexican military academies are famous for the level of discipline they instill. An American officer, a graduate of a U.S. military academy, wrote that the dominant value would be the individual's willingness to subordinate himself totally to those in authority over him and the expectation that submission would be rewarded and independence would be severely punished. An officer's primary motivation would be to secure the rewards that the system has to offer.[17]

Colonel Steven Wager, one of the most knowledgeable Mexican military analysts, argued:

> Most of the political influence the military has attained since World War II has derived from its crisis management role, which has been fairly limited. However, that role has more often served as a double-edged sword for the army, rather than the distinct advantage some experts have perceived. Since the unfortunate incidents during the student uprisings in 1968, military leaders have been reluctant to participate in crisis situations, preferring to leave police actions to local and state authorities. The irony is that only by defending the state in a major crisis can the army substantially augment its power and prestige within the Mexican system.[18]

For these reasons and many others, the military is clearly subordinate to the civilian political leadership in Mexico. This does not mean that it has little or no influence on the government. The military has served the government in many capacities other than those traditionally subscribed to by the military in the United States.[19] The Mexican military's primary responsibility has not been national defense; rather, it has operated in many realms as an internal police force devoted to national security.[20] Not only does it provide the government with political intelligence, but it also has been used to maintain electoral peace, to settle contentious strikes, and, in the 1980s and 1990s, to carry out antinarcotics raids.

The activities that will most affect the military's relationship to the state and increase or decrease its potential influence over the decision-making process are its roles in the anti-drug-trafficking campaign and in maintaining public security, which have emerged in the 1990s as national security issues of significant proportions.[21] The United States not only has generated demand for illegal drugs, but by restricting sea and land routes through the Caribbean, the Drug Enforcement Agency has increased the number of locations in Mexico used in drug transshipments from Latin America. The alleged connection of drug trafficking and drug monies to the assassinations of the PRI's presidential candidate, the Tijuana police chief, and Cardinal Posadas in Guadalajara indicates the depth to which drug-related corruption has penetrated the Mexican political establishment.[22] In response to growing levels of crime and drug-related violence, President Zedillo established a National Public Security Council in 1996, giving for the first time "Mexico's military a role in decision making and policy-setting in important domestic public security matters."[23]

Salinas also fired his navy secretary midway through his administration when it became apparent that naval officials were using military installations and ports to transport drugs. Zedillo had to remove his first highly touted drug czar, General Jesús Gutiérrez Rebollo, just weeks after his appointment, when it became apparent that he too was in the pay of a drug cartel. The degree to which various units of the military are compromised by drug corruption increases their autonomy from civilian authorities and their own superiors, provokes interagency rivalries, and hastens the decline of military institutional integrity. Given the amounts of money involved and the constant demand from the United States, this is a serious, deeply troubling issue that will not disappear in the foreseeable future. It contributes heavily to political instability and to problems in the military–civilian relationship and the societal–institutional relationship generally.

The expanded military role in national security matters raises international and human rights issues too. In 1997 and 1998, according to the *Washington Post*, some 1,067 Mexican officers were trained at United States bases, and the Central Intelligence Agency instructed 90 officers in intelligence-gathering courses to enhance their participation in counter-narcotics activities. Critics charge that equipment supplied to the armed

forces for anti-drug trafficking use can be used indiscriminately against ordinary citizens or guerrilla sympathizers.[24]

Drug corruption and its consequences will be the most intractable
problem facing Mexico's leaders for the remainder of this century, but the
country's most immediate political issue refocusing attention on civil–
military relations is the attack by the Zapatista Army of National Liberation (EZLN) on January 1, 1994, on army encampments in the highlands
of Chiapas. Although the military had provided accurate intelligence on
the Zapatistas' activities long before their surprise attack, civilian intelligence authorities in the Secretariat of Government either chose to ignore
that information or convinced themselves that they could delay resolving
festering conflicts in the region, despite evidence to the contrary. The response of the Mexican military was swift and repressive and led to numerous allegations of human rights abuses and summary executions. However, because of the extraordinary Mexican and foreign media coverage,
President Salinas quickly reined in the military. The military responded
with extreme force to the Zapatista attacks, but it has not been anxious to
suppress large groups of Mexicans in response to mishandled civilian policies since the debacle of the 1968 student massacre. This decision has led
military leaders to demand a larger voice in formulating government security policy, rather than merely acting as a tool for resolving civilian mistakes.[25] According to one analyst, a high-ranking army officer publicly declared that the army would not attack the Zapatistas unless the EZLN
attacked first and more important, it would do so only if Congress approved.[26] The military lost the public relations war to the Zapatistas in
1994, damaging in the process its institutional and self-image. Thus, because of the price it paid for civilian failures, it is likely to ask for and receive a larger role in the policy process under the Zedillo administration.

Although the situation with the Zapatistas remains unsettled, army
troops have had to respond to a smaller but more widespread guerrilla organization, the People's Revolutionary Army (ERP), which emerged in the
summer of 1996 and is now operating in numerous states, as far north as
the border state of Tamaulipas. Accordingly, the military not only will demand a higher price from the government for its continued loyalty, but perhaps more important, because of the increasing political pluralization and
the declining civilian legitimacy, it may want autonomy from the state, at
least from a PRI-controlled state. The pluralist environment and the increasing strength of some opposition parties do offer the military this option for the first time in Mexico's recent history of forming alliances outside the government, thereby placing in jeopardy its traditional relationship
with civil authorities.

The Church

Although Mexico legally established and, in practice, enjoys freedom of religion, Mexicans, as we noted in Chapter 4, are overwhelmingly Catholic, products of a Catholic, Christian culture.[27] The Catholic Church exercised extraordinary political influence in Mexico and elsewhere in the region during the colonial period and continued to do so in the nineteenth century and part of the twentieth.[28] The pattern was broken at about the same time that the government began to reduce military influence significantly. The restrictive provisions in the 1917 constitution were implemented.

The church, unlike the military, operated as an institution fully independent of the government yet severely hampered in theory and practice by the constitution. The state reached an informal understanding with the church after 1930 that in effect allowed it to carry out its spiritual and pastoral functions within the purview of all churches in return for its remaining publicly quiet about political and social issues. The understanding remains in effect to this day and in practice was fairly well followed by both parties until the early 1980s.

The church's role as an interest group is limited because of the antichurch rhetoric that is incorporated into the public education of each child in Mexico. The church and clergy were at a disadvantage compared with some other groups in the corporatist arrangement because of the legal limbo they occupied. For example, the church as an institution had no legal standing until 1992, the only institution of the five sectors under discussion so characterized. Before 1992, clergy of all faiths did not have a legal right to vote, although many actually did.[29]

As Chapter 4 pointed out, Mexicans nonetheless remain very religious: Many are practicing Catholics, and most have a high regard for clergy and the church as an institution. Because respect for the church is high and opposition political organizations have not provided adequate channels for people to express their political demands, some Mexicans have turned to the church for guidance and, more important, as an institutional vehicle to convey their political frustrations.

The church, as is true of other groups, such as businessmen, does not speak with a single voice. Despite its image as a centralized, hierarchical institution, it is decentralized at the level of individual dioceses, of which there are seventy-three in Mexico. Dioceses and archdioceses are territorial subdivisions that serve as organizational units, and each is governed by a bishop or archbishop. Collectively, these men are the extremely autonomous hierarchy of the church. In recent years numerous bishops have spoken out publicly on issues affecting their dioceses.

It is apparent from recent events in Mexico that the geography and the social and economic composition of a diocese often affect the attitude and orientation of its priests and bishops. The most extreme example of this is, of course, Bishop Samuel Ruiz in Chiapas, whose clergy represents rural, indigenous interests in San Cristóbal de las Casas. Ruiz's firm stance in defense of the Indians, both before and after the Zapatista uprising, engendered criticism as well as support within episcopal ranks.[30] One of the issues that has increasingly disturbed many bishops is electoral fraud. Numerous bishops believe it is their responsibility to take stands on matters of social and political consequence, a belief that has produced implicit and explicit criticism of government actions.[31] One bishop commented:

> One point that is important to make which is independent of the present condition in Mexico is that the Church, both the bishops and priests, consider it necessary to socialize the people about their civic obligations regardless of what the political situation might be. The people are very ignorant of their civil responsibilities. From a moral point of view, we need to create a sense of consciousness. All of this can be badly interpreted by the government, which may see us wanting to reestablish political privileges we have had historically. For us, however, it is obvious that we have no desire to make policy decisions that are handled presently by the government. We only believe we have a responsibility to defend the people. Who else is there?[32]

Some bishops have strengthened their positions by joining together to explain their views. The most memorable instance in the past decade was that of the northern bishops, led by Archbishop Adalberto Almeida of Chihuahua; they condemned election fraud in Chihuahua in 1986 and called on the administration of Miguel de la Madrid to annul the results and hold new elections.[33] The bishops threatened to stop saying mass until the government responded to their demands. Although the pope intervened to prevent their carrying out the threat, the bishops' public posture, in direct violation of the constitution, illustrated their potential influence.

The leadership of the church in Mexico in terms of policy influence is the episcopate—the body of bishops, archbishops, and cardinals—which in conference recommends policies on issues ranging from the purely theological to foreign debt, the maldistribution of income, and drugs. The episcopal meetings result in the publication of pastoral letters and enunciations of recommended positions.

President Salinas moved, as part of his modernization plans, to make the Catholic Church a more open actor in the political system. Although many politicians resisted any changes in the constitutional restrictions of the church, Salinas believed the relationship was outdated and had to be refashioned. Demonstrating his new posture, he invited leading clergy to attend his inauguration in December 1988 and then appointed a former political figure as his personal representative to the Vatican. He also made Pope John Paul a welcome guest in Mexico in the summer of 1991, creating even closer relations between the government and the church. In 1992, Salinas revised several major constitutional provisions, one of which now permits recognition of all churches as legal entities. However, the reforms did leave several major constitutional issues unresolved, among them "religious education in public schools, access to electronic means of mass communication, [and] fiscal measures for religious associations."[34]

The church generally does not openly lobby for its political positions; rather, it requests and receives audiences with the state officials. Typically, party presidential candidates meet with bishops during their campaigns.[35] Church personnel also meet with various members of the executive branch on matters of mutual concern. On the state level, bishops frequently meet with state governors and collaborate with the government on social welfare projects. Although relations are good as a rule and have improved considerably since 1989, at the local level in certain instances, such as in the southern state of Chiapas, they may be quite conflictual. Chiapas has witnessed the deportation of priests, armed attacks on the bishop, conflicts among various religious groups, and the intervention of various outside national and international actors, including the Vatican envoy. The San Cristóbal de las Casas diocese has become deeply embroiled in the Chiapan conflict, involving indigenous peasants, mestizo ranchers, the government, paramilitary groups, and the army.

Many analysts continue to underestimate the potential social and political influence of the Catholic Church. But recent research shows that only a small minority of Mexicans want the church to pursue nonspiritual activities. Nevertheless, it is also clear that the church is regarded as a legitimate institution to express the general populace's frustrations with the government's social, economic, and political failures, particularly the issues of electoral fraud and human rights abuses.

President Salinas effectively legitimized the church's institutional role.[36] Although some observers believe the constitutional reforms decrease the church's autonomy, in practice the state actually legitimized it, decreasing the negative impact of the liberal heritage and allowing the church a greater part in nonspiritual matters. Although the church is very unlikely to confront the state on secular matters, it has become a more influential actor and will make its voice heard on national issues as societal dissension heats up.[37] The church is not successful in fomenting dissent; rather, it mirrors its constituency's frustrations. Indeed, it may well become an important channel for people's frustrations with the government's severe austerity measures.

Business

The private business sector combines some of the corporatist features of a governmental institution, the military, with those of an autonomous institution, the Church. As pointed out earlier, an array of its organizations present its demands to the government. The most important quasi-governmental organizations, established by the government itself, are a group of federations that include the National Chamber of Industries (Canacintra, or CNIT), the National Chamber of Commerce (Concanaco), and the National Federation of Chamber of Industries (Concamin). These organizations have been considerably weakened since 1996, when the Supreme Court ruled against obligatory chamber membership, leaving them insufficient revenues from membership fees and dependent on Commerce Department subsidies. The most important autonomous organizations, in addition to Coparmex, are the Mexican Insurance Association (AMIS), the Mexican Council of Businessmen (CMHN), and, before the nationalization of the banks in 1982, the Mexican Bankers Association.

When Cárdenas established some of these quasi-governmental business groups, the private sector was rather weak. As it has grown, it has not only developed other organizations to represent its own interests but has often taken positions on economic policies different from those advocated by the government.[38] The private sector, however, has labored under conditions similar to the constraints on the church, although not nearly as extreme. The government has allowed labor, professional organizations, and peasants to be formally represented in the party, but it has purposely excluded the private sector. It has done so because private-sector interests have not coincided with the rhetoric of the postrevolutionary leadership, even if in reality their interests have been shared.

Business groups do not easily fit into the corporatist model used by some scholars to describe Mexico's political system. This is so because the quasi-governmental organizations are not the most important means for expressing private-sector demands. Again, the significance of *informal* channels to express those demands becomes apparent. One prominent businessman described the actuality:

> Sometimes it is the business groups which approach the government concerning policy questions, and in other situations it is the government which takes the initiative with the private sector through the individual chambers.

It is really what you might call a corporatist situation in which the government and the private sector are tied together as far as interest representation. The difference between our system and that in your country is that here we try to influence directly the minister of the appropriate secretariat rather than going through the legislative branch. Normally, even though we try to directly influence the minister in charge, we first go through the chamber before approaching the individual personally.[39]

Recognizing the advantage of collective representation, at least on certain issues, businessmen created a unitary body to represent the top organizations: the Businessmen's Coordinating Council (CCE). The CCE, however, is not representative of its own members, even though it speaks for them. By far the most important business organization is the semisecret CMHN, which is made up of some thirty-eight prominent capitalists. The members meet frequently with both cabinet members and the president. Yet as members of the CMHN have revealed, rarely does it make demands on the government or the president; rather, membership in the elite organization is the instrument by which individual access to the president or the appropriate government official is gained.

Unofficial organizations have also exerted some influence. Until the 1970s, business and government maintained a relatively stable and symbiotic relationship, although tensions did exist.[40] By the end of Luis Echeverría's administration in 1976, these tensions were increasing as the government began to expand its economic role, buying up privately operated enterprises and initiating policies that ran counter to private-sector interests. This culminated in the 1982 decision by President José López Portillo (1976–1982) to nationalize privately owned banks. There followed a significant break between the private sector and the government and the former's great distrust of the latter.[41]

President Miguel de la Madrid worked assiduously in the 1980s to repair the damaged relationship and partially succeeded. Nevertheless, smaller independent business groups under Coparmex's vociferous leadership advocated a more energetic political activism for businessmen, including open support for opposition parties. These groups began to campaign for candidates of the National Action Party, and members even ran for state and local offices, especially in northern Mexico.[42] Their position was symbolized in the 1988 presidential race when a successful northern businessman, a former president of both Coparmex and the CCE, opposed Salinas on the PAN ticket. Their commitment became more intense and had positive results in the 1992 Chihuahua gubernatorial campaign, in which many of their members supported the PAN's victorious candidate, Fernando Barrio.

PAN is not the only party which has made inroads in the traditional government–business alliance. Dissident members of Canacintra, opposed to the entire formal, corporatist arrangement between business organizations and the state, found a strong ally in the PRD. As one observer argues, "PRD officials saw an opportunity to broaden the party's base of support to include one faction of business. Thus, the PRD integrated the private sector dissendents' anti-corporatist campaign with their own on-going criticisms of the state's liberal economic policies and authoritarian practices."[43]

Businessmen, more than any other group in Mexico with the exception of the political leaders themselves, have the capability of influencing government decisions, but especially in the economic realm, they have not been able to do so consistently or to a meaningful degree. This can be seen most vividly in the private sector's open criticism of Zedillo's austerity policy, thereby jeopardizing its success. Government economic policy, which has favored business's interests more frequently than those of organized labor, has emerged as much from the self-interest or preferences of government leaders as from private-sector pressures.

A student of private-sector political activity concluded, based on a case study of Chihuahua, this overt participation of entrepreneurs in the electoral arena has changed the traditional relationship between business and government.[44] The author believes—and this pattern appears to have been repeated in the 1995 elections in Jalisco, where the PAN also emerged victorious —that the entrepreneurs' support was crucial to the PAN's successes and strengthened the opposition generally. As individual businesses or business groups become directly tied to the electoral process and to the fortunes of opposition-party candidates, they acquire powerful political capital that they can use to negotiate with the state. In turn, the state must pay closer attention to business's demands, especially given the increasing electoral competitiveness and business's greater ability to determine the outcome of elections. This greater activity marks a significant change in entrepreneurial political behavior and, if adapted elsewhere in Mexico, will cause major alterations in state-group relations.

Organized Labor

Of all the groups with political influence in Mexico, organized labor best meets the criteria of an ideal, corporatist group. One of the contributing causes of the Mexican Revolution was the suppression of the working class under the Porfiriato. General Obregón recognized the political importance of labor and relied on labor's support in his struggles against President Venustiano Carranza. The labor movement started to grow in the 1920s, and in the next decade membership in labor organizations reached 15.4 percent of the economically active workforce. It has not grown in percentage terms since 1940 and by 1970 began to decline.[45]

Organized labor in Mexico is quite different from that in the United States. The first distinguishing characteristic is the preponderance of government employees, most of them federal, who account for more than a third of all organized workers. The second characteristic is that organized labor is made up of unions called confederations, similar to the chambers of the business organizations. Nearly half of organized laborers are members of these broad confederations. The third differentiating characteristic of labor is the lesser presence of purely industrial-based unions such as those of miners, electricians, and petroleum workers.

The most important labor organization, the Mexican Federation of Labor (CTM), was established under President Cárdenas. He and his successors maintained a close relationship with union leaders that amounted to government control.[46] The control was cemented by incorporating the CTM as the foundation of one of the three sectoral pillars of the National Revolutionary Party—a role that continues to this day. The CTM was led from the 1940s to 1997 by Fidel Velázquez, giving him considerable stature and influence in the labor movement.[47] More than any other characteristic, organized labor's status within the party places it in the semi-corporatist fold. Unlike business, the church, or even the military, which is incorporated into the state itself, organized labor has had a prominent role in the government party. Between 1979 and 1988, for example, 21 to 25 percent of the PRI's candidates were labor leaders, most commonly from the CTM.[48] This does not mean that it influences the decision-making process but, rather, that its relationship with the government, through the party, is formalized, legitimized, and visible.

A small but growing percentage of unions in Mexico are independent of government control. One of the most interesting consequences of the North American Free Trade Agreement's (NAFTA) labor provisions is the impact on labor–government relations generally, and specifically on legitimizing independent organizations. In 1997, for the first time in history, a PRI-affiliated union was decertified in favor of an independent union among the 2,700 assembly (maquiladora) plants.[49] In some cases their leadership has been able to obtain better benefits for members than have government-controlled unions. On the other hand, studies of independent unions in Mexico reveal that democratically elected leaders typically do not better represent the demands of the rank and file than do the designated leaders in government-controlled unions.

The government has used unions to prevent the mobilization of large-scale opposition. "The government treats labor as a firm parent would a teenager. When it needs support in family crises and labor quickly provides it, it rewards the action. But when labor strays away from the family fold, it is scolded in a variety of ways. The government, not organized labor, controls the relationship."[50] The most common technique used by the government's firm hand is promoting new unions and leaders to keep established unions in line. As independent unions increase in numbers, and as opposition parties gain strength, the government will no longer be able to use this technique so effectively. The dominance of the CTM is waning. Within two months of Fidel Velasquez's death in 1997, other leaders formed the National Workers Union (UNT), an umbrella organization composed of 110 unions and two million workers, to oppose the CTM. Organized labor has failed to achieve political and economic influence in Mexico because of its subordination and because it represents only a small proportion of all workers. Unions have also remained weak and dependent on government because most of their members do not pay dues; state-controlled unions actually receive subsidies from the government.[51]

One of the most important groups in Mexico, and the largest single organization in the union of government workers, is the National Teachers Union (SNTE). A study of it provides interesting data on its techniques for conveying demands to the private sector and the government (see Table 6-1). Mexican unions must convince the government that their demands are legitimate; otherwise, they cannot legally strike. Determinations of legality are made by conciliation and arbitration boards, on which the gov-

Table 6-1 Means Used by Organized Labor in Mexico to Convey Demands: National Teachers Union

Union Means of Action	Percentage of Total
Partial strike	20.71
Meetings, marches, demonstrations	20.71
Strike	16.82
Indefinite strike	6.47
Parade in front of public buildings	5.82
Call for a demonstration	5.82
Rejection of salary increases	5.50
Denunciations in press conferences	5.12
Block streets and highways	4.20
Occupy educational institutions	3.55
Block access to offices	2.58
List of demands to authorities	1.94
Hunger strikes	.64

Source: Este País, June 1991, 32–34; based on an analysis of 237 newspaper articles, January–April 1991.

ernment representative holds the deciding vote. The strike is only one means of conveying demands; marches and demonstrations have become increasingly common. But strike threats bring pressure to bear on both government and private-sector management.

Because teachers were federal employees when the data were compiled, it is revealing to examine how the government itself responds to labor demands (see Table 6-2). Rarely does it actually raise salaries; rather, it provides low-cost benefits—such as discounts for married teachers at government stores—or relies on dialogue or promises to resolve complaints. If it decides not to negotiate, the government then takes a hard line, either refusing to discuss the issues or threatening to fire striking teachers.

Organized labor, although part of the declining government corporatist structure, did not favor the nomination of Carlos Salinas or Ernesto Zedillo as the PRI presidential candidate. In fact, in the case of Salinas, the leadership of the powerful petroleum workers union encouraged its members to support the opposition. Only a short time after his inauguration Salinas had the head of the union arrested and charged with a number of criminal violations. Salinas also engineered a change in the leadership of the teachers union. Critics wanted him to eliminate the cozy relationship between organized labor and government to bring about economic and political liberalization. Instead, Salinas established control over recalcitrant union leaders. Since taking office, Zedillo has not shown any inclination to alter this relationship.

The current relationship between labor and the state extends well beyond labor's failure to choose a favored candidate as the PRI presidential nominee. The economic liberalization policies introduced by Miguel de la Madrid in the mid-1980s and expanded by Salinas have had "profound im-

Table 6-2 Government Responses to Organized Labor Demands: National Teacher Union

Government Response to Union Demands	Percentage of Total
Married teachers will receive discounts	42.02
Dialogue	14.49
Shut off dialogue	13.04
Promise to resolve issues	8.69
No funds available	8.69
Will fire teachers who miss three days	7.24
Offer a small salary increase	2.89
Reject violent actions	1.44
Reject actions	1.44

Source: Este País, June 1991, 32.

plications for the state-labor alliance which has been so central to the Mexican regime" since the formation of the corporatist strategy.[52] As Ruth Berins Collier observed, the established relationship, based on the state's protection of labor, has now lost its logic. Although it is clear from economic data that labor never benefited in real terms from rising wages, the government did provide subsidies for consumer goods and housing and job security. And of course, the government included labor representation in the legislative branch. The activities of the PRD, which espouses an economic philosophy decidedly more favorable to labor interests, offer a political alternative to both organized and unorganized working-class groups allied with the PRI.

In terms of impact on government policy, labor has little to say. In the 1980s, real wages fell dramatically, and labor was not able to obtain increases even equal to inflation. In fact, the minimum wage in 1998 in real terms is less than it was in 1970. In the only studies of actual policy decisions in which labor and the private sector had a part, the private sector came out on top.[53] Still, the private sector believes that labor had the greater say in economic policy than business did, primarily because labor is represented formally in the party structure and business is not. This inaccurate perception implies the psychological and symbolic importance of such formal standing and of government *rhetoric*, which favors the interests of the working class.

Intellectuals and the Media

The intellectual community has an amorphous relationship with the government. Some of its formal organizations are patronized by the state; others are independent. None speaks for the intellectual community, but they do provide some public prestige. The most salient quasi-governmental organization is the National College, whose members are prominent in all fields, including law, sciences, humanities, social sciences, and fine arts.

The relationship of the intellectual community to the state is much more a product of the relationship between the government and intellectual employment than between the government and intellectuals' organizations. Three sectors of the economy employ the vast majority of intellectuals: government, academia, and publishing. Unlike intellectuals in the United States, Latin American intellectuals—Mexican intellectuals among them—have a long history of employment in public life, either in a federal bureaucracy, especially the Secretariats of Foreign Affairs and Education, or in various political posts as governors, party leaders, and cabinet members.[54]

The lack of employment opportunities in Mexico has encouraged intellectuals to work for the government. This means that the government does not have to incorporate intellectuals formally into institutional relationships with the state because the majority have been state employees since the 1920s. Many intellectuals, desirous of maintaining greater autonomy, have sought employment in the most prestigious universities, especially those in Mexico City. They hold teaching and administrative positions at the National Autonomous University, the Autonomous Technological Institute of Mexico, the Ibero-American University, and at the Colegio de México. Intellectuals have advantageous ties to the government because many were classmates of future politicians and others have been their teachers. Politicians often identify prominent intellectuals as having been their most influential professors.

If intellectuals influence societal ideas, they do so through the written word. Intellectuals in Mexico, as in the United States and other countries, establish magazines to circulate their views. Magazines dedicated to particular schools of thought are typically the product of a group of people who share certain ideological principles. One Mexican described the phenomenon:

> There are some good papers and excellent magazines here, but each one tends to be controlled by some group or interest. All of these, such as *Excélsior*, or the publications of the Colegio de México and the Fondo de Cultura Económica, are publications of elite groups. It is very difficult for a person who writes to publish in them if [he or she does] not belong to the group in control of that publication. . . . These groups exist because most intellectuals are receptive to ideas paralleling their own preferences. . . . Actually there are very few independent intellectuals in Mexico, or intellectuals who have not formed groups.[55]

Some of the more prominent contemporary intellectual groups in Mexico include those of the late Octavio Paz, who contributed to his journal *Vuelta*, Héctor Aguilar Camín, who directs the popular monthly *Nexos*, and Federico Reyes Heroles, who edits *Este País*, Mexico's first magazine devoted to survey research, but with a strong intellectual bent. Other groups are associated with newspapers, and many intellectuals earn a portion of their income contributing essays to editorial pages.

The intellectual community has increasingly sought new channels in the electronic media, mainly in television. Some prominent Mexican figures, including Enrique Krause, Octavio Paz, and Rolando Cordera, have used this medium to reach a larger audience and to discuss controversial political and social topics. The proliferation of public opinion polls, the association of some leading figures with these survey research efforts, and most important, their analysis of the findings in both the print and electronic media extend the intellectuals' influence to the electoral arena, as polling results become identified with the party and the candidate.[56]

The government's relationship to the intellectual community is also reflected in its attitude toward the media and censorship.[57] Although freedom of speech obtains throughout Mexico, freedom of the press depends on the medium. Radio and television programming comes under strict supervision. Book publishing is very open, though with a bit of censorship. Publishers generally use self-censorship. An example occurred at *The News*, an English-language daily controlled by *Novedades*, whose publisher, Rómulo O'Farrill Jr., censored its staff in both 1992 and 1993.[58] There are some notable cases of the government's pressure on publications that criticized its policies. One such publication, the daily newspaper *Uno Más Uno*, lost its independence in a move engineered by the Salinas government; it has since followed a pro-Salinas line. The government briefly attempted to use the same strategy against *Este País*. In other situations the government has threatened to cancel or has actually canceled advertising in offending publications. Most leading publications receive 30 to 40 percent of their revenues from government advertising; accordingly, this indirect subsidy encourages caution among its beneficiaries.[59]

The influence of censorship and self-censorship on politics can be better understood by exploring the media's coverage of various parties in the electoral process. A number of studies examined both television and print media coverage of the candidates in the 1994 elections. These studies found qualitative biases in the media's presentation of the various parties or candidates, and in addition, the quantitative biases in the coverage were extreme. For example, in a study of two leading television news programs, *24 Horas* and *Hechos*, from January to April 1994, the authors discovered that on *24 Horas* the amount of time given to the PRI candidate compared with that given to his major rivals was in a ratio of 46 to 1. The parties did better, but on both programs, the PRI received far more attention than did the PAN or the PRD.[60] The same was true of the print media, which gave the PRI candidate 44 percent of their coverage, compared with 24 percent and 20 percent for the PRD and the PAN, respectively.

Overall, despite these conditions, media professionalism is on the upswing. *Reforma*, a major Mexican daily owned by a Monterrey-based publisher, accepts no government advertising and has strict journalistic guidelines. Televisa, a private television monopoly with an openly declared government bias in the past, not only has faced intense competition from the Azteca chain, but its leadership changed significantly in 1997.[61]

Table 6-3 The Impact of Media on Voter Preferences in Mexico, 1997

Viewer Preference	Percent Favoring PRI	Percent Voting for PRI
Televisa Viewers	28	13
Televisión Azteca Viewers	14	14
All Viewers	21	14

Source: Adapted from Chappell Lawson, "Does it Matter? What a Free Press Could Mean in Mexico," in *Media and New Democracies: Mexico's Fourth Estate*, ed. Sallie Hughes and Roderic Ai Camp (forthcoming, 1999).

The impact of this changing pattern in television coverage is starkly illustrated by Chappell Lawson's examination of 402 voters in Mexico City during the contentious 1997 race for head of the Federal District. Lawson interviewed the respondents when the candidates were announced, after a debate on television, and immediately following the elections. He discovered a marked change among Televisa viewers who initially favored PRI. More than half of those voters abandoned the PRI for another party's candidate. (See Table 6.3.) Televisa coverage, balanced among the leading candidates, significantly altered the outcome of the election.

The dependence of intellectuals and journalists and the institutions that employ them, on the largesse of the state, affects their relationship to the government. Some intellectuals have successfully pursued independent careers as economic opportunities have expanded, a practice that may be on the rise, but still is unusual. Sectors of the intellectual community continue to rely heavily on the government to support their activities and to recognize their merits, thus legitimizing government in the eyes of the educated Mexican.

VOICES OF DISSENT

Whether or not Mexico's political model is a more or less orthodox example of a corporatist structure, the government has never successfully incorporated all potentially influential groups into its fold, nor all members of the groups just discussed. Indeed, many of those who oppose the government politically were formerly its supporters. These include both intellectuals and political opposition leaders.

Mexico has allowed dissent but has successfully controlled its level and tone for some time. The government has had a structural advantage in terms of continuity of leadership and the dominance of its machine, the

PRI, over the voting process. In an underdeveloped economy, the state's economic resources are overwhelming, and in Mexico those resources have been used to disarm and co-opt dissidents, be they peasant leaders, lawyers, labor organizers, or intellectuals. Yet the state, including the presidency and the federal bureaucratic leadership—contrary to its impression as a monolithic and all powerful institution—demonstrates in practice that it is "a heterogeneous concoction of social classes and political factions holding little consensus over critical issues."[62] Co-optation is the process by

---

Cooptation: the process by which the government successfully incorporates an individual person or group into its ranks.

---

which the government incorporates an individual person or group into its ranks. Groups find it difficult to counter government influence over their leaders. Few people can resist the attraction of political power or money, and the government often rewards cooperation with prestigious posts. Some persons accept the posts for financial reasons; others because of the possibility of working within rather than outside the system.

On the whole, the government has dealt well with contending groups, maneuvering them against one another when it believed that was necessary or creating intragroup competition to diminish the strength of a single recalcitrant leader or organization. The attitudes of each administration toward various groups and individual leaders have varied. President Salinas changed overall government-group relations, giving greater attention and consequently prestige to business, the military, and the church, and less attention to labor.

Nongovernmental Organizations

Mexico has witnessed a flowering of popular movements since 1989. This is not a new phenomenon. Many groups with political, economic, and social interests grew out of the general malaise of the 1968 student movement and the subsequent government repression, and such organizations were given an additional boost in Mexico City after the 1985 earthquake. Also, after 1968, women were given more influential roles in these organizations, particularly in urban areas. In the 1988 presidential elections, many of these movements began linking themselves more closely to political parties.[63]

Critical voices have been a presence among most of these groups for decades. But a set of organizations over which the government has been unable to exercise much control has been nongovernmental organizations. Nongovernmental organizations range in scope from civic action groups, similar to the League of Women Voters in the United States, to religiously affiliated human rights advocacy organizations.

As the 1994 presidential elections approached, many civic organizations were formed specifically to observe and evaluate the electoral process. Among the most notable of these organizations was an umbrella group, the *Alianza Cívica,* or Civic Alliance, which coordinated dozens of other organizations. Directed by Sergio Aguayo, a leading Mexican intellectual and human rights activist, Civic Alliance represented Mexicans seeking democratic change, in particular clean and fair elections. It recruited election observers from four hundred nongovernmental and civic groups to watch five thousand polling places. Even intellectuals became involved in the electoral outcome, when a loosely organized elite, calling itself the San Angel group, acted as a watchdog.

The political changes introduced since the 1988 presidential elections, as well as President Salinas's dismantling of certain features and structures of established state–group relations, contributed to the increasing growth and strength of nongovernmental organizations and to links with peer groups in other countries, ranging from environmental to human rights allies. Human rights organizations in Mexico, both independent and affiliated with the Catholic Church, were especially effective in obtaining media attention and support for their agendas, thereby becoming important actors in the political and social arenas.

Some analysts believe that President Salinas attempted to respond to many of the local nongovernmental groups and to reformulate the relationship between these grassroots organizations and the government through his Solidarity program, by channeling large amounts of federal revenues into local projects.[64] In reality, most nongovernmental groups are characterized by their lack of partisan political attachments. They also have created a network of channels from which to work outside the party system altogether. Finally, they have contributed significantly to an expansion of international influences in Mexico.[65]

Guerrillas

The failure of Mexican administrations—local, state, and national—to resolve many long-standing problems, particularly in rural communities, came to a head on January 1, 1994, with far-reaching national and international consequences. A different kind of popular movement, willing to use force to obtain redress for decades of abuse and exploitation of indigenous peasants in the highlands of Chiapas, emerged in the form of the Zapatista Army of National Liberation (EZLN), which launched guerrilla attacks and seized villages near San Cristóbal de las Casas.[66]

The Zapatistas' beliefs are laid out very clearly in their official paper, *El Despertador Mexicano*, and cover many issues, including women's rights. Their principal focus is on agrarian and economic reform, and some of their requests echo the voice of their inspiration, Emiliano Zapata, such as limits on land ownership and the redistribution of excessive land holdings.[67] The rebellion had at least three underlying causes: disappointment with the government for changing the provisions for agrarian reform in Article 27 and ignoring peasants as a client group, the peasants' declining economic status in the rural community, and their exclusion from the political process.[68]

The enigmatic spokesperson for the EZLN, Subcomandante Marcos, later identified as Rafael Sebastián Guillén, a former university professor and non-Indian, captured the national and international media's attention.[69] It immediately became clear that although most Mexicans opposed the guerrillas' use of force, they sympathized strongly with their goals. The EZLN uprising influenced the pace of electoral change for the remainder of 1994, leading to more electoral reforms favorable to the opposition parties, and it also set the tone for this period as one of increasing political instability and violence, especially after the PRI presidential candidate, Luis Donaldo Colosio, was assassinated. The rebellion also demonstrated to other popular movements that even small, well-organized groups can have tremendous political influence. The Zapatistas also demonstrated the importance of the electronic media, illustrating their ability to defeat the military and the government in the media war, and the means by which such a group could affiliate itself with NGOs nationally and internationally through e-mail. It maintains an updated web site.[70]

Although the government and the Zapatistas signed an agreement in February 1996, the San Andrés accords, President Zedillo has not implemented these provisions. Among the provisions, the government agreed to permit the Indian communities to establish local governments, to educate themselves using indigenous languages, and to mandate indigenous representation in legislative bodies. The negotiations remain stalemated as of early-1999.

The continued lack of resolution of the Zapatista issue, the high-level presence of troops in the region, and the activities of paramilitary groups, often in the employ of local economic interests and political officials, have contributed to increased violence in Chiapas. Most notably, a paramilitary group in the employ of a local PRI leader attacked the village of Acteal in

December 1997, murdering forty-five indigenous people, including children. The national and international reaction to these blatant acts of violence and human rights abuses led to President Zedillo replacing his secretary of government, the cabinet figure responsible for internal security and negotiating peace with the EZLN, in early 1998, and also to the resignation of the governor of Chiapas.[71]

The emergence of the Zapatistas produced an environment more favorable to other groups willing to use violence to achieve their goals. In the summer of 1996, an organization calling itself the People's Revolutionary Army (ERP) initated attacks on isolated police outposts and military patrols in the southern state of Oaxaca and elsewhere in central Mexico. They have been traced back to dissident leftist groups founded in the 1960s, and to an organization associated with Lucio Cabañas, a guerrilla leader killed in Guerrero in the 1970s. Unlike the Zapatistas, the ERP has been unwilling to negotiate with the government. Small affiliated groups have continued their attacks in seventeen different states. Other armed groups are also operating in many rural regions.

CONCLUSION

From the leadership's viewpoint, Mexico developed a successful corporatist structure for engaging and controlling the society's most important interest groups. The corporatist system had never been comprehensive or complete but had channeled many political demands through quasi-governmental institutions. It is not an ideal corporatist system but it is nevertheless essential to the workings of the political process.

Various groups in Mexico, including the military, the Church, business, labor, intellectuals, and the media, have maintained somewhat different relations with the government, depending on the legal and institutional role given to them by society. Interestingly, whether their relationship is established and visible or more autonomous and independent, the informal channels that their leaders use carry more weight in the decision-making process than do the formal channels. The political system has used and abused interest-group institutions to mobilize the rank and file for their own purposes rather than, for the most part, to hear group demands.

The groups having the most institutionalized relationship with the government through their incorporation in the party structure have had the least influence, on the whole, on the decision-making process. Groups excluded from the party, such as business, the Church, and the military, have influenced the decision-making process more heavily. Of the major interest groups in most Western polities, business has had the most influence on Mexican government policies, primarily in the area of economics. The relationship between business and the government has been symbiotic, benefiting both.

The state itself has often pursued its own policies, not in response to demands or pressures from any particular group, but because of self-interest or its interpretation of societal interests.[72] In this sense, the state has been an actor in the decision-making process. It has had the greatest potential for influencing the outcome of policy making because it operated in a semiauthoritarian environment and it mediated among the more traditional, competing interests.

Mexico has been able to sustain its peculiar brand of corporatism because, as one careful student discovered, it was able to "balance (imperfectly and with dire fiscal consequences) demands from below for social justice with economic growth."[73] But the pluralistic influences introduced into the political system have restricted the government's ability to perform these tasks in the future. It remains to be seen, however, if nongovernmental organizations or nonviolent popular movements can go beyond making social demands to serving as a direct bridge to political change, establishing organizational and policy alternatives.[74] Mexico is witnessing the breakdown of the authoritarian structures and a change in the rules of the game while at the same time it has debilitated and weakened the mediating structures between interest groups and the state. Some of these groups are also undergoing internal changes, thus further complicating their relationship with the state.

NOTES

1. For the Mexican version, see Ruth Spalding, "The Mexican Variant of Corporatism," *Comparative Political Studies* 14 (July 1981): 139–61.

2. Nora Hamilton, *The Limits of State Autonomy: Post Revolutionary Mexico* (Princeton, N.J.: Princeton University Press, 1982), describes this early pattern. Presidents Adolfo López Mateos (1958–1964) and Luis Echeverría (1970–1976) also responded more strongly to working-class interests.

3. For an interpretation that identifies cracks in the corporatist edifice in the mid-1980s, see Howard J. Wiarda, "Mexico: The Unravelling of a Corporatist Regime?" *Journal of Inter-American Studies and World Affairs* 30 (Winter 1988–1989): 1–28.

4. Luis Rubio, "Economic Reform and Political Liberalization," in *The Pol-*

itics of Economic Liberalization in Mexico, ed. Riordan Roett (Boulder, Colo.: Lynne Rienner, 1993), 35–50.

5. James Sánchez Susarrey, "Corporativismo o democracia?" *Vuelta* 12 (March 1988): 12–19.

6. Blanca Heredia, "Clientelism in Flux: Democratization and Interest Intermediation in Contemporary Mexico," paper presented at the National Latin American Studies Association, Guadalajara, 1997.

7. Robert J. Shafer, *Mexican Business Organizations* (Syracuse, N.Y.: Syracuse University Press, 1973), explains these requirements in some detail.

8. Judith A. Teichman, *Policymaking in Mexico: From Boom to Crisis* (Boston: Allen & Unwin, 1988).

9. Miguel Basáñez, *La lucha por la hegemonía en México, 1968–1990*, 8th ed. (Mexico City: Siglo XXI, 1990), 35ff.

10. Abraham Lowenthal and J. Samuel Fitch, *Armies and Politics in Latin America*, rev. ed. (New York: Holmes & Meier, 1986), 4ff.

11. Franklin D. Margiotta, "Civilian Control and the Mexican Military: Changing Patterns of Political Influence," in *Civilian Control of the Military: Theories and Cases from Developing Countries*, ed. Claude E. Welch Jr. (Albany: State University of New York Press, 1976).

12. Gordon C. Schloming, "Civil-Military Relations in Mexico, 1910–1940: A Case Study" (Ph.D. diss., Columbia University, 1974), 297.

13. Jorge Lozoya, *El ejécito mexicano (1911–1965)* (Mexico City: El Colegio de México, 1970), 64.

14. James W. Wilkie, *The Mexican Revolution: Federal Expenditure and Social Change Since 1910*, 2d ed. (Berkeley and Los Angeles: University of California Press, 1970), 100–6.

15. Merilee Grindle, "Civil-Military Relations and Budget Politics in Latin America," *Armed Forces and Society* 13 (Winter 1987): 255–75.

16. Roderic Ai Camp, "Militarizing Mexico, Where is the Officer Corps Going?," RAND Corporation, Santa Monica, 1997.

17. Michael J. Dziedzic, "Mexico's Converging Challenges: Problems, Prospects, and Implications," unpublished manuscript, U.S. Air Force Academy, April 1989, 34.

18. Stephen J. Wager, "The Mexican Military Approaches the 21st Century: Coping with a New World Order," *Special Report* (Carlisle, Pa.: U.S. Army War College, 1994), 15.

19. See Roderic A. Camp, *Generals in the Palacio: The Military in Modern Mexico* (New York: Oxford University Press, 1992), for an analysis of these roles.

20. Phylis Greene Walker, "The Modern Mexican Military: Political Influence and Institutional Interests" (master's thesis, American University, 1987), 76.

21. For evidence of this, see José Luis Reyna, "Narcotics as a Destabilizing Force for Source Countries and Non-Source Countries," in *The Latin American Narcotics Trade and United States National Security*, ed. Donald A. Mabry (Westport, Conn.: Greenwood Press, 1989), 123–35.

22. The most pessimistic view, backed by considerable evidence of corrup-

tion in the Salinas and de la Madrid administrations, reaching the top levels, is offered in Christopher Whalen's "México: El narcosistema," *Dinero*, November 1994, 162–76.

23. Eric L. Olson, "The Evolving Role of Mexico's Military in Public Security and Antinarcotics Programs," Washington Office on Latin America, May 1996, 4.

24. Douglas Farah and Dana Priest, "Mexican Drug Force Is U.S.-Bred," *Washington Post*, February 26, 1998, 1A.

25. I present these arguments in my "The Sword and the Cross, New Battlefields in Chiapas?" "Enfoque," *La Reforma*, February 20, 1994, 16–20.

26. Stephen J. Wager, "The Mexican Military: The Dilemma of Functioning in a One-Party System," in *Beyond Praetorianism: The Latin American Military in Transition*, ed. Richard Millett and Michael Gold-Bliss (Miami: North-South Center Press, 1996), 125.

27. Soledad Loaeza, "La iglesia católica y el reformismo autoritario," *Foro Internacional* 25 (October-December 1984): 142.

28. The relationship is outlined in Karl Schmitt, "Church and State in Mexico: A Corporatist Relationship," *Americas* 40 (January 1984): 349–76.

29. For an excellent example, see Matt Moffet, "In Catholic Mexico, a Priest's Power Is Limited to Prayer," *Wall Street Journal*, December 6, 1989.

30. The best analysis of church involvement in base communities and the internal and external consequences of Bishop Ruiz's role in Chiapas can be found in Michael Tangeman (longtime correspondent for the *Catholic National Review*), *Mexico at the Crossroads, Politics, the Church, and the Poor* (Maryknoll, N.Y.: Orbis Books, 1994). For the political involvement of CEBs, see Elsa Guzmán and Christopher Martin, "Back to Basics Mexican Style: Radical Catholicism and Survival on the Margins," *Bulletin of Latin American Research* 16, (1997): 351–66.

31. For examples of the potential political conflict, see Claude Pomerlau, "The Changing Church in Mexico and Its Challenge to the State," *Review of Politics* 43 (October 1981): 540–59.

32. Interview with Abelardo Alvardo Alcantara, auxiliary bishop of Mexico City, June 2, 1987.

33. Dennis M. Hanratty, "The Church," in *Prospects for Democracy in Mexico*, ed. George Grayson (New Brunswick, N.J.: Transaction Books, 1990), 118.

34. Roberto Blancarte, "Religion and Constitutional Change in Mexico, 1988–1992," *Social Compass* 40 (1993): 567.

35. Interviews with former presidents José López Portillo and Miguel de la Madrid, Mexico City, summer 1990.

36. For an excellent description of church-state relations under Salinas before the reforms, see Allan Metz, "Mexican Church-State Relations Under President Carlos Salinas de Gortari," *Journal of Church and State* 34 (Winter 1992): 111–30.

37. Evidence of this, based on numerous interviews with higher clergy, can be found in my *Crossing Swords: Politics and Religion in Mexico* (New York: Oxford University Press, 1997).

38. The best analysis in English of these industrial groups is by Dale Story,

Industry, the State, and Public Policy in Mexico (Austin: University of Texas Press, 1986).

39. Roderic Ai Camp, *Entrepreneurs and Politics in Twentieth Century Mexico* (New York: Oxford University Press, 1989), 141–42.

40. John Womack, "The Spoils of the Mexican Revolution," *Foreign Affairs* 48 (July 1970): 677–87.

41. Saúl Escobar Toledo, "Rifts in the Mexican Power Elite, 1976–1986," in *Government and the Private Sector in Contemporary Mexico*, ed. Sylvia Maxfield (La Jolla, Calif.: Center for U.S.–Mexican Studies, UCSD, 1987), 79.

42. Graciela Guadarrama S., "Entrepreneurs and Politics: Businessmen in Electoral Contests in Sonora and Nuevo León," in *Electoral Patterns and Perspectives in Mexico*, ed. Arturo Alvarado (La Jolla, Calif.: Center for U.S.–Mexican Studies, UCSD, 1987), 83ff.

43. Kenneth C. Shadlen, "Small Industry and the Mexican Left: Corportism, Neoliberalism, and Political Activism," paper presented at the National Latin American Studies Conference, Guadalajara, 1997, 28.

44. See Yemile Mizrahi, "Changing Political Traditions in Mexico: The Emerging Role of Entrepreneurs," paper presented at the National Latin American Studies Association, Atlanta, March 1994, 15; her major study, "A New Conservative Opposition in Mexico: The Politics of Entrepreneurs in Chihuahua (1983–1992)" (Ph.D. diss., University of California at Berkeley, 1994); and her "La nueva relación entre los empresarios y el gobierno: el surgimiento de los empresarios panistas," *Estudios Sociológicos* 14, (1996): 493–515.

45. Howard Handleman, "The Politics of Labor Protest in Mexico: Two Case Studies," *Journal of Inter-American Studies and World Affairs* 18 (August 1976): 267–94.

46. George W. Grayson, *The Mexican Labor Machine: Power, Politics, and Patronage*, Significant Issues Series 19 (Washington, D.C.: CSIS, 1989), 12.

47. For background, see Kevin J. Middlebrook, "State-Labor Relations in Mexico: The Changing Economic and Political Context," in *Unions, Workers, and the State in Mexico*, ed. Kevin J. Middlebrook (La Jolla, Calif.: Center for U.S.–Mexican Studies, UCSD, 1991), 1–26.

48. Juan Reyes del Campillo, "El movimiento obrero en la Cámara de Diputados (1979–1988)," *Revista Mexicana de Sociología* 52 (July-September 1990): 139–60.

49. Sam Dillon, "Mexican Factory to Recognize Independent Union Severing Ties to Government," www.NYT.com, December 14, 1997.

50. Roderic A. Camp, "Organized Labor and the Mexican State: A Symbiotic Relationship?" *Mexican Forum* 4 (October 1984): 4.

51. Kevin J. Middlebrook, "The Political Economy of State-Labor Relations in Mexico," paper presented at the National Latin American Studies Association, Washington, D.C., March 1982, and "The Sounds of Silence: Organised Labour's Response to Economic Crisis in Mexico," *Journal of Latin American Studies* 21 (May 1989): 195–220.

52. Ruth Berins Collier, *The Contradictory Alliance, State-Labor Relations*

and Regime Change in Mexico (Berkeley: International and Area Studies, University of California, 1992), 156.

53. Susan K. Purcell, *The Mexican Profit-Sharing Decision: Politics in an Authoritarian Regime* (Berkeley and Los Angeles: University of California Press, 1975).

54. Fred P. Ellison, "The Writer," in *Continuity and Change in Latin America,* ed. John J. Johnson (Stanford, Calif.: Stanford University Press, 1964), 84.

55. Roderic A. Camp, *Intellectuals and the State in Twentieth-Century Mexico* (Austin: University of Texas Press, 1985), 131.

56. For discussions of its influence, see Juan Carlos Gamboa, "Media, Public Opinion Polls, and the 1994 Mexican Presidential Election," in *Polling for Democracy, Public Opinion and Political Liberalization in Mexico,* ed. Roderic Ai Camp (Wilmington: Scholarly Resources, 1996), 17–36.

57. Albert L. Hester and Richard R. Cole, eds., *Mass Communications in Mexico* (Brookings, S.D.: Association for Education in Journalism, 1975).

58. The details of these machinations are fully explained by Jeffrey Staub (a former reporter for the paper), in "Self-Censorship and the Mexican Press," *Mexico Policy News,* no. 9, fall 1993, 30–34. Background information on these relationships can be found in Ilya Adler, "Press-Government Relations in Mexico: A Study of Freedom of the Mexican Press and Press Criticism of Government Institutions," *Studies in Latin American Popular Culture* 12 (1993): 1–29.

59. Marvin Alisky, "Government Mechanism of Mass Media Control," paper presented at the Southeast Council of Latin American Studies, Tampa, April 1979.

60. See Mexican Academy of Human Rights, "The Media and the 1994 Federal Elections in Mexico, a Content Analysis of Television News Coverage of the Political Parties and Presidential Candidates," May 19, 1994, 3.

61. For the impact of *Reforma,* see Murray Fromson, "Mexico's Struggle for a Free Press," in *Communications in Latin America: Journalism, Mass Media, and Society* (Wilmington: Scholarly Resources, 1996), 115–37.

62. Diane E. Davis provides the most thorough and recent case study of policymaking in Mexico, focusing particularly on the Federal District Department and government strategies in Mexico City. See *Urban Leviathan, Mexico City in the Twentieth Century* (Philadelphia: Temple University Press, 1994), 320.

63. These and other arguments are developed by contributors to Joe Foweraker and Ann L. Craig, eds., *Popular Movements and Political Change in Mexico* (Boulder, Colo.: Lynne Rienner, 1990); and Maria Lorena Cook, Kevin J. Middlebrook, and Juan Molinar Horcasitas, eds., *The Politics of Economic Restructuring, State-Society Relations and Regime Change in Mexico* (La Jolla, Calif.: Center for U.S.–Mexican Studies, UCSD, 1994). For human rights, see Edward L. Cleary, "Human Rights Organizations in Mexico: Growth in Turbulence," *Journal of Church and State* 37 (Autumn 1995): 793–812.

64. For example, see Paul Haber's statement that "it was the single most important element of the Salinas strategy for establishing new forms of political relations with important urban popular movements." "The Art and Implications of

Political Restructuring in Mexico: The Case of the Urban Popular Movements," in *The Politics of Economic Restructuring*, ed. Cook et al., 191–292.

65. For an excellent summary of the changes wrought by NGOs, see Douglas A. Chalmers and Kerianne Piester, "Nongovernmental Organizations and the Changing Structure of Mexican Politics," in *Changing Structure of Mexico: Political, Social and Economic Prospects*, ed. Laura Randall (New York: M.E. Sharpe, 1996) 253–61.

66. Some of the best background information on this movement can be found in Thomas Benjamin, *A Rich Land a Poor People, Politics and Society in Modern Chiapas* (Albuquerque: University of New Mexico Press, 1989); and Tom Barry's perceptive exploration of the agrarian issues in *Zapata's Revenge: Free Trade and the Farm Crisis in Mexico* (Boston: South End Press, 1995).

67. *El despertador mexicano*, no. 1, December 1993, 1–20.

68. See George A. Collier's "The New Politics of Exclusion: Antecedents to the Rebellion in Mexico," *Dialectical Anthropology* 19 (May 1994): 1–44. Other explanations, focused on its being a response to postmodernism, can be found in Carlos Arriola, *Chiapas 1994: The Enemies of Modernity* (Mexico City: M. A. Porrúa, 1994); and Roger Burback, "Roots of the Postmodern Rebellion in Chiapas," *New Left Review*, May-June 1994, 113–24.

69. Revealing portraits of Marcos can be found in Alma Guillermoprieto, "The Unmasking," as well as her earlier essay in the *New Yorker*, March 13, 1995, 40–47; and Ann Louise Bardach, "Mexico's Poet Rebel," *Vanity Fair*, June 1994, 69–74, 130–35.

70. See Ruth Urry, "Rebels, Technology, and Mass Communications: A Comparative Analysis of EZLN and FMLN Media Strategy," Tulane University, 1996.

71. For a brief discussion of such groups, see Mary Beth Sheridan, "Pro-PRI Gangs Breed Fear, Potential Chaos in Chiapas," *Los Angeles Times*, January 25, 1998, 1A.

72. For support of this view, see Rose J. Spalding, "State Power and Its Limits: Corporatism in Mexico," *Comparative Political Studies* 14 (July 1981): 139–64.

73. Viviane Brachet-Marquez, *The Dynamics of Domination, State, Class, and Social Reform in Mexico, 1910–1990* (Pittsburgh: University of Pittsburgh Press, 1994), 182–83.

74. Katherine M. Bailey, "Civic NGOs in Mexican Politics: A New Democratizing Force," Master's thesis, Tulane University, 1998. This argument can be found in Jonathan Fox and Luis Hernández, "Mexico's Difficult Democracy: Grassroots Movements, NGOs, and Local Government," *Alternatives* 17 (Spring 1992): 193.

7

Who Governs? The Structure of Decision Making

> Once the Mexican president and his advisers are in agreement regarding the wisdom of making the decision, the president publicly associates himself with it by making a formal announcement or an executive-sponsored legislative proposal, or both. All important decisions are formally initiated by the president, and the president both claims and receives full credit for the decision, whether or not the idea for the decision was originally his. Because of the patrimonial nature of staff arrangements, all individuals who participate in the decision-making process supposedly do so at the president's will and serve in the capacity of his subordinates. In return for receiving the delegated power to serve, they attribute all credit for their accomplishments to their patrimonial leader, the president.
>
> SUSAN K. PURCELL, *The Mexican Profit-Sharing Decision*

Every political system devises a set of structures and institutions to facilitate political decision making. Studies of decision making reveal that there are a number of interrelated steps in the process. The steps begin with a problem requiring a political solution and pass through a series of institutions in which the problem is ignored or resolved, often legislatively. Some institutions primarily channel demands from society through the political system. Other institutions contribute to the selection and election of political leadership. Still others carry out the solutions proposed by the political system.

Each political model performs the steps in decision making differently, although many models have certain similarities. For example, in the United States, the legislative branch plays a critical role in the formulation of laws and as a focus of interest-group activity. In the United Kingdom, although Parliament plays a critical role in approving legislation, most of its formulation and lobbying are done through the executive branch. The cabinet, however, is a product of the legislative branch; that is, its members are members of Parliament, and so election to Parliament determines who will make many government decisions.

Mexico, as has been suggested earlier, evolved a political system that formally resembles that of the United States but centralizes much greater authority in the executive branch. The powers of the executive branch combined with the dominance of a leadership group represented by a single party—the PRI and its antecedents—has led to a government dominated by the executive, largely in the person of the president. Which institutions are the most salient, and what functions do they perform?

THE EXECUTIVE BRANCH

The seat of the Mexican government is Mexico City, in the Federal District, a jurisdiction with certain similarities to the District of Columbia in the United States. Mexico City, however, unlike Washington, D.C., combines the qualities of New York City, Chicago, and Los Angeles, for Mexico's political capital is also its intellectual and economic capital.

The executive branch of the government houses two types of agencies: those that have counterparts in most First and Third World countries, such as departments of foreign relations and national defense, and others that are idiosyncratically Mexican, sometimes called decentralized or parastatal agencies, somewhat analogous to the Tennessee Valley Authority in the United States. Parastatal agencies are a product of Mexican nationalism, Mexicanization, and state expansion from the 1940s through the 1980s, culminating in the nationalization of private, domestically owned banks in 1982.[1]

The preeminent parastatal agency in Mexico, recognized internationally, is Petroleos Mexicanos (Pemex), the national petroleum company. Pemex was born when President Lázaro Cárdenas nationalized foreign-owned petroleum companies in 1938.[2] Since then the government has controlled the development of petroleum resources, including exploration and drilling, and the domestic retailing of petroleum products. Because of the vast Mexican oil reserves and their rapid exploitation in the 1970s and 1980s, Pemex became Mexico's number-one company. Its sales at their apex accounted for more than three-quarters of export revenues.

Among the fifty leading firms (excluding banks) in Mexico during the 1980s, a fourth were government owned. Other important government entities included the Federal Electric Commission, which develops and distributes electricity; the National Bank of Foreign Commerce, designed to promote trade; the National Company of Public Commodities (Conasupo), a distributor of basic foodstuffs to low-income Mexicans; Sidermex, a basic-steel producer; the National Finance Bank (Nacional Financiera), a developmental bank; and many other companies in utilities, communications, transportation, minerals, fertilizers, and so on. These agencies had semicabinet status, and the president announced his appointees to them simultaneously with those of formal cabinet members.

The formal cabinet has nineteen agencies: Attorney General of the Republic; Secretariat of the Comptroller General; Secretariat of Fishing; Secretariat of Agrarian Reform; Secretariat of Tourism; Mexican Institute of Social Security; Secretariat of Agriculture and Hydraulic Resources; Secretariat of Communications and Transportation; Secretariat of Foreign Relations; Secretariat of Government; Secretariat of Energy, Mines and Government Industries; Secretariat of Health and Welfare; Secretariat of Commerce and Industrial Development; Secretariat of Labor and Social Welfare; Secretariat of National Defense; Secretariat of the Navy; Secretariat of Social Development; Secretariat of Public Education; and Secretariat of the Treasury and Public Credit.

An examination of the major agencies suggests some interesting aspects of Mexican policy issues and the importance of specific economic problems. For example, the historic impact of agrarian issues and agrarian reform after the revolution can be seen in the fact that *two* cabinet-level agencies are devoted to agriculture, one specifically to agrarian reform, and until recently, hydraulic resources were the purview of a separate agency. Nevertheless, it would be misleading to say that any president since Lázaro Cárdenas has given priority to agrarian issues. In fact, the desire of the Salinas administration to eliminate land-tenure problems generated by village-held land titles (*ejidos*), incorporated in constitutional reforms of Article 127, may mean the eventual disappearance of the Secretariat of Agrarian Reform. A second agency of special importance is Tourism, which has had departmental status since 1959, indicative of the industry's impact on the economy. The current secretary has asked President Zedillo to give the agency more responsibilities. The most recently reconstituted secretariat is that of Social Development, in response to its political and economic importance. It administered Salinas's highly touted solidarity program, giving its head control over extraordinary resources and opportunities to establish personal contacts at the grassroots level. Luis Donaldo Colosio, its first secretary, used these opportunities to great personal advantage.

The agencies of greatest standing in the executive branch are those with long histories. In the 1920s, 1930s, and 1940s, the Secretariat of National Defense carried far more weight than it does today, not because of its impact on day-to-day policies but because it often was the source of presidential leadership, given the control exercised by revolutionary generals. With the centralization of power in the hands of the president and, as we have seen, the importance of individual, federal bureaucratic agencies as sources of political recruitment, some relationship exists between decision-making influence and the degree to which individual agencies are the source of high-level personnel. In the 1950s and 1960s, the Secretariat of Government, an agency devoted to internal political affairs, replaced the Secretariat of National Defense as a source of presidential leadership and as a major voice in policy decisions.[3]

Despite the roles played by the Secretariat of Defense and the Secretariat of Government, the Secretariat of the Treasury wielded considerable influence, and its head received much attention in each cabinet. President Cárdenas enhanced both Treasury's authority and its leader by permitting him to act as an arbiter in the allocation of funds to other agencies and to state governors in connection with the federal revenue-sharing program.[4] Thus, other than the president, the treasury secretary became the key figure in the distribution of economic resources, as well as in the determination of the direction of financial policy.

Economic agencies in the government gained substance with the onset of hard times. By the 1980s, the Secretariat of Programming and Budgeting (combined with Treasury in 1992), the Secretariat of the Treasury, and the Bank of Mexico (the federal reserve bank) became the troika in setting economic policy.[5]

The most interesting of these three agencies, and the most politically influential during its short life (1977–1992), was the Secretariat of Programming and Budgeting, which produced three consecutive presidents: de la Madrid, Salinas, and Zedillo. More important, it produced a cadre of important political-technocrats who have dominated the Salinas-Zedillo camarillas, their political generation, and economic decision making.[6] It is ironic, therefore, that this agency and the presidents it produced both expanded statist economic intervention in the form of hundreds of government-owned enterprises—whose budgets the new secretariat managed, and then presided over its eventual disappearance as a budgeting agency.[7] To streamline cabinet coordination and facilitate policymaking, Miguel de la Madrid organized subcabinet groups along policy lines, including an economic cabinet. These groups were more active under Salinas, and he added another category, national security, giving it heightened visibility. It includes the Secretariats of Government, Foreign Relations, National Defense, and the Attorney General of the Republic.

Groups in Mexican society who want some part in national policy decisions must make their concerns and interests known to the executive branch at the highest possible level. Yet as Daniel Levy observed, this is difficult to accomplish:

> As most important legislation is initiated and carried through to approval by the president, hardly any opportunity exists for effective interaction between citizens and their representatives during the lawmaking process. However, groups and individuals may occasionally influence the way in which laws and policies are actually implemented. A common element of day-to-day politics in Mexico is the presentation of demands to local and state governments, to departments of the federal bureaucracy, and even directly to the president.[8]

The cabinet secretary is the key figure in initiating policy proposals, and his staff thoroughly studies the issues and collects information relevant to the formulation of policy. He may be responding to a presidential request or pursuing matters associated with his agency's mandate under broad guidelines outlined to him by the president and the presidential advisers.[9] The persons who have access to the president himself are even more successful in influencing decisions than are those whose highest-level contacts are cabinet figures.

Because the decision-making structure is so hierarchical and the president exercises so much influence (or is expected to exercise authority over the system), considerable pressure is put on channels of access to the presidency. The president's private secretary, who functions as a chief of staff and whose position is essentially a cabinet-level appointment, has the complete confidence of the president. Because he acts as a gatekeeper in denying or granting requests to see the president, he performs a crucial role in the decision-making process.

Salinas emphasized two positions in his administration, positions that reflected the nature of the decision-making process. To coordinate the cabinet and keep closer control over policy initiatives, the president appointed a coordinator of the technical cabinet subgroups who reported directly to him. Zedillo followed this same pattern. Unlike his predecessor, however, he has not chosen to exercise a similar level of authority. In the first two-thirds of his administration, the president appears to be more strongly influenced by his individual cabinet secretaries.

Part of any decision-making process is informing the public about policy decisions. Salinas understood public opinion better than any recent Mexican president. Consequently, he gave much thought to the position of head of social communication for the presidency, the Mexican version of the U.S. presidential press secretary. But more than coordinating presidential press conferences, a rarity in Mexico, the press secretary attempts to shape media coverage of presidential actions, policy initiatives, and policy outcomes.

Salinas used other party, governmental, and semigovernmental agencies as "spin doctors" for both the domestic and foreign media. His government also understood the importance of public opinion polls and hired its own pollsters, who used data that presented the administration or the president in a favorable light. Salinas, however, introduced a significant but dangerous variable in government decision making: image building as a public relations tool. The president himself became, in part, a victim of his own creation shortly after Zedillo succeeded him, when a major devaluation decision and its consequent economic results were blamed on the former president. Salinas, who had maintained extraordinarily high approval ratings through the end of his administration, suddenly found himself an outcast in his own country, less than four short months into the next administration.[10] Zedillo, on the other hand, has taken decisions which were not popular with Mexicans or with his own party, such as his austerity program. Nevertheless, his persistence in his economic strategy, despite failures in other policy arenas, has contributed to a gradual but steadily increasing level of popularity, which tapered off in 1998.

The few studies of Mexican decision making have attempted to classify the role of the presidency in the decision-making process.[11] Although there is no question that decision making is centralized and that the president personally has greater influence over the outcome of policies than does the U.S. president, because more than 90 percent of legislation prior to 1994 came from his office, he cannot in most cases arbitrarily make a policy decision—nor is it likely he would want to do so. For example, in her recent study of Federal District Department decisions affecting the capital, Diane Davis discovered that even the president often failed to get his way.[12] The worst fears of critics of the Mexican semiauthoritarian decision-making process were borne out in 1982 when President José López Portillo announced without warning the nationalization of the banks. The circumstances surrounding the decision have been well documented, and according to the few people López Portillo consulted, he did not consider the views of any of the groups that would be affected.[13] The fact that a single political actor, in consultation with two or three others, could make a decision that would have major reverberations throughout the economy and bring relations between the private sector and the state to a breaking point demonstrates the dangers inherent in centralized power.[14] This can also occur in the political realm, as illustrated in the manner in which the incumbent president has been able to designate his own successor. This power was magnified in 1994, when the PRI's presidential candidate was assassinated, and the president had to decide quickly, and very much in the public eye, on a successor, without the charade of the party itself making such a choice. Salinas's choice of Ernesto Zedillo thus only exacerbated the divisions within the party and government leadership.

Typically, however, presidents do not operate in solitary splendor; their consultations tend to be more private and hidden from public view than in the United States, where lobbying goes on in front of the scenes as well as behind them. One of the characteristics of the decision-making process is that often it is the executive branch itself that takes the initiative in regard to affected parties rather than vice versa. In other words, the role of interest groups is often reactive, not proactive. This pattern is changing as Mexico's system becomes increasingly plural and as President Zedillo tries to establish new ground rules for decision making. President Zedillo has publicly committed himself to making his cabinet more representative, initially appointing the attorney general from the PAN and bringing more women into his party. He also has made clear his desire to minimize the president's intervention in the PRI's candidate selection process and to strengthen the judicial and legislative branches. Although in the first year of his administration Zedillo was perceived as "weak," part of this perception is due to the fact that he wants to reduce presidential powers in support of democratization, but at the same time, the Mexican people share an expectation of a president as decisive, energetic, and even strong.

Presidentialism, which has been the cornerstone of the Mexican system, becomes a liability in a transition from a semiauthoritarian to a democratic model. The origins of this pattern are both constitutional, although this has been exaggerated, and experiential.[15] As Miguel Centeno has suggested, certain structural changes, such as the reelection of congresspersons, would allow Mexico to construct a democratic model from below, rather than impose it through executive fiat.[16] The political crisis which Mexico faces can be attributed, in part, to the structural role of the presidency.[17]

THE LEGISLATIVE BRANCH

Mexico's national legislature is bicameral, with the Chamber of Deputies and the Senate. Deputies are elected on the basis of roughly equally populated districts, of which there are three hundred. In 1970 one hundred seats were added for deputies selected from party lists based on the proportion of the votes cast for the parties. The purpose of the increment was to increase the opposition's representation, owing to the overwhelming dominance of the PRI in the regular legislative seats. In the reforms in the 1980s, another hundred seats were added; now three hundred deputies represent districts and two hundred represent parties. These party deputies are elected at large, based on the proportion of votes received in five regions containing forty seats. As one astute observer concludes: "In terms of democracy . . . , proportional representation exacts a heavy cost for minimal benefits. Formulas which ensure minority representation, while bringing opposition to the legislature, are at best distorting and at worst antidemocratic."[18] This system breaks the link between voters and their representatives. Even more surprising, all three parties are using these relatively "safe seats" to elect party leaders to the Chamber.

The Senate, which has fewer powers than the Chamber of Deputies, has two senators from each state and the Federal District, a total of sixty-four, and in 1994 added sixty-four additional seats, thirty-two to be assigned to the party with the second highest vote count in each state in 1994, and the remaining thirty-two as national proportional representation seats in 1997, for a grand total of 128. Senators are elected for six-year terms, all of which will come up for election in 2000. The Chamber of Deputies and the Senate each have numerous committees, some with names like those in the U.S. Congress. But because deputies and senators cannot be reelected to consecutive terms, seniority does not exist, at least regarding committees, for all members are new to a particular legislature. Some critics argue that one means of enhancing legislative powers in Mexico is to allow consecutive reelection, which would permit members to develop stronger ties with their constituencies. Interestingly, many Americans would like to see a limit set on congressional terms. Mexican legislators proposed eliminating the reelection prohibition in 1995, but it remains in place.

An examination of the committee structure reveals that in many cases congressional leaders attempt to place persons on committees relevant to their expertise and/or interest. For example, in the past military officers on leave or retired were appointed to the National Defense Committee, or legislators representing the peasant unions were assigned to the committees dealing with agriculture.

The legislative branch has long been controlled by the PRI, whose members have accounted for more than 90 percent of the district seats in the Chamber of Deputies and, until 1988, all Senate seats (see Table 7-1). Until 1997, the president appointed a congressional leader (equivalent to the

Table 7-1 Representation in the Legislative Branch, Mexico, 1991–2000

	Deputies									Senators						
	District Seats			Party Seats			Total			State Seats[c]		Party Seats[b]		Total		
Party[a]	1991	1994	1997	1991	1994	1997	1991	1994	1997	1991	1994	1994	1997[d]	1991	1994	1997
PRI	290	277	165	31	23	74	321	300	239	61	64	32	13	61	96	77
PAN	10	18	64	80	101	57	90	119	121	1	0	24	9	1	24	33
PRD	0	5	70	40	66	55	40	71	125	2	0	8	8	2	8	16
PFCRN	0	0	0	23	0	0	23	0	0	0	0	0	0	0	0	0
PARM	0	0	0	14	0	0	14	0	0	0	0	0	0	0	0	0
PPS	0	0	0	12	0	0	12	0	0	0	0	0	0	0	0	0
PT	0	0	1	0	10	6	0	10	7	0	0	0	1	0	0	1
PVEM			0			8			8				1			1
Total	300	300	300	200	200	200	500	500	500	64	64	64	32	64	128	128

[a]PRI = Institutional Revolutionary Party, PAN = National Action Party, PRD = Democratic Revolutionary Party, PFCRN = Cardenista Front for National Reconstruction Party, PARM = Authentic Party of the Mexican Revolution, PPS = Popular Socialist Party, PT = Labor Party, PVEM = Green Party.
[b]The Senate did not have proportional representation seats until 1994–1997.
[c]The state seats were all elected in 1994.
[d]Only 32 seats were allocated in 1997.

majority leader in the U.S. Congress), who headed all the state delegations. Each state's delegation in the Chamber was usually headed by someone who had served before or by a rising star who was given the post for the first time. Many deputies from the PRI complained that decisions were made in an authoritarian fashion by the leadership and that as individuals they played a minor role.[19] Since the opposition won control of the Chamber of Deputies in 1997, the deputies have elected their own leader, in this case Porfirio Muñoz Ledo, a prominent PRD politician. Opposition members now chair and serve on the various committees as well. The Senate also has a leader, and the senior senators from each state form the internal governing body. The Senate has taken on a more plural character since 1994, when the PAN and PRD obtained thirty-two party seats, 25 percent of the total, but even after the 1997 elections, it remains in the hands of PRI.

Earlier discussion indicated that the legislative branch had little to say in the decision-making process, unlike the U.S. Congress. The reason for this is that each legislator who is a member of the government party was beholden to the political leadership, and indirectly the president, for his or her position. If such a legislator wants to pursue a public career, he or she must follow presidential directives. Although Zedillo announced that he would no longer select the PRI's legislative candidates, only a small minority of PRI deputies have shown any sign of believing that declaration and breaking ranks. In the most unpopular legislative decision in many years, approving the president's austerity package in March 1995, only two PRI deputies voted against it. They were greeted with cries from party loyalists to resign. This pattern is beginning to change, both because PRI has lost control of the Chamber and because some PRI legislators have begun to form their own internal groups, such as the "Galileo movement," in pursuit of independent policy goals.[20]

The role of the legislative branch in the Mexican decision-making process has changed dramatically since late 1997, after a coalition of parties, led by the PRD and PAN, took control of the Chamber of Deputies. In the past, congress primarily examined presidential legislative initiatives and made recommendations to the executive branch for alterations. Although theoretically it could have rejected a presidential initiative, most presidential legislation was approved, typically overwhelmingly (see Table 7-2). Today, however, not only have the opposition parties significantly altered executive proposals, but they have focused increased attention on bills proposed by the Chamber itself. The open debates on policy issues have generated a more contentious legislative environment. A subgroup from the PRI legislators, formed in the 1994–1997 session, known as the *Bronxistas*, shout down their opponents.[21]

Table 7-2 Legislative Initiatives in Lower House, 1997

Origin	Submitted	Passed	Success Rate (%)
Executive	90	89	99
PRI	16	3	19
PAN	74	7	10
PRD	36	1	3
PT	1	0	0

Source: Review of the Economic Situation of Mexico, September, 1997, 366.

The legislative branch remains in a weakened position via-à-vis executive policy initiatives since it requires the opposition parties to retain a unified front when voting on major or controversial legislation. For example, the PAN voted with the PRI, instead of with the PRD and the Green and Labor parties, on the federal spending bill in December 1997.[22]

Beginning with the administration of José López Portillo, the legislative branch began a practice common to the British Parliament: Cabinet secretaries are required to come before the Chamber at least yearly and report on their various activities. Although the Chamber was powerless in reality to alter cabinet decisions or to withhold resources, discussions of the reports and opposition pronouncements were covered in the media. Today, visiting cabinet officials are regularly grilled and publicly criticized. The Chamber has become a significant forum where public policy is debated, and those points of view are presented on the evening news and in the press.

The Senate does not initiate legislation but, rather, approves or disapproves of certain executive branch appointments—just as the U.S. Senate does with presidential appointments—and must approve certain bills emanating from the Chamber of Deputies. Because most senators are still elected under the same conditions as former PRI deputies, they are not likely to reject a presidential appointment. There have been some cases, however, when this has occurred, most notably in connection with military promotions. All career military officers above the rank of colonel are promoted by the president, subject to the pleasure of the Senate. In the early 1950s the Senate actually rejected an abuse of presidential authority involving promoting officers who had not met the required time in grade according to military law.[23] Recent presidents have not violated their authority in this regard.[24]

The legislative branch also serves to legitimize executive legislation. One of the potential consequences of the elections since 1988, when opposition parties began obtaing a significant representation in the Chamber of Deputies, was that the government lost its ability to amend the constitution; the PRI did not have two-thirds of the seats in the lower chamber, the number necessary to do so. Mexican presidents and the executive branch have used constitutional amendments to give major, controversial legislation an extra measure of legitimacy. The opposition's gains since 1988 prevent the government from using this technique without first achieving a coalition.

A proposed change by the Zedillo administration would considerably strengthen the opposition's voice in the Chamber of Deputies and significantly increase the importance of the judicial branch. According to the *Diario Oficial*, on December 31, 1994, Article 105 of the constitution was modified to grant the equivalent of 33 percent of the members of the Chamber of Deputies, the Senate, or local state legislators the right, within thirty days of passing a law, to question the constitutionality of such legislation before the supreme court.[25] Although the law will go into effect only when the implementing legislation is approved, the fact that it was proposed and signed by Zedillo indicates his seriousness about changing the balance of power and strengthening the other branches.

There are two important structural conditions which contribute to the legislative branch's weaker policy-making position compared to Mexico's executive. The first of these, mentioned above, is the continued prohibition on consecutive reelection, which limits the expertise among legislators.[26] The second condition is the limited budget devoted to congressional staff. The Chamber has approximately sixty researchers for five hundred legislators, and like their employers, many leave at the end of three years. By contrast, the executive branch has several thousand full-time permanent staff.[27]

The legislative branch is also a training ground for future political leaders and an important source of political patronage. It has been used to reward people prominent in quasi-governmental interest groups and among the labor, peasant, and popular, professional sectors.[28] Among opposition parties, it remains the only national venue for their leaders. Although professional people predominate among the legislators, peasant and labor leaders, as well as women, who might not obtain higher political office in the executive branch, are well represented. Even more important, the legislative branch provides upward mobility to a different type of politician: those who are more likely to have come from a working-class background, from the provinces (because of the district representation), from electoral careers, and with less formal education (see Table 7-3). Women, too, as in

Table 7-3 Legislators and Executive-Branch Officials, 1991–1994

Background Variable	Legislators (%)	Executive Branch Officials (%)
Gender		
Female	7	6
Education		
Preparatory or less	19	1
Career Experience		
Political parties	87	41
Unions	61	17
Elective posts	61	8
Parents' Occupation		
Peasant	5	1
Laborer	3	1
Birthplace		
Federal District	16	52

Source: Diccionario biográfico del gobierno mexicano (Mexico: Presidencia de la República, 1992); based on 1,162 officials and 550 legislators.

many European countries, are best represented in this branch of government. In short, greater percentages of persons who are excluded from executive branch careers, even at the departmental level, can find places in the legislative branch. The fact that some channels are open to these kinds of Mexicans, who in many background characteristics correspond more closely to the population in general, is important to social mobility and leadership fluidity.

The legislative branch also is a school for political skills. Among national government institutions, opposition leaders and parties are represented only in the legislative branch. Their electoral wins beginning in 1988 substantially increased their political influence, forcing government leadership to compromise on several policy issues related to electoral reform.[29] Negotiating skills will be more and more valued in the decision-making process as the opposition parties continue their progress in vote getting. Most officials in the executive branch have little or no experience in such skills; hence persons whose careers have brought them through the legislative bodies are likely to be in greater demand in the future. Zedillo's own attempts at expanding pluralism in the executive branch and decentralizing decision making are increasing the legislative branch's influence. For example, Zedillo's first attorney general, Fernando Antonio Lozano, was the head of the PAN delegation in the 1991–1994 session.

THE JUDICIAL BRANCH

A major principle in the U.S. government structure is the balance of power. The founding fathers were concerned that the executive branch might take on dictatorial aspects and hence sought to apportion power among the executive, legislative, and judicial branches in such fashion that none would dominate. The Mexican judicial system is structurally patterned after that found in the United States. It has local, state, and national levels, the last comprising a court of appeals and a supreme court.

A judicial branch influences the decision-making process when it is independent of legislative and executive authority, and when it can legislate through judicial rulings. The U.S. Supreme Court can declare a law unconstitutional, after which Congress can devise other legislation to achieve its goal if it so wishes. U.S. courts hand down rulings that bear on future cases and also on legislation regarding the issues involved.

Legislating through judicial precedent is not a viable procedure in Mexico. For the supreme court to establish a binding precedent, it must repeatedly reach identical conclusions about precisely the same issues. This rarely, if ever, occurs. Although the supreme court has some independence, justices do not sit for life, and their appointments have been political. Presently, the Supreme Court consists of eleven justices who may serve terms of up to fifteen years. They are appointed by the president with two-thirds approval of the Senate. District and circuit court judges are chosen by a six-member Council of the Federal Judiciary. The proposed changes in Article 105, allowing one-third of the members of congress to request a constitutional review of new federal legislation, or one-third of the members of state legislatures to make a similar request for state laws, potentially enhances its influence.[30] The high bench typically rules on appeals of individual persons, not on matters of constitutionality, and they do not venture into political issues. The lower levels of the legal system are tainted by corruption and outside political manipulation. An absence of consistency and integrity makes it difficult, if not impossible, for the average citizen to resort to the system to protect his or her rights. The criminal justice subsystem has incorporated the use of torture in obtaining confessions.[31] These circumstances combine to create a lack of respect for the law, a crucial element in a viable, legal system.

President Zedillo, recognizing this, has attempted to make respect for the law a crucial element in his presidency. By initially appointing an attorney general from the opposition and reopening three major cases, the president signaled his intent to reinvigorate the legal process. The arrest of President Salinas's brother as the alleged intellectual instigator of the murder of PRI official José Ruiz Massieu sent a clear message that even a president's family could not act with legal impunity. But since these major cases remain unresolved, and noted cases of corruption have been discovered throughout the criminal justice and drug enforcement agencies, the rule of law remains an unreached goal.

THE PRI

Many analysts of Mexican politics commonly refer to the government as the PRI or, frequently, the PRI government. The label implies that the PRI, which is the political party of the government, exercises policymaking authority over the system. Nothing could be further from the truth. As pointed out in the previous chapter, the PRI plays a significant role in institutionalizing semicorporatist structures and in the relationship between certain groups and the government. In fact, the PRI acts as a channel in decision making for the least influential groups. Its own leadership has little if any impact on the making of policy, as Dale Story found:

> The Party [the PRI] clearly does not control the reins of political decision-making, nor is it even a coequal to the state. Yet most national elites are at least Party members, and more significantly, the Party is a very critical institution serving the executive branch of government, in particular the office of the presidency. Especially with national elites becoming so technocratic, the PRI provides the president with the necessary political legitimacy, the symbolic aura of the Revolution, and the machinery for running campaigns, winning elections, and maintaining contacts with the masses.[32]

As an institution, the PRI does not have policy influence over the members of the legislative or executive branches. Although its role is very visible in the legislative branch because until 1997 its members were the leaders of both chambers, they do not report to the party leadership. Even if they were to do so, the party leadership is selected by the president, thus placing the party under the thumb of the executive branch.

For example, of the members of the first PRI executive committee during the Zedillo administration, the president, secretary general, and press secretary owe their posts to the president. The president of PRI was responsible for the appointment of only two committee members, the electoral and social promotion secretaries (see Table 7-4). Only three members have held prominent posts in the executive branch; the remainder are former governors, deputies, senators, and labor union leaders. The Party has relied on the executive branch for financial support; generally the Secretariat of Government allocated the funds. Electoral reforms have eliminated this subsidy. Still, support is difficult to measure because it involves more than money. The government, through its contacts, provides many other resources, such as lodging, transportation, and meals for those doing party business. Individual candidates receive little direct financing from the party, but it does pay for party, as distinct from candidate, advertising, indirectly promoting the fortunes of the individual politician.[33] Party leadership has sought out new means of support, emulating some of the techniques long used by the PAN.

The PRI, as a party vehicle, does not even have much influence over executive branch officials, who are the most active in the decision-making process. Many of the officials have few formal ties to the party; in fact, a number of top officials have never been members of any party. Credentials other than active party experience are of greater value to an individual person's career. That may change if party rules requiring active PRI organizational experience before an individual can become a party candidate for governor or president remain in effect.

The PRI does not function autonomously. Its dependence on the government and on executive branch leadership in the past effectively eliminated any direct influence it might have had on the decision-making process, especially in connection with economic and social policy issues. Nevertheless, in terms of recent political reforms, officials who have made their careers within the PRI, particularly at state and local levels, have be-

Table 7-4 Zedillos' First PRI National Executive Committee

President:	María de los Angeles Moreno
Secretary General:	Pedro Joaquín Coldwell
Organization:	Jorge López Tijerina
Electoral:	Tristán Canales
Regional Coordination:	Arnoldo Ochoa
Information:	Heriberto Galindo
International Affairs:	Alejandro Carrillo Castro
Social Promotion:	Guadalupe Gómez Maganda
CNC:	Hugo Andrés Araujo
CTM:	José Ramírez Gamero
Popular Sector:	Mariano Palacios Alcocer
Territorial Movement:	Carlos Sobrino

Source: "Enfoque," *Reforma*, March 5, 1995, 6.
CVC = National Peasant Federation, CTM = National Workers Federation.

gun to express themselves as a viable interest group regarding executive-branch decisions affecting the party's strength and growth. The executive branch has demonstrated its superiority in the decision-making process in imposing solutions on party problems. This was illustrated clearly in 1995. The president removed one PRI gubernatorial candidate soon after his in-auguration in Chiapas after the PRI had claimed victory in this hotly con-tested election over the PRD. Whether or not the PRI had won fairly, the president imposed his will on the party leadership, making clear their sub-ordination to presidential authority.

Nevertheless, signs of change are apparent. In the case of Tabasco, in order to obtain the PRD's support for a national political pact, the federal government tried to impose a negotiated settlement on the newly elected PRI governor, Roberto Madrazo. Madrazo, skillfully drawing on local PRI leaders and supporters, successfully resisted his forced resignation, which had taken the form of a resolution imposed by the federal executive branch. In early 1995, in a meeting between the governors and President Zedillo, the governor of Puebla told the president that the governors would no longer submit to presidential intervention in state affairs. In mid-1998, the gov-ernor of Morelos resigned. It is unclear, however, the degree to which the president or the federal government determined his decision to leave office.

Opposition victories at the local level are forcing structural changes on the party. Therefore, to survive, the party must compete successfully against PAN and PRD candidates and seek out new means of financing. Once the PRI's monopoly on executive officeholding—on both the local or state levels—is broken, it will limit the PRI's ability to rely on com-paratively unlimited resources from local businessmen and other interests, who can no longer count on favors from a PRI out of power. Thus, oppo-sition-party victories have led to significant changes in the PRI and in its relationship to society. Finally, the party, encouraged by President Zedillo, began experimenting with the internal selection of candidates, experiments that were used in the municipal and state elections in Guanajuato and Jalisco in late 1994 and early 1995, and again in 1998, through party primaries.

Although the focus of this chapter is on decision making at the na-tional level, the changing structure of electoral competition and the nu-merous successes of the PAN and PRD imply far-reaching changes in this pattern at the state and local level, and subsequently through the national congress. Thus, it is important to recognize the role of not just the PRI in decision making but increasingly that of PAN and the PRD. PAN now ad-ministers numerous state bureaucracies, and the PRD is in charge of the Federal District government, formerly a major national cabinet agency. As Victoria Rodríguez and Peter Ward wrote in their important work, the opposition parties have been confronted with the task of governing, as distinct from the task of winning office.

> Invariably the personnel coming to power in representation of the successful parties lack experience or background in urban governance. In the case of non-PRI parties, we have seen how public officials have had to be recruited from the private sector and how this, in turn, shaped their performance while in office. This problem is accentuated by the shortness of terms and by the constitutional no reelection clause. Although junior personnel may show some continuity in office, the rule in the past has been for all senior officers to change with the election of a new municipal president.[34]

Despite fraud, the PRI has shown its ability to adapt and survive. If the political leadership wishes to rely on the PRI to continue legitimizing its authority through the electoral process, as the opposition strengthens, then the PRI bureaucracy will gain in influence in the political arena. Party officials who make their political careers in the party bureaucracy and in elective office, will develop and express their own interests, as do officials in the federal bureaucracy, attempting to have a say in decisions that affect their institutional future as well as their political careers.

CONCLUSION

Decision making in Mexico is still controlled through the executive branch, centralized in the person of the president. As economic problems have overshadowed all other issues, the influence of the economic cabinet has expanded. The decision-making process listens to demands more through informal internal channels than through formal public channels. As the analysis of interest groups in Chapter 6 demonstrates, leaders from various sectors seek out individual decision makers in the executive branch, typically the cabinet secretary or, if they have access, the president.

The degree of centralization of decision-making power in the president and the executive branch affects the whole government process. Not only does a president have a huge reservoir of political authority, but most Mexicans expect—indeed, react positively to—his exercise of his powers. Salinas was praised for his decisiveness during his administration, when he used his decision-making authority to rebuild lost confidence in the presidency. Zedillo, on the other hand, has been criticized for appearing indecisive.

The reliance on informal channels of influence favors certain groups over others. Business interests have been more successful than labor or peasants in having their point of view heard. The government does not stress listening to demands made through formal channels; rather, it concerns itself with how its policies are received and its image. The powers exercised by the executive branch since the revolution have left Mexico with weak legislative and judicial institutions. Not only did the state grow in size throughout most of this period, reversed only since 1988, but its power lay within the executive branch. Because ambitious politicians understand this, competition for careers in the executive is more intense than in the other branches. In fact, the imbalance discouraged formation of an active, independent opposition, which contributed to the leadership's cooptive capability. The increasing pace of recent opposition victories and President Zedillo's willingness to relinquish his presidential authority over party affairs are promoting changes in the pattern of decision making, allocating much greater influence to the legislative branch, strengthening federalism, and altering the influence of various actors.

NOTES

1. For an analysis of how this sector has functioned, see the case study by William P. Glade, "Entrepreneurship in the State Sector: Conasupo of Mexico," in *Entrepreneurship in Cultural Context*, ed. Sidney Greenfield et al. (Albuquerque: University of New Mexico Press, 1979), 191–222.

2. For background, see George Grayson, *The Politics of Mexican Oil* (Pittsburgh: University of Pittsburgh Press, 1980); Edward J. Williams, *The Rebirth of the Mexican Petroleum Industry* (Lexington, Mass.: Heath, 1979).

3. Miguel Alemán, 1946–1952; Adolfo Ruiz Cortines, 1952–1958; Gustavo Díaz Ordaz, 1964–1970; and Luis Echeverría, 1970–1976, are presidents indicative of this changing institutional influence and the rise of civilian leadership; they came from the Secretariat of Government.

4. See the introduction by Antonio Carrillo Flores in Eduardo Suárez, *Comentarios y recuerdos, 1926–1946* (Mexico City: Porrúa, 1977).

5. For background on the rise of the Secretariat of Programming and Budgeting, see John J. Bailey's excellent "Presidency, Bureaucracy, and Administrative Reform in Mexico: The Secretariat of Programming and Budgeting," *Inter-American Economic Affairs* 34 (Summer 1980): 27–59.

6. Miguel Angel Centeno and Sylvia Maxfield, "The Marriage of Finance and Order: Changes in the Mexican Political Elite," *Journal of Latin American Studies* 24 (February 1992): 84.

7. Julie A. Erfani, *The Paradox of the Mexican State, Rereading Sovereignty from Independence to NAFTA* (Boulder, Colo.: Lynne Rienner, 1995), 127ff.

8. Daniel Levy and Gabriel Székely, *Mexico, Paradoxes of Stability and Change*, 2d ed. (Boulder, Colo.: Westview Press, 1987), 49–50.

9. For case studies in education, hydraulic resources, and agricultural policy, see Guy Benveniste, *Bureaucracy and National Planning: A Sociological Case Study in Mexico* (New York: Praeger, 1970); Martin H. Greenberg, *Bureaucracy and Development: A Mexican Case Study* (Lexington, Mass.: Heath, 1970); Merilee S. Grindle, *Bureaucrats, Politicians, and Peasants in Mexico: A Case Study in Public Policy* (Berkeley and Los Angeles: University of California Press, 1977). A new examination of oil policy formulation concluded that "conflict, lobbying, and coalition building between patron-client pyramids, or bargaining" were typical. See María de la Luz Valverde, "A Heuristic Model of Mexican Public Policymaking," paper presented at the Latin American Studies Association, Los Angeles, 1992, 19.

10. For example, the PRI headquarters from 1988 to 1994 had a special section that provided information to foreign scholars; the government sent copies of its favored newspaper, *El Nacional*, to various academics; and the embassy mailed data on election results and speeches of party officials.

11. See, for example, Purcell, *The Mexican Profit-Sharing Decision*, 4; Roderic Ai Camp, *The Role of Economists in Policy-Making: A Comparative Case Study of Mexico and the United States* (Tucson: University of Arizona Press, 1977), 9; Judith A. Teichman, *Policymaking in Mexico: From Boom to Crisis* (Boston: Allen & Unwin, 1988).

12. Diane E. Davis, *Urban Leviathan, Mexico City in the Twentieth Century* (Philadelphia: Temple University Press, 1994), 316.

13. Carlos Tello, *La nacionalización de la banca en México* (Mexico City: Siglo XXI, 1984).

14. Roderic Ai Camp, *Entrepreneurs and the State in Twentieth Century Mexico* (New York: Oxford University Press, 1989), 128–33.

15. Jeffrey Weldon, "The Political Sources of *Presidencialismo* in Mexico," in *Presidentialism and Democracy in Latin America*, ed. Scott Mainwaring and Matthew Shugart (Cambridge: Cambridge University Press, 1997), 225–58.

16. Miguel A. Centeno, "The Failure of Presidential Authoritarianism: Transition in Mexico," in *Politics, Society, and Democracy: Latin America*, ed. Scott Mainwaring et al. (Boulder: Westview Press, 1997), 44.

17. Lorenzo Meyer, "La crisis del presidencialismo mexicano," *Foro Internacional* 36 (January 1996): 11–30.

18. For excellent background on the legislative structure, see Michael C. Taylor, "Constitutional Crisis: How Reforms to the Legislature Have Doomed Mexico," *Mexican Studies* 13 (Summer 1997): 319.

19. The best description of how the committee system functions and the role of the Chamber of Deputies prior to pluralization is Rudolfo de la Garza, "The Mexican Chamber of Deputies and the Mexican Political System" (Ph.D. diss., University of Arizona, 1972). The best analysis to date is Alonso Lujambio's excellent *Federalismo y congreso en el cambio político de México* (Mexico: UNAM, 1995).

20. *Reforma*, September 22, 1997, 1.

21. Sam Quiñones, "Legislative Rowdies," *Mexico Business*, July 1997, 79–80.

22. *El Financiero International Edition*, December 22, 1997, 5.

23. Senado, *Diario de los debates*, 1953, 5–6.

24. Personal interviews, Mexico City, 1990–1991.

25. *Diario Oficial*, December 31, 1994, 2–6.

26. For a discussion of this issue, see my "Mexico's Legislature: Missing the Democratic Lockstep," in *Legislatures and the New Democracies in Latin America*, ed. David Close (Boulder: Lynne Rienner, 1995), 17–36.

27. Sam Quiñones, "Politicians Learning to Play Nice," *US–Mexico Business*, November 1997, 20–22.

28. See Peter H. Smith, *Labyrinths of Power: Political Recruitment in Twentieth-Century Mexico* (Princeton, N.J.: Princeton University Press, 1979), 217ff.

29. For background, see Robert A. Pastor, "Post-Revolutionary Mexico: The Salinas Opening," *Journal of Inter-American Studies and World Affairs* 32 (Fall 1990): 1–22.

30. Pilar Domingo, "Democratization Without Separation of Powers? The Case of the Mexican Supreme Court," paper presented at the National Latin American Studies Association, Washington, D.C., 1995.

31. Americas Watch, *Human Rights in Mexico: A Policy of Impunity* (New York: Human Rights Watch, 1990), 1; *Unceasing Abuses, Human Rights One Year After the Introduction of Reform* (New York: Human Rights Watch, 1991).

32. Dale Story, *The Mexican Ruling Party: Stability and Authority* (Stanford, Calif.: Hoover Institution, 1986), 131–32. For a historical exploration of its founding, see Carl Henry Marcoux, "Plutarco Elías Calles and the Partido Nacional Revolucionario: Mexican National and Regional Politics in 1928 and 1929" (Ph.D. diss., University of California at Riverside, 1994).

33. Interview with a candidate for federal deputy, Mexico City district, 1985.

34. Victoria Rodríguez and Peter Ward, eds., *Opposition Government in Mexico* (Albuquerque: University of New Mexico Press, 1994), 226. This is the first major work that explores fully the consequences of opposition-party victories at the local and state levels.

8

Expanding Participation:
The Electoral Process

> The period from 1968 onward has been characterized by many
> authors as one of "transition," as Mexico moves away from the
> traditional political and social order built around Revolutionary
> principles. But does this political transition also constitute a de-
> mocratic one? While recognizing that it is not feasible to re-
> spond definitely to this question, the progress in opening the
> electoral space to recognize more victories of the opposition at
> the state and local levels seems to indicate that at least as far
> as local elections and access to political office are concerned,
> Mexico may well be on its way to consolidating its democra-
> tization. The test, naturally, will be whether this urban electoral
> pattern can be transferred to the national level. As some ana-
> lysts have argued, the consolidation of democracy in Mexico
> will only become evident when a candidate of the opposition
> wins the presidency of the Republic. That seems, indeed, a
> rather ambitious yardstick by which to measure a democratic
> transition.
>
> VICTORIA RODRIGUEZ, "Opening the Electoral Space in Mexico"

A little over a decade ago, most political analysis would have given little
space to elections and electoral politics in Mexico. Although elections have
been a feature of the political landscape since the time of Porfirio Díaz,
with the exception of Francisco Madero's election in 1911, they never functioned as the crucial determinant of political leadership or furnished a policy mandate.

Beginning in the mid-1970s, elections took on a new dimension. At
first, the uncharacteristic emphasis could be tied to the desire of some establishment figures to strengthen the PRI's image and that of the political
system by promoting the opposition's fortunes. In other words, the government itself, through a series of electoral reforms, tried to stimulate the

179

opposition. It provided opposition parties with an incentive to challenge the PRI's dominance by increasing their potential rewards but without extending the possibility of real victory. The single-party dominance of the system and election results was brought home when the National Action Party (PAN), frustrated by the futility of opposition, refused to nominate a candidate to run against José López Portillo in the 1976 presidential race.

ELECTORAL REFORMS

Some government strategies believed it was smart politics to increase opposition representation in the Chamber of Deputies through implementation of a plurinominal deputy system (deputies selected on the basis of their party's total national vote); others were committed to actual reforms. The latter, who hoped to democratize the elections, believed that genuine competition would strengthen the political model and increase participation, a change for which they believed Mexicans were ready. One of the architects of these earlier reforms, Secretary of Government Jesús Reyes Heroles, introduced enabling legislation in 1977 under José López Portillo (1976–1982).[1]

The 1977 reforms, incorporated into the Federal Law of Political Organizations and Electoral Processes (LOPPE), altered several constitutional provisions. The law increased majority districts for federal deputies (similar to United States congressional districts) from approximately two hundred to exactly three hundred seats. It also specified that an additional one hundred seats be assigned to opposition parties in the Chamber of Deputies through a complex mathematical formula that allocated seats proportional to each party's national vote totals. Under the party-deputy arrangement in effect from the 1964 through the 1976 national elections, opposition parties

---

Majority districts: legislative districts of roughly equal populations whose congressional representative wins the largest number of votes cast within the district.

---

were allocated thirty to forty seats, also on the basis of each party's national vote totals. From the mid-1960s to the mid-1970s the opposition, combining party and majority deputies, averaged about 17 percent of the seats in the lower house but none in the Senate. The 1977 law, however, set aside *all* one hundred seats for this purpose, requiring them to be divided proportionately among the opposition parties. In effect, this meant that opposition parties, after the LOPPE went into effect, garnered approximately 26 percent of the seats in the lower house and were guaranteed a minimum of one-quarter of all the seats.

The 1977 reforms, while giving some encouragement to opposition parties, providing them with more seats in the Chamber of Deputies and allowing them greater access to the media during campaigns, lost their impetus after 1979, when Reyes Heroles left his post. Both the reforms in the early 1960s, which first introduced the party deputy system, and the 1977

Proportional representation: a system for allocating legislative seats to parties on the basis of the national or regional vote cast for all of the party's legislative candidates.

---

electoral law, which created the plurinominal deputy system, stabilized opposition gains at a given level during the life of the legislation. In other words, opposition representation within the two periods (1964–1976 and 1979–1985) remained stable at approximately 17 and 26 percent respectively, suggesting—at least on the basis of official tabulations—that the opposition parties experienced little growth.

When President de la Madrid took office in 1982, he seemed to indicate a new posture toward the opposition. Specifically, his administration initially tolerated intense electoral competition at the local level. Wayne Cornelius argued:

> Even more significantly, de la Madrid established a new policy regarding municipal elections: henceforth, municipal-level victories by opposition party candidates would be recognized, wherever they occurred. During the first ten months of his administration, the PRI conceded defeat in municipal elections held in seven major cities, including five state capitals and Ciudad Juárez, a large city on the U.S.–Mexican border. Virtually no electoral fraud was reported in these key municipal contests of 1983. As one high-ranking PAN official recalled, "It was like Switzerland up there. There was no interference in the voting, and the ballot count was absolutely clean."[2]

In 1986 de la Madrid introduced his own electoral law, which had significant consequences in the 1988 presidential elections, the first to test it. The 1986 electoral code included the following provisions:

1. The winning or majority party is never to obtain more than 70 percent of the seats in the lower chamber.
2. Three hundred deputies are to be elected by a relative majority based on individual congressional districts (similar to the United States).
3. The seats allotted to deputies on the basis of a proportional percentage

of their total national vote are to be increased from 100 to 200, increasing
the total number of seats from 400 to 500 (300 by district and 200 by
proportional representation).

4. Opposition parties may obtain 40 percent of the seats without winning
a single majority district (200 of the 500 seats).

5. The party winning the greatest number of majority seats is to retain a
simple majority in the entire chamber; that is, the party is to be allotted
seats through the proportional representation system sufficient to obtain
an absolute majority in the lower house.

6. Half the Senate is to be renewed triennially instead of the entire chamber every six years (the first change in senatorial elections since 1934).[3]

Compared with the two earlier laws, these reforms reduce the proportion
of the majority party (the PRI) in the Chamber of Deputies, which ranged
from 83 percent to 74 percent, to 70 percent or less. The 1986 law also reduced the overall importance of majority districts, which were generally
won by the PRI (usually 95 percent or more, see Table 8-1). Again, the
law increased the opposition's presence in the Chamber of Deputies, but it
was an increase *allocated by the government*, rather than an increase that
the government permitted the opposition to earn.

It can be argued that economic and political conditions did more to
boost opposition fortunes and to give elections greater political importance
in Mexico than did internal reforms during this interim. As the economic
crisis worsened in the early 1980s, the opposition on the state and local
levels thrived. Opposition-party candidates were winning local-level executive positions and seats on municipal councils. The PAN in particular was
placing its members in important city posts in state capitals.

The declining legitimacy of the presidency, in combination with the
declining legitimacy of the government itself, began to take a toll by the
1985 and 1986 elections. Although some of the smaller leftist parties were
beneficiaries of these trends, the party capturing the greatest number of local seats was the PAN. The PRI worked hard to recoup the losses, in some
cases by using such techniques as missing ballot boxes, duplication of registered voters, counting votes of citizens who had not voted, last-minute
disqualifications of opposition poll watchers, and last-minute changes in
the location of polling booths.[4]

The imposition of PRI victories on the subnational level reached a
high point with the gubernatorial and local elections in the state of Chihuahua, a next-door neighbor of Texas. Ciudad Juárez, one of Mexico's
largest cities, lies on the border and is traditionally a PAN stronghold. The
PRI claimed victories in the state capital and in Ciudad Juárez, as well as

Table 8-1 Seats in the Chamber of Deputies by Party, 1949–2000

Year	PRI	PAN	PPS	PARM	PDM	PSUM	PST	PRT	PMT	PRD	PFCRN	PT	PVEM
1949	142	4	1	—	—	—	—	—	—	—	—	—	—
1952[b]	152	5	2	—	—	—	—	—	—	—	—	—	—
1955	155	6	1	—	—	—	—	—	—	—	—	—	—
1958[b]	153	6	1	1	—	—	—	—	—	—	—	—	—
1961	172	5	1	—	—	—	—	—	—	—	—	—	—
1964	175	2	1	—	—	—	—	—	—	—	—	—	—
Party	—	18	9	5	—	—	—	—	—	—	—	—	—
1967	177	1	0	0	—	—	—	—	—	—	—	—	—
Party	—	19	10	5	—	—	—	—	—	—	—	—	—
1970	178	0	0	0	—	—	—	—	—	—	—	—	—
Party	—	20	10	5	—	—	—	—	—	—	—	—	—
1973	189	4	—	1	—	—	—	—	—	—	—	—	—
Party	—	21	10	6	—	—	—	—	—	—	—	—	—
1976	195	—	—	2	—	—	—	—	—	—	—	—	—
Party	—	20	12	9	—	—	—	—	—	—	—	—	—
1979	296	4	—	—	—	—	—	—	—	—	—	—	—
Plurinominal	—	39	11	12	10	18	10	—	—	—	—	—	—
1982	299	1	—	—	—	—	—	—	—	—	—	—	—
Plurinominal	—	50	10	0	12	17	11	—	—	—	—	—	—
1985	289	9	—	2	—	—	—	—	—	—	—	—	—
Plurinominal	—	32	11	9	12	12	12	6	6	—	—	—	—
1988[c]	233	38	4	5	—	—	—	—	—	15	5	—	—
Plurinominal	27	63	27	23	—	—	—	—	—	11	46	—	—
1991	290	10	—	—	—	—	—	—	—	—	—	—	—
Plurinominal	31	80	12	14	—	—	—	—	—	40	23	—	—
1994	277	18	—	—	—	—	—	—	—	5	—	—	—
Plurinominal	23	101	—	—	—	—	—	—	—	66	—	10	—
1997	164	65	—	—	—	—	—	—	—	70	—	1	—
Plurinominal	74	57	—	—	—	—	—	—	—	55	—	6	8

Source: Adapted from Héctor Zamitiz and Carlos Hernández, "La composición política de la Cámara de Diputados, 1949–1989," *Revista de Ciencias Politicas y Sociales* 36 (January–March 1990): 97–108.

[a]PRI = Institutional Revolutionary Party; PAN = National Action Party; PPS = Popular Socialist Party; PARM = Authentic Party of the Mexican Revolution; PDM = Democratic Mexican Party; PSUM = Mexico's United Socialist Party; PST = Socialist Workers Party; PRT = Revolutionary Workers Party; PMT = Mexican Workers Party; PRD = Democratic Revolutionary Party; PFCRN = Cardenista Front for National Reconstruction Party; PVEM = Green Party.

[b]Three other seats were won by members of the Federación de Partidos Populares Mexicanos and the Partido Nacionalista Mexicano.

[c]Three deputies were classified as independents, and one deputy among the PRD majority transferred his loyalty to the PRD after being elected on the PRI ticket.

in the state gubernatorial race.[5] The scope of fraud was so great and citizen resistance so palpable that prominent intellectuals and Catholic bishops denounced the results in a full-page ad in Mexico's leading daily, *Excélsior*, and called for the election to be annulled. As mentioned earlier, northern bishops announced they would cancel masses if the federal government did not respond. The Vatican delegate to Mexico, at the prompt-

ing of Mexico's secretary of government, persuaded the clergy to withdraw
their threat.

The overall political environment laid the groundwork for the most
significant change in the PRI and led to the events that characterized the
1988 presidential election, a benchmark in Mexican electoral politics. Certain persons in the establishment leadership, in disagreement with the economic direction of the de la Madrid government and the timidity of his reforms, attempted a reform of the party's structure. In 1986 they constituted
themselves as the Democratic Current. Among the most prominent members were Cuauhtémoc Cárdenas, a former governor of Michoacán and son
of President Lázaro Cárdenas, the major political figure in the 1930s, and
Porfirio Muñoz Ledo, a former cabinet official and president of the National Executive Committee of the PRI. The group and other party figures
and intellectuals kept up a running criticism of the government's failure to
implement genuine democratic reforms. Although at first tolerated, their
dissenting voice became intolerable to the party and government leadership during the 1987 presidential succession. Their party memberships were
revoked.

Cárdenas, Muñoz Ledo, and other PRI dissidents formed the Democratic Front for National Reconstruction (FDN), selecting Cárdenas as its
presidential candidate. Because the FDN joined the race too late to have
its credentials legally recognized, one of the PRI's tiny splinter parties, the
Authentic Party of the Mexican Revolution (PARM), selected Cárdenas as
its nominee, thus giving the FDN a place on the ballot. The FDN's formation occurred at a time when internal contention over the selection of
the PRI's candidate broke into the open. Carlos Salinas de Gortari, the programming and budget secretary, was seen by most observers as a man who
would continue de la Madrid's economic philosophy. This suggested that
the PRI's populist wing, represented by such persons as Cuauhtémoc Cárdenas, would not have a presence in his administration.[6] The fact that Salinas had no prior electoral or grassroots political experience marked the ascendancy of the technocratic leadership within the PRI.[7]

THE 1988 AND 1994 PRESIDENTIAL ELECTIONS

The 1988 presidential election illustrated a longtime pattern in electoral
politics: The strongest opposition movements are often led by dissidents
from within the PRI. As will be seen in the brief histories of several major opposition parties, most were founded by persons who abandoned gov-

ernment leadership because of policy and personal disagreements. This was true of the PAN and the Popular Socialist Party (PPS).

The 1988 presidential election took place when the government and the PRI were at a low in terms of their legitimacy among the people. The selection of Salinas as the PRI candidate, the least popular choice among party leaders, further eroded the PRI's position. Given these conditions, the opposition began a vigorous campaign against Salinas. The PAN selected a charismatic businessman from the north, Manuel J. Clouthier, who provided energetic, if somewhat bombastic, leadership during the contest. Cárdenas was off to a rocky start, but with his name recognition, notably in rural Mexico, he began to build a following. Three leftist parties, which typically have attracted only small numbers of Mexican voters (see Table 8-1), eventually joined Cárdenas's battle against the PRI candidate: the Popular Socialist Party (PPS); the Cardenista Front for National Reconstruction Party (PFCRN), formerly the Socialist Workers Party (PST); and the Mexican Socialist Party (PMS). Of the eight parties on the 1988 presidential ballot, four supported Cárdenas.

To most analysts' genuine surprise, the populist and leftist Cárdenas alliance generated a widespread response among Mexican voters. Cárdenas, according to official tallies, received 31 percent of the vote, the highest figure given to an opposition presidential candidate since the revolution; Salinas obtained 51 percent, barely a simple majority; and Clouthier captured 17 percent, the typical PAN percentage in a presidential election. Contrary to most observers's expectations, the Left, not the Right, altered the face of the election. In other words, the 1982 voters who defected from the PRI six years later cast their ballots for Cárdenas, not the PAN.

It is important to remember that the 1988 election took place under the 1986 law, which allowed, for the first time, the majority party (the PRI) to increase its representation in the Chamber of Deputies from some of the 200 plurinominal seats. The PRI needed to implement the provision because it obtained only 233 majority district seats, 18 short of a simple majority of 251. It allocated itself 27 plurinominal seats, which added to the 233 majority district seats gave it a slight majority (260 out of 500). Table 8-2 illustrates the extraordinary shift in the parties' representation in the legislative branch. Up to 1988 the highest percentage of seats obtained by the opposition, combining majority districts and plurinominal seats, was 28 percent. In 1988, however, the opposition achieved 48 percent of the total, a 71 percent increase in three years.

Most observers of the 1988 election believe that the PRI engaged in fraudulent practices. Some—PRD figures among them—believe that Cárdenas actually won. Most, however, although agreeing with charges of

Table 8-2 Percentage of Total Vote Won by Candidates for Congress by Major Party, 1961–1997

Election Year	Party[a]												
	PRI	PAN	PPS	PARM	PDM	PSUM	PST	PRT	PMT	PRD	PFCRN	PT	PVEM
1961	90.2	7.6	1.0	0.5	—	—	—	—	—	—	—	—	—
1964	86.3	11.5	1.4	0.7	—	—	—	—	—	—	—	—	—
1967	83.3	12.4	2.8	1.3	—	—	—	—	—	—	—	—	—
1970	80.1	13.9	1.4	0.8	—	—	—	—	—	—	—	—	—
1973	69.7	14.7	3.6	1.9	—	—	—	—	—	—	—	—	—
1976	80.1	8.5	3.0	2.5	—	—	—	—	—	—	—	—	—
1979	69.7	10.8	2.6	1.8	2.1	4.9	2.7	—	—	—	—	—	—
1982	69.3	17.5	1.9	1.4	2.2	4.4	1.8	1.3	—	—	—	—	—
1985	65.0	15.5	2.0	1.7	2.7	3.2	2.5	1.3	1.5	—	—	—	—
1988	50.4	17.1	10.5	6.2	0.4	3.6[b]	—	0.4	—	—	10.5	—	—
1991	61.4	17.7	1.8	2.1	1.1	—	—	0.6	—	8.3	4.4	—	—
1994[c]	50.3	25.8	0.7	0.9	0.4	—	—	—	—	16.1	1.1	2.9	—
1997	39.1	26.6	0.3	0.7	—	—	—	—	—	25.7	—	2.5	3.8

Sources: Delal Baer, "The 1991 Mexican Midterm Elections," CSIS Latin American Election Study Series (October 1, 1991), 31; federal election data. Mexican Embassy, Washington, D.C.; Instituto Federal Electoral, *Elecciones federales 1994* (August 28, 1994).
[a]PRI = Institutional Revolutionary Party; PAN = National Action Party; PPS = Popular Socialist Party; PARM = Authentic Party of the Mexican Revolution; PDM = Democratic Mexican Party; PSUM = Mexico's United Socialist Party; PST = Socialist Workers Party; PRT = Revolutionary Workers Party; PMT = Mexican Workers Party; PRD = Democratic Revolutionary Party; PFCRN = Cardenista Front for National Reconstruction Party; PT = Labor Party; PVEM = Green Party.
[b]Votes for the PSUM in 1988 were for the Mexican Socialist Party (PMS).
[c]Several minor parties, obtaining fewer than 2 percent of the vote, are not reported in these figures.

fraud, believe that Salinas actually did win—but that his percentage of the total vote was lower.

The 1988 elections appeared to suggest the end of Mexico's one party-dominant system, the increased importance of pluralism in the political culture, and, as suggested in Chapter 7, the greater importance of the legislative branch, where the PRI would have to negotiate with the opposition to obtain alliances sufficient to gain passage of major legislation. Although the 1988 elections were a departure from a pattern, the 1991 congressional elections temporarily dampened expectations of an augmentation of opposition strength.

The PRI claimed 61.4 percent of the vote in the 1991 elections, a step back from 1988's brink but still within the pattern of decline since 1961 (see Table 8-2). These elections wrought changes. First, whereas the PRI was on the verge of becoming merely a plurality party, controlling the electorate through the largest number of votes rather than exceeding a majority, it recovered its majority status. Second, the PAN basically remained at the same level as in 1982 and 1988, retaining its position as the second-ranking party, the key opposition party for three decades. Third, the PRD, the major beneficiary of PRI defectors in 1988, was the primary source of PRI returnees in 1991. The PRD did not win a majority of votes in a single state in 1991, including those it had dominated in 1988 (Michoacán, México, Morelos, and the Federal District). Overall, its vote declined from nearly a third in 1988 to only 8 percent. Finally, instead of increasing the legislative branch's importance, the PRI's renewed dominance reinforced its weakness.

The 1994 elections established a new benchmark in the Mexican electoral process. First, the political context was more challenging and less stable than in 1988. Beginning with the surprise uprising of the Zapatista Army of National Liberation on January 1, 1994, followed two months later by the assassination of PRI's presidential candidate in Tijuana, Baja California, on March 23, in midcampaign (the first presidential candidate to be assassinated since 1929), the fear of political instability became widespread among all social classes. Among urban Mexicans polled in February 1994, 42 percent believed that the situation in Chiapas would lead to important changes. Two months later, shortly after Colosio's murder, 30 percent of urban Mexicans perceived the country's situation as very grave, and 39 percent as grave.[8] Second, before these events, the congress introduced several significant reforms into the COFIPE, including eliminating the right of the plurality party to guarantee itself a simple majority, preventing any party from winning more than 315 of the 500 seats in the Chamber of Deputies, doubling the number of seats in the Senate from 64 to 128, establishing the Federal Electoral Institute (IFE) as the arbiter of all federal elections, introducing campaign-spending limits, and improving access to media. Third, these events led to the formation of the Pact for Peace, Justice, and Democracy by eight political parties to promote electoral reforms, later approved by the congress. In addition to these changes, the congress altered the composition of the IFE, giving to six "citizen" councillors, who had no party affiliation, the balance of power in the eleven-member body.[9]

The election results themselves were widely anticipated not only in Mexico but abroad as well. Although public opinion polls taken immediately before election day predicted a PRI victory, what was not expected was the extraordinary turnout, 78 percent, of registered voters, the highest ever recorded in Mexico and well above national averages elsewhere; the active participation of independent voters; and the proportion of independent voters casting ballots in favor of the PRI. Most analysts had expected the PRI to win with only 45 percent of the vote, but Zedillo captured approximately the same percentage of voters as did his predecessor (50 percent). Moreover, most Mexicans believed that the PRI actually won these elections, which was an important change in the credibility of the electoral process.[10]

The presence of international and trained national observers from numerous civic and nongovernmental organizations helped validate the outcome, despite the evidence of some fraud, the lack of secrecy in casting actual ballots, and many technical violations. In retrospect, most critics agreed that although the voting on election day itself was among the cleanest in recent Mexican history, the larger electoral context, including financing and access to media, created an unfair playing field favoring the PRI's fortunes.[11]

The 1994 presidential elections also demonstrated an ideological trend toward the center-right, even though half the voters cast their ballots for someone other than the PRI candidate. Diego Fernández de Cevallos, the PAN presidential contender, obtained 26 percent of the vote, firmly establishing the PAN as Mexico's second party. These elections also confirmed the declining fortunes of the PRD, whose candidate, Cuauhtémoc Cárdenas, was unable to capitalize on his earlier popularity in 1988, earning a distinct third place with 17 percent of the vote. The PAN also continued to do very well in the north, as it did in 1988, although it lost those states in which it won its first gubernatorial elections.

These losses also demonstrated that the opposition by no means had a lock on repeated electoral victories and that the PRI, because of the differing local circumstances, could recover. Finally, the pollster for *Reforma*, Mexico City's leading independent newspaper, found that uneducated voters, fearful of violence, voted in significantly larger numbers for the PRI. This finding also was evident in an August 12 poll taken shortly before the election, in which 54 percent of the citizens questioned agreed that they would "prefer that PRI win to continue the advances that have been achieved," compared with only 36 percent who favored change directed by an opposition party.[12]

In the 1988 and especially the 1991 and 1994 elections, Mexico's proximity to the United States played a special role. In 1988 the government became increasingly sensitive to charges of pervasive election fraud from abroad, especially from the United States media.[13] By 1991 Mexico's conduct in the electoral arena came under severe scrutiny in the U.S. Congress and in the media as discussions of the North American Free-Trade Agreement (NAFTA) continued. American critics of the agreement charged that the United States should not be a party to it in light of Mexico's antidemocratic practices. Even with NAFTA going into effect on January 1, 1994, the United States' interest, governmental and public, remains high.

The 1997 congressional and state gubernatorial elections reinforced more strongly the declining fortunes of the PRI and reversed PRI's recovery in the 1994 presidential elections. In 1996, the PRI-controlled congress passed further electoral reforms.[14] Among these, the IFE was further modified, becoming completely independent of government control. The General Council increased from six to nine independent citizens, party representatives were removed as voting members, and an independent was appointed head of IFE. As Armand Peschard suggests, perhaps most important among these reforms was the decision to allocate larger amounts of public monies for campaign expenditures, approximately 264 million dollars, 30 percent distributed equally among eight contending parties, and 70 percent according to their share of votes in the 1994 election.[15] The IFE also provides free television and radio advertising, also allocated on the same 30/70 percent formula. Finally, for the first time in many years, majority congressional districts were reallocated to correspond more closely to shifting demographic patterns. The most important changes were in the Federal District, which lost 25 percent of its seats (from forty to thirty); Chiapas, which increased its seats by the same percentage (from nine to twelve); México, which gained two seats, replacing the Federal District as the most populous entity in Mexico; and Guanajuato, which also gained two additional seats.

Despite the fact that the 1997 elections involved congressional and gubernatorial races only, 58 percent of the electorate voted, an unusually high figure for midterm elections. More important, in response to the economic crisis, the government austerity program, conflicts within the PRI, and severe social problems, particularly urban crime and violence, the opposition won the largest number of congressional seats ever, 136 of the 300 majority districts.[16] Combined with their plurinominal seats, the four opposition parties, PAN, PRD, PT (the Labor Party), and PVEM (the Green Party), controlled 262 of the 500 seats and, for the first time, the Chamber of Deputies. The PRD also made a significant comeback, as did the party's standard-bearer, Cuauhtémoc Cárdenas, who, with 48 percent of the vote, handily defeated both PRI and PAN as the first elected head of government of the Federal District since the 1920s. The PRD replaced PAN in congress as the number-two party. The PAN, which barely lost its position as the number-two party nationally, increased its strength in congress and won two important gubernatorial races, one in the important industrial border state of Nuevo León and the other in the central state of Querétaro, a traditional PRI stronghold.

The 1997 elections confirm the importance Mexican citizens attribute to the electoral process, which has increasingly become more competitive and clean. Nevertheless, Mexicans continue to remain skeptical, despite growing opposition victories. More than half of all Mexicans (56 percent) considered these elections to have been fradulent.[17] Attitudes toward elections are crucial to Mexican conceptions of democracy. When asked what was most important to achieve a better democracy, nearly two-thirds of all Mexicans said clean elections.[18] Perhaps this explains why many Mexicans do not believe democracy exists in their country.

TRENDS IN MEXICAN ELECTIONS: OPPOSITION FORTUNES

As noted in Chapter 7, many variables affect voters' perceptions of the parties. However, if we analyze the Mexican opposition in the aggregate rather than analyze each component party, we discover some universal characteristics. Among the variables most influencing opposition strength since the 1940s are location, relations with the government, level of development, and urbanization.[19]

Opposition to the PRI and its antecedents has a long history, despite the predominance of the government party since the late 1920s. Opposition has often coalesced around individual candidates and temporary party organizations, such as those of José Vasconcelos in 1929 and General Miguel Henríquez Guzmán in 1952, but opposition tendencies have remained strong in certain states and regions for many decades, indicating a permanence extending beyond any single issue or personality. For example, examination of the 1946, 1952, 1982, and 1988 presidential elections, when the opposition was strongest, indicates that the opposition consistently obtained at least 30 percent or more of the vote in seven states: Baja California, the Federal District, Guanajuato, Jalisco, México, Michoacán, and Morelos. In the 1991 elections, except for Jalisco and Morelos, the opposition attracted more than 40 percent of the vote; and in the Federal District and Baja California, more votes than the PRI. In 1994, the opposition dominated in Mexico, Jalisco, Morelos, the Federal District, and Michoacán, where it won more than half of all votes cast. It also won more than 45 percent of the vote in Guanajuato. However, in the case of Baja California, despite the PAN's gubernatorial control, it lost badly. In part, the PRI's strength there in 1994 can be attributed to the fact that Zedillo is from Mexicali. In 1997, the opposition won the majority of seats in Baja California, the Federal District, Guanajuato, Jalisco, México, Michoacán, and Morelos, as well as Nuevo León, Querétaro, and Sonora.

There are many reasons for the long opposition to the PRI in these states. For some—Baja California, the Federal District, Nuevo León,

Sonora, and México—growth, income, urbanization, and development are important, as they are among the seven states with the highest per capita income. (see Table 8-3.) Economic growth is likely to have the most influence on opposition strength over the long term. It has been argued that economic growth and development are statistically related to election results.[20] In the United States we know, for example, that when the economy does poorly, support for the president and his party generally declines; this was so for President Bush in the fall of 1991 and into 1992. In Mexico, however, although strong economic performance in the short term increases voter satisfaction with the government, when economic performance translates into higher standards of living, those who live in regions benefiting most have voted for the opposition, contrary to expectations.

The region of the country that has best demonstrated the surprising voting behavior over time is the Federal District, which has always been among the high-per-capita-income states and has always recorded sizable votes for the opposition. The PAN has done extremely well in the capital for many years, as did the PRD during the 1988 presidential and 1997 congressional elections. To illustrate the relationship between economic development and support for the opposition, we can group Mexico's states according to per capita income and the percentage of votes for and against the PRI (see Table 8-3). In each election year since 1976, whether we are dealing with presidential or legislative candidates, the total percentage of votes for the PRI in high-income states is much lower than the national average. On the other hand, the PRI obtains a disproportionate amount of its support from low-income states.[21]

Table 8-3 PRI Vote by State Per Capita Income Level, 1976–1994

	Election Year						
Jurisdiction[a]	1976 (%)	1979 (%)	1982 (%)	1985 (%)	1988 (%)	1991 (%)	1994 (%)
Nation	87	74	68	68	50	61	50
Low-income states	92	81	82	81	75	71	52
Medium-income states	93	78	73	68	56	66	49
High-income states	78	55	55	52	37	53	48

Sources: Adapted from Paulina Fernández Christlieb and Octavio Rodríguez Araujo, *Elecciones y partidos en México* (Mexico: El Caballito, 1986), 218, 223–24; Joseph Klesner, "Changing Patterns of Electoral Participation," in *Mexican Politics in Transition,* ed. Judith Gentleman (Boulder, Colo.: Westview Press, 1987), 1930, 1935; *El Día,* July 16, 1988, 8; Instituto Federal Electoral, 1991 election data, district computations, courtesy of Luis Medina, Mexican Embassy, Washington, D.C.; 1994 data, Instituto Federal Electoral, August 28, 1994.

[a]High-income states = Baja California, Baja California Sur, Chihuahua, Federal District, México, Nuevo León, and Sonora; low-income states = Chiapas, Hidalgo, Oaxaca, Puebla, San Luis Potosí, Tlaxcala, Yucatán, and Zacatecas; medium-income states = the remaining states.

What is most extraordinary about the 1994 election results, however, is a reversal of the long-term pattern of fewer votes for the PRI in high-income states. For the first time since 1976 (see Table 8-3), there was very little difference in the vote the PRI obtained in low-versus high-income states and, equally important, almost no difference between its national vote and the vote it earned among all state groupings by income. The variation in these figures is only 2 to 4 percent. In an exit poll of 5,635 voters taken on election day, 53 percent considered Mexico's economic situation to have improved under Salinas. Of those voters, 68 percent cast their ballots for the PRI, indicating the continued importance of a positive perception of economic conditions and partisanship. Voters who wanted to demonstrate their displeasure with the government party or believed it was time for the opposition to win—about a fourth of all Mexicans surveyed—overwhelmingly voted for the PAN, PRD, and several other smaller opposition organizations.[22]

Why is the opposition stronger in states benefiting economically under PRI leadership? A number of reasons stand out. One, the PRI is much better organized in rural areas, and low-income states typically are the most agrarian. The PRI accentuated this relationship through resources allocated by Pronasol (Solidarity) and by Procampo, a peasant-subsidy program.[23] Two, educated Mexicans, who are more sophisticated about participation and more likely to vote for an opposition candidate, live in greater numbers in high-income states. Three, supervision of voting in urban centers, often located in the high-income states, is characterized by fewer reports of fraud and hence fairer.

The data in Table 8-4, in combination with the geographic distribution of higher- and lower-income populations, continue to support the traditional pattern, but in 1994 these differences were not extreme, except among the poorest versus all other income groups. A possible explanation for the decline in differences among income groups in support of the opposition probably has more to do with certain conjunctural political events—the Chiapas uprising and the assassinations—which generated a "fear" factor. A large minority of voters, who voted in large numbers for the PRI, considered this party to be the best option or voted for it because it was a known quantity.

Long-term development trends, therefore, tend to favor the opposition, not the government's party. This pattern has implications for policy because the federal government, which collected more than 85 percent of tax revenues until 1998, decides how they are to be distributed. In terms of direct investment, the government typically has favored the most economically developed states. Ironically, then, the government has reinforced

Table 8-4 Opposition Support in the 1994 Presidential Elections

	Parties	
Variable	Opposition (%)	PRI (%)
Gender		
Men	51	49
Women	47	53
Age		
18 to 29	52	48
30 to 59	48	52
60+	45	55
Education		
Preparatory and beyond	59	41
Secondary	51	49
Primary	42	58
None	36	64
Occupation		
Government employee	45	55
Private-sector employee	58	42
Independent professional	50	50
Self-employed blue collar	49	51
Student	65	35
Housewife	45	55
Unemployed	52	48
Household income		
Below poverty level	46	54
Low and middle income	55	45
High income	51	49
Wealthy	55	45

Source: New York Times, August 24, 1994, 1.

the pattern by directing financial goods to the regions that support the PRI the least.[24]

Geographic location is important to other states. For Baja California, Sonora, and Nuevo León, proximity to the United States has played an important role. It is difficult to link empirically that proximity with Mexican voters' support for the opposition. There is little doubt, however, as we suggested earlier, that where Mexicans live affects their views of the United States and its political system, and their political values.[25] In fact, surveys show that the closer Mexicans live to the United States and the more they travel to it, the greater their admiration is.[26] Many of the prominent figures in the PAN are products of the border culture, including its 1988 presidential candidate, who attended high school in San Diego. In fact, Mexicans living in the United States repeatedly have requested the right to vote by absentee ballot, a request consistently denied. Observers argue that the government refusal is based on the high probability that the overwhelming majority would support opposition parties.[27]

A geographic trend that is becoming a stronger and, in the view of some scholars, disturbing pattern in the democratic transition is the division of votes among the PRI, PAN, and PRD. Joseph Klesner contends that "instead of a three-party system, two separate party systems seem to be developing in Mexico. In the north and west, the PAN and the PRI compete. In the areas south and east of the capital, excepting Yucatán, the PRD is the PRI's main adversary."[28] This regional separation remains, borne out by the 1997 congressional races. PAN did not win a single district in fourteen out of thirty-two states. PRD did not win a single district in twenty-two out of thirty-two states.[29] Such a development will accentuate regionalism and geographic partisanship, making national unity more difficult.

Historical experience has also had much to do with the level of opposition support in various states, generally in connection with poor relationships. For example, Morelos, a state just south of Mexico City, gave birth to the most important agrarian movement during the 1910 Revolution, led by Emiliano Zapata. Zapata and his followers never pursued goals compatible with those of the Mexican government, even after the revolution's initial success in 1911 or its more institutional phase after 1916. Hence, tensions have always existed between the peasants in Morelos and national political leadership.

Strong opposition in Guanajuato, Jalisco, and Michoacán stem from the importance of Catholicism and church-state relations in those states during the 1920s. When the federal government strictly applied constitutional provisions relative to religion, it provoked resistance from staunch Catholics and some clergy in the region, including these three states. This movement in defense of religious rights became known as the Cristero rebellion. Memories of the events are still fresh in the minds of the people who were children in the 1920s. The region contributes heavily to the priesthood and hierarchy, and a disproportionate number of bishops are graduates of the Morelia seminary in the heart of Michoacán.

Geography, level of development, income, and urbanization, among other variables, add to the historic importance of opposition. Although none of the opposition parties yet has had the strength enough to best the PRI nationally, the foundation to do so has existed for many decades. The time will come when one of them, or some new opposition party, possibly in 2000, wins primacy among the electorate.

The collective strength of the opposition can be measured in terms of the population it presently governs. After the 1997 elections, its elected officials held offices responsible for 57 percent of the population, and all of

Table 8-5 Control Over Elective Offices by Political Parties, 1997

Positions	PAN	PRI	PRD	Other	Totals
Governors	6	25	1	0	32
Senators	33	77	13	5	128
Deputies	122	239	125	14	500
Legislators	244	541	143	63	991
Mayors	308	1,642	251	191	2,392
Population	31,913,000	39,146,113	17,496,207	2,033,360	90,588,680
% Population	35	43	19	2	99

Source: Instituto Federal Electoral, 1997.

these representatives were selected at the state and local level. (See Table 8-5.)

OPPOSITION PARTIES: THEIR ORIGINS AND FUTURE

The most important opposition party in Mexico, and the longest-lived in terms of putting up promising candidates, is the National Action Party, founded in 1939 by Manuel Gómez Morin, a former national figure in government economic policymaking, and Efraín González Luna, a lawyer and Catholic activist. As is true of so many of the opposition parties, leadership often came, at least initially, from disgruntled establishment elites. In some cases it is persons who have had their own political ambitions cut short; in other cases it is a question of policy differences. The PAN's formation is an example of the latter's bringing together diverse individuals who were against the statist, populist economic policies of President Lázaro Cárdenas (1934–1940).

The PAN first put up candidates against the PRI on the local level. Although it had supported several opposition presidential candidates, it did not run its own candidate until 1958. It has put up a candidate in every election since then except 1976, when it protested the PRI's monopoly and electoral fraud by withdrawing from the presidential contest. Ten years after its founding, it captured less than 3 percent of the legislative seats (Table 8-2). After the first electoral reforms went into effect in 1964, it began obtaining roughly 10 percent of the seats, assisted by its share of party deputies. Its representation stabilized around that figure until 1988, when it doubled its share to 20 percent. In the 1991–1993 legislature it fell to 18 percent but rebounded to 24 and 26 percent in 1994 and 1997, respectively.

The PAN ideological banner has shifted over time. Initially, party leaders, many of whom were well connected financially or had ties to Catholic Action youth or other Catholic movements, were described as conservative, in some cases reactionary, pro-business, and pro-church. By the 1960s the party evolved gradually into a Mexican variant of a Christian Democratic organization.[30] However, like the PRI and especially the left-of-center parties, the PAN suffered from internal dissent. At various points its leadership has wavered between those desirous of playing more or less by the rules of the political game, as set down by the government, and those who advocated a more aggressive stance vis-á-vis the PRI.

The new PAN activists, sometimes referred to as neo-Panistas, have taken a more conservative stance ideologically and have often allied themselves with combative businessmen willing to run under the PAN banner. As Soledad Loaeza suggested in her analysis of the 1988 presidential election, the neo-Panistas broke new ground "by challenging the unwritten rules of Mexican politics—in particular, the idea that industrialists should not participate in politics."[31] When President Salinas took some of the thunder out of traditional PAN issues, like statism, labor corruption, and outmoded church-state relations, the PAN centered its major criticism on political modernization, notably genuine electoral reform, a popular issue with the electorate. Yet the PAN's leadership, even when faced with vehement internal dissension, eventually supported an electoral law introduced by Salinas, a law it believed would ensure integrity in voter registration and balloting. The 1989 reform also made it extremely difficult for smaller parties to put up coalition candidates, as Cárdenas had done under the National Democratic Front in 1988.

The PAN's growth nationally has never been dramatic. It has remained the major opposition party, except during the 1988 presidential race, but its strength from 1982 to 1993 stabilized at approximately 17 percent. In 1994, it established a stronger presence, accounting for half of all opposition votes cast, a fourth of the electorate. National figures and figures from each of the three hundred majority districts suggest the regional quality of PAN support. Its organizational strength and the narrowness of its platform have made it viable primarily in urban centers. Indeed, it would be accurate to call the PAN a regional, urban party. In 1988, the first time that the PAN won more than 10 percent of the legislative majority districts, the thirty-eight seats it obtained were in the major cities, including Ciudad Juárez; Mexico City; León; Guadalajara, the capital of Jalisco; several districts in the industrialized section of the state of México; San Luis Potosí and Mérida, both state capitals; and Culiacán. In fact, four-fifths of its legislative seats were in just five Mexican cities. The PAN repeated the same pattern in 1994, but more than half its eighteen seats were from Jalisco and five from the north. Two-thirds of the districts it captured were from León, Guadalajara, and Mérida. In 1997, when it won sixty-five seats, more than half were from Jalisco, Guanajuato, México, Baja California, and Nuevo León.

The PAN's potential for the future, even with more stringently applied electoral reforms, is stronger at the local and state levels than nationally. One region where this growth is likely to occur is the north, where many owners of small and medium-size businesses are pressing for a more open voice in partisan politics.[32] As data in the previous chapter indicate, only a small percentage of prospective voters express sympathy for the PAN. A stronger national future is also made less likely by the fact that at least under Zedillo and Salinas, the PRI's ideology has absorbed many of its economic ideals, rendering the PAN's program less distinctive. People who vote for the PAN do so because they want a change from the PRI,[33] and after 1995, specifically a change in the management of government economic policy.

The PAN expanded and deepened its national strength at the regional, grassroots level, winning numerous mayoralty elections in small towns, then in capital cities. It then became the first opposition party to win a governorship, defeating PRI in Baja California in 1989. PAN complaints about alleged fraud in the Guanajuato gubernatorial race in 1991, echoed in the U.S. media, led the government to force the resignation of the PRI candidate. He was replaced by an interim governor, also a Panista. In 1992, PAN won the governor's post in Chihuahua. The PAN's greatest potential to establish a foothold, however, was in Jalisco, where in 1994 it swept federal legislative posts and then in early 1995 defeated the PRI for the governorship and most other local offices. It repeated its electoral victory in Baja California in 1995, and by mid-1998 was governing in six states. Although PAN has never garnered more than 27 percent of the vote nationally, its charismatic presidential front-runner, governor Vicente Fox of Guanajuato, may be the person to push it to a national victory.

The only other major opposition is the Democratic Revolutionary Party. The PRD has a short history; it constructed itself on a foundation of smaller leftist parties that had flowered during the 1970s. Elements of the Mexican Communist Party (PCM), founded in 1919, and the Mexican Socialist Party (PMS), founded in 1987, provided the formal organizational basis. The PRD came into being after the 1988 presidential election. Many of its founders, as in the case of the PAN, were PRI dissidents.[34] Some of its members in the Chamber of Deputies and in the Senate previously held political posts as Priistas or as leftist-party members. In fact, so many figures have resigned from the PRI to become contenders for PRD candidacies in gubernatorial races in 1998, that is provoked a negative reaction among many PRD leaders.

The PRD's ideology is difficult to characterize because the party's ranks are an amalgam of political groups professing views ranging from Marxist to populist. Some issues prominent in the PRD platform and that distinguish it from the PRI include electoral reforms, fiscal reforms, broad social programs, women's rights, and free education. In short, the PRD advocated the diversification of economic relations, increased political pluralism in the electoral arena, programs to mitigate the negative effects of NAFTA, and thoroughgoing electoral reforms. Typically, it has favored economic policies that cater less to business interests and advocated the traditional importance of the state in economic affairs.[35]

The results of the 1988 election were deceptive in terms of PRD strength. The immense popularity of candidate Cárdenas's father among many sectors of the population made it difficult to distinguish support for Cuauhtémoc Cárdenas as a symbol of his father from support for the principles of his coalition. Those who vote for the PRD, as in the case of the PAN, are primarily interested in change. But the PRD, even more than the PAN, owing to its origins in a loosely connected alliance of small parties, has found it difficult to maintain its cohesion. One of the parties in the original alliance, the Cardenista Front for National Reconstruction, has pursued an independent course since 1988.

Some observers have noted a decided strategy by the PRI in its electoral contests with the PRD to maintain the PAN's strength and to focus on defeating the PRD. The strategy, it is argued, became apparent in 1989, after the PAN won the governorship of Baja California, and the PRI claimed surprising victories in local and state legislative districts in Michoacán, Cárdenas's home state. By 1991 PRD electoral strength had declined precipitously to only 8 percent of the vote, a distant third to the PRI and the PAN (Table 8-1). The PRD faced electoral conditions involving fraud, and many of its active supporters were physically threatened, injured, or killed. In fact, PRD members constitute the single largest group of victims in national and international Human Rights Commission reports. The PRI also was successful in 1994 in convincing many voters to associate electoral violence with the PRD. That fact, combined with Cárdenas's poor performance in the first televised presidential debate, ensured PRD's third-place position.

The 1997 midterm elections offered both Cárdenas and the PRD an opportunity to revive its electoral fortunes. Cárdenas became the party's standard-bearer in the most significant race, that of the newly elected head of the Federal District, Mexico's most influential urban center. Changing his campaign style and benefiting from deteriorating social and economic conditions, as well as a poor campaign by his PAN opponent, Cárdenas easily defeated PRI's candidate. Using the Federal District's thirty congressional seats as a base, the party swept to victory in twenty-nine districts and recaptured its original strength in México, Michoacán, and Morelos, states where it did well in 1988. Although it won nearly the same percentage of votes as PAN nationally, 26 percent, it did slightly better in the plurinominal regions, thus receiving more seats and giving it second place after PRI in the Chamber of Deputies. However, given the greater depth of support for PAN nationally, PRD should continue to be ranked as the third most important party. Cárdenas will use his position as head of the Federal District to make a third run for the presidency in 2000.

Voter support for the Left is even weaker nationally than voter support for the Right, expressed through the PAN. Voter strength since 1998 has wavered considerably in the 1991, 1994, and 1997 elections. In 1988, PRD, with the exception of Michoacán, could not translate its strong presidential showing into legislative victories. The PRD was not able to reverse this pattern in 1994, winning only five of the three hundred district seats. Voters made clear immediately before the election that neither the candidate nor the PRD's ability to solve Mexico's problems had gained much support. As Barry Carr had predicted, unless the leftist parties were able to translate their 1988 election victories into grassroots labor and agrarian organizations, they would not create a base sufficient to sustain future electoral successes.[36] The deteriorating economic situation in 1995 and 1996, the dramatic rise in crime, and the dissension within PRI ranks allowed PRD the opportunity to compete vigorously in 1997. To increase its appeal, it will need to expand well beyond the states where it presently is strong, to moderate its internal conflicts, and to broaden its ideological base.

CONCLUSION

Election trends in Mexico, with the exception of the 1988 presidential election, demonstrate some remarkably consistent patterns. Despite the continued monopoly of the PRI as the national government electoral vehicle and the PRI resurgence in the 1991 elections, because of grassroots efforts of opposing groups, it has continued to decline slowly in overall support, leaving an opening for present and future opposition parties. If economic modernization raises the standard of living of individual Mexicans as well as of geographic regions, it is likely in the long run to give impetus to support for opposition parties, given increased voter sophistication and the difficulties in perpetrating fraud in urban centers. Opposition control at the local level—if translated into effective governing and increasing party strength—can improve the political culture, favoring greater receptivity to democracy.[37] Analysts dispute the degree to which local opposition influences are more important than national pressures to change from the top down, but there is no question that a bottom-up process is at work too.[38] Historically, higher-income regions, those benefiting most from government policies, have voted against the PRI, not for it. Although the PRI continues to appeal to a wide range of income groups and is the only party demonstrating depth nationally in terms of its base of support, it has many vulnerabilities.

Two conditions prevent opposition parties from capitalizing fully on the PRI's weaknesses. The first is the relationship between the party and the government. Although government performance is generally associated in competitive, democratic systems with the success or failure of its party, Mexico's PRI can ride out these ups and downs economically and otherwise because of advantages gained through its symbiotic relationship to the government. The most important advantages are financial benefits, more indirect than direct, and the human resources that accrue to the party through the government. For example, in a presidential campaign, army troops and officers are assigned to the PRI candidate and carry out many logistical activities. Furthermore, the PRI gains from tremendous coverage in the media; studies show that it receives far more attention from the press than do any of the other parties.[39] Its ability to furnish transportation to reporters, provide them with favors, and give them first-rate communication facilities all lead to PRI dominance over the media. Opposition control of the legislative branch, and its increased scrutiny of agency budgets, has limited and will eventually eliminate these subsidies. Most important, PRI monopolization of government offices provides it with a reward system unmatched and unattainable by any other party. If the same kinds of "goodies" applied to legislative positions, given the fact that 455 PAN members held legislative office between 1943 and 1994, opposition parties could offer more attractive rewards to their leaders and rank and file. Instead, the rewards they can offer are few and less worthwhile politically. The structural prohibition of no consecutive reelection also prevents the opposition from developing an experienced leadership. Since their opportunities in the national executive branch are few, this is a greater obstacle for the PAN and PRD than it is for the PRI.[40]

The second inhibiting condition is intertwined with the first: the extraordinary difficulty attached to bringing a major opposition entity into being. From an ideological point of view, Mexico needs another centrist party, perhaps even center-right, that would accord with the desires of the electorate, as revealed to pollsters. Even if such an organization did materialize, it would not be likely to sustain itself beyond a single election, owing to the first condition just described. Until a leader can capture the imagination of many voters, can appeal to the ideological center, and can appeal to all social backgrounds, the PRI political hegemony is secure. Only when elections are almost universally deemed honest and fair will citizens become more interested in the process and its outcome. The 1994 presidential and 1997 legislative elections demonstrated very clearly this possibility.

Perhaps the single most interesting variable altering the outcome of the 1994 presidential elections was the May 12 televised presidential debates, watched by an estimated thirty million Mexicans. The debates demonstrated that a single, public encounter—highly publicized and well covered in the mass media—makes it possible for an opposition candidate to capture the imagination of the voters, and thereby to reduce the PRI's overall media advantage. In the Mexican case, it did this so decisively that it permanently changed the fortunes of the PRD and the PAN, giving a huge boost to the PAN candidate, Diego Fernández Cevallos.

Immediately before the debate, 16 percent of the electorate said they would vote for the PAN. The day after, this figure more than doubled to 39 percent, placing the PAN in first place in the minds of committed voters. Cárdenas, who had been in second place with the support of 20 percent of the voters, lost almost half this support, to only 12 percent. Zedillo also fell from first to second place, down to 37 percent from a high of 49 percent. There was no doubt that Fernández Cevallos swept the debate, but more important, 28 percent of the voters indicated that they had changed their vote. No other single event in 1994, including the assassination of Luis Donaldo Colosio, changed voter preferences so much. The viewers gave Fernández Cevallos their strongest marks for his speaking ability and self-confidence. But in regard to qualities related to governing—which in the long run contributed to Zedillo's victory—including experience, ability to solve economic problems, and moral leadership, Zedillo remained well ahead of the other two candidates.[41]

It is also well to remember that even with the extraordinary advances of PAN and the PRD at all levels—local, state, and national—the opposition parties by no means are secure in each of their posts. In other words, research demonstrates that despite their initial popularity, they frequently fail to convince voters to return them to office in the next election.[42] The reasons for voter disenchantment are often the same as those given for citizen dissatisfaction with PRI: incompetence, unfulfilled campaign pledges, and corruption. Thus, PRI's ability to make a comeback depends not only on its performance but on that of its opponents, once they have garnered elective office. PRI's victory over PAN in the 1998 Chihuahua gubernatorial race, returning the state to the government party, illustrates this new pattern of electoral competition.

NOTES

1. For background, see John Bailey, "Can the PRI be Reformed," in *Mexican Politics in Transition*, ed. Judith Gentleman (Boulder, Colo.: Westview Press, 1987), especially, 74–94.

2. Wayne Cornelius, "Political Liberalization in an Authoritarian Regime: Mexico, 1976–1985," in *Mexican Politics in Transition*, ed. Judith Gentleman (Boulder, Colo.: Westview Press, 1987), 22.

3. María Emilia Farias Mackey, *The Reform of Electoral Policy* (Mexico: Congreso de la Unión, 1987), 8–9. A detailed analysis of the motivations behind these changes are available in Silvia Gómez Tagle's "Electoral Reform and the Party System, 1977–90," in *Mexico, Dilemmas of Transition*, ed. Neil Harvey (London: Institute of Latin American Studies, 1993), 64–90.

4. Daniel Levy and Gabriel Székely, *Mexico: Paradoxes of Stability and Change*, 2d ed. (Boulder, Colo.: Westview Press, 1987), 68.

5. For detailed background, see Delal Baer, "The 1986 Mexican Elections, The Case of Chihuahua," CSIS Latin American Election Study Series (Washington, D.C.: Georgetown University, September 1986); and Vikram Khub Chand, "Politicization, Institutions, and Democratization in Mexico: The Politics of the State of Chihuahua in National Perspective" (Ph.D. diss., Harvard University, 1991).

6. For background, see Peter H. Smith, "The 1988 Presidential Succession in Historical Perspective," in *Mexico's Alternative Political Futures*, ed. Wayne Cornelius, Judith Gentleman, and Peter H. Smith (La Jolla, Calif.: U.S.–Mexico Studies Center, UCSD, 1989), 399ff.

7. Roderic Ai Camp, "Mexico," in *Latin America and Caribbean Contemporary Record*, ed. James M. Malloy and Eduardo A. Gamarra (New York: Holmes & Meier, 1990), B300.

8. MORI de México weekly poll for *Este País*, February 23 and April 20, 1994.

9. These and other changes are outlined in detail in George Grayson's excellent summary, *A Guide to the 1994 Mexican Presidential Election*, CSIS Election Studies Report (Washington, D.C.: CSIS, 1994), 8–10; and in John Bailey, *The 1994 Mexican Presidential Election*, CSIS Election Studies Series (Washington, D.C.: CSIS, 1994).

10. An excellent summary of opinions and discussion concerning the significance of the 1994 elections can be found in "Mexico's Electoral Aftermath and Political Future," summary of a conference at the Mexican Center, University of Texas, Austin, September 2–3, 1994; and in Enrique Calderón Alzati and Daniel Cazés, eds., *Las elecciones presidenciales de 1994* (Mexico: UNAM, 1996).

11. Numerous criticisms of the shortcomings of the 1994 election, before and during election day, can be found in Human Rights Watch/Americas, "Mexico at the Crossroads" 6 (August 1994): 1–24; Civic Alliance, "The Quality of the Election Day Process, August 21, 1994," September 19, 1994; "The Prospects for a Free, Fair and Honest Election in Mexico," A Report to the Business Coordinating Council, August 15, 1994; and Washington Office on Latin America, "The 1994 Mexican Election: A Question of Credibility," Washington, D.C., August 15, 1994; and the Instituto Federal Electoral, "Main Criticisms to the Electoral Roll and the Nominal Lists" (Mexico City: IFE, 1994).

12. Belden and Russonello, "Mexico 1994, A National Poll of the Mexican Electorate," Washington, D.C., August 10, 1994.

13. Leonardo Ffrench Iduarte, "The Mexican Presidential Election in the Mass Media of the United States," in *Sucesión Presidencial: The 1988 Mexican Presidential Election*, ed. Edgar W. Butler and Jorge A. Bustamante (Boulder, Colo.: Westview Press, 1991), 218.

14. For an excellent analysis, see Joseph Klesner, "Electoral Reform in Mexico's Hegemonic Party System: Perpetuation of Privilege or Democratic Advance? Paper presented at the American Political Science Association meeting, Washington, D.C., 1997.

15. Armand Peschard-Sverdrup, *The 1997 Mexican Midterm Elections, Post-Election Report*, Western Hemisphere Election Study Series (Washington, D.C.: CSIS, 1997), 6.

16. Partisans of all three parties ranked personal security, economic crisis, and unemployment as the principal issues in the elections. *Este País*, July 1997, 37.

17. Ulises Beltrán et al., *Los mexicanos de los noventa* (Mexico: UNAM, 1996), 37.

18. *Este País*, May 1998, 16.

19. See my "Mexico's 1988 Elections: A Turning Point for Its Political Development and Foreign Relations," in *Sucesión Presidencial: The 1988 Mexican Presidential Elections*, ed. Edgar W. Butler and Jorge A. Bustamante (Boulder, Colo.: Westview Press, 1991), 98ff.

20. Barry Ames, "Bases of Support for Mexico's Dominant Party," *American Political Science Review* 64 (March 1970): 153–67.

21. For the most comprehensive analysis of these and other variables, see Joseph Klesner, "Electoral Reform in an Authoritarian Regime: The Case of Mexico" (Ph.D. diss., MIT, February 1988); for 1988, Antonia Martínez Rodríguez, "Que hable México: último gobierno priista?" *Revista de Estudios Políticos* 63 (January–March 1989): 251–58; and for 1991, see Joseph Klesner, "Realignment or Dealignment? Consequences of Economic Crisis and Restructuring for the Mexi-

can Party System," in *The Politics of Economic Restructuring, State-Society Relations and Regime Change*, ed. Maria Lorena Cook, Kevin J. Middlebrook, and Juan Molinar (La Jolla, Calif.: Center for U.S.–Mexican Studies, UCSD, 1994), 159–94.

22. *New York Times*, August 23, 1994, 1, 8.

23. The most careful analysis of the relationship between government spending and PRI support between 1988 and 1991 found only a marginally significant connection. Kathleen Bruhn, "Social Spending and Political Support," *Comparative Politics* (January 1996): 151–77.

24. Roderic Ai Camp, "A Reexamination of Political Leadership and Allocation of Federal Revenues in Mexico, 1934–1973," *Journal of Developing Areas* 10 (1976): 100–2.

25. Alberto Hernández Hernández, "Political Attitudes Among Border Youth," in *Electoral Patterns and Perspectives in Mexico*, ed. Arturo Alvarado (La Jolla, Calif.: Center for U.S.–Mexican Studies, UCSD, 1987), 216.

26. William J. Millard, *Media Use by the Better-Educated in Major Mexican Cities* (Washington, D.C.: U.S. International Communications Agency, 1981); Alberto Hernández Medina and Luis Narro Rodríguez, eds. *Cómo somos los mexicanos* (Mexico City: CREA, 1987).

27. Comments, Symposium on Mexican Electoral Reform, Institute of Latin American Studies, University of Texas, March 1991, Austin.

28. Joseph Klesner, *Mexican Studies* 11 (Winter 1995): 137–50.

29. *Review of the Economic Situation in Mexico*, September, 1997, 363.

30. Donald Mabry, *Mexico's Acción Nacional: A Catholic Alternative to Revolution* (Syracuse, N.Y.: Syracuse University Press, 1973). For an update on the reasons for its growth, see Leticia Barraza and Ilán Bizberg, "El Partido Acción Nacional y el régimen político mexicano," *Foro Internacional* 31 (January–March 1991): 418–45.

31. Soledad Loaeza, "The Emergence and Legitimization of the Modern Right, 1970–1988," in *Mexico's Alternative Political Futures*, ed. Wayne Cornelius, Judith Gentleman, and Peter H. Smith (La Jolla, Calif.: Center for U.S.–Mexican Studies, 1989), 361.

32. See Yemile Mizrahi, "The New Conservative Opposition in Mexico: The Political Radicalization of Northern Entrepreneurs," paper presented at the National Latin American Studies Association meeting, April 1991.

33. Gallup Organization, exit poll, August 18, 1991. This was the first exit poll permitted by the Mexican government.

34. The evolution of the Democratic Current and the formation of the original electoral front, as described in detail by Cuauhtémoc Cárdenas in a lengthy interview with Carlos B. Gil, *Hope and Frustration: Interviews with Leaders of Mexico's Political Opposition* (Wilmington, Del.: Scholarly Resources, 1992), 155ff. This is the first work of its kind on Mexico and provides a broad sense of opposition views.

35. Javier Farrera Araujo and Diego Prieto Hernández, "Partido de la Revolución Democrática: Documentos básicos," *Revista Mexicana de Ciencias Políticas y Sociales* 36 (January-March 1990): 67–95. For a comparison with the PAN

and other parties, see Federico Reyes Heroles, ed., *Los partidos politicos mexicanos en 1991* (Mexico City: Fondo de Cultura Económica, 1991).

36. Barry Carr, "The Left and Its Potential Role in Political Change," in *Mexico's Alternative Futures*, ed. Wayne Cornelius, Judith Gentleman, and Peter H. Smith (La Jolla, Calif.: Center for U.S.–Mexican Studies, 1989), 381.

37. Yemile Mizrahi provides an excellent case study of this process in support of that thesis in "Conciliation Against Confrontation: How Does the Partido Acción Nacional Rule in Chihuahua?" CIDE, October 1994.

38. For views on this issue see Victoria Rodríguez, "Urban Elections in Democratic Latin America," in *Urban Elections in Democratic Latin America* ed. Henry Dietz and Gil Shidlo (Wilmington: Scholarly Resources, 1998), 177; Steven Barracca, "A Tale of Two Political Cultures: Local Elections in Yucatán, Mexico," paper presented at the National Latin American Studies Association, Guadalajara, 1997; and Kathleen Bruhn, "PRD Local Governments in Michoacán: Implications for Mexico's Democratization Process," paper presented at the National Latin American Studies Association, Guadalajara, 1997.

39. See "Espacio a los partidos en la prensa, 1988–1990," *El Nacional*, June 22, 1991, 1.

40. Emma Campos concluded that only 11.5 percent of the 455 Panista deputies were reelected, and two-thirds of those, only once. See "Realmente se reeligen los diputados? El caso del PAN," unpublished paper, ITAM, 1994.

41. See Indemer/Louis Harris, "Public Opinion Reaction to Mexican Presidential Debate," May 12, 1994; MORI, "Encuesta," *Macrópolis*, May 16, 1994, 10. Two months later, half of all voters considered Zedillo the "most able to govern." Belden and Russonello, "Mexico 1994."

42. For a discussion of the pragmatic consequences of holding versus obtaining office, see Yemile Mizrahi, "Dilemmas of the Opposition in Government: Chihuahua and Baja California," *Mexican Studies* 14 (Winter 1998):151–89.

9

External Politics: Relations with the United States

As in previous decades, Mexico's foreign relations during the 1990s will be conditioned by internal as well as external factors. On the one hand, the external environment is subject to a process of profound transformation, with direct implications for potential foreign activity in our country and for potential expansion of Mexican participation in world markets. The fiscal, trade, and skills deficits of the United States, its relative weakening in the world economy, the leadership role that Japan and Germany play, the formation of regional blocs, détente and the transmogrification of the Eastern European economies, and finally the developing countries' loss of relative importance—all these will affect Mexico's foreign relations and pose behavioral alternatives about which fundamental decisions must be made.
JESÚS SILVA HERZOG, "Mexico's External Relations in the 1990s"

Throughout this book, beginning with Chapter 2, I have emphasized the impact of the United States on Mexico and the historical relations of the two countries. Although my focus has been on domestic politics, the pervasive influence—if only psychological—of the United States, in addition to politics of place, culture, and economics, has helped mold indirectly and implicitly, Mexican political behavior. This does not mean that Mexico is not concerned with foreign relations elsewhere in the region, particularly with Central America or Europe and the Pacific Rim. Rather, the dominance of the United States in foreign policy issues important to Mexico usually outweighs the latter's interests in other external actors. As the next chapter makes clear, Europe's rejection of Mexico's request for investment and aid in the late 1980s, in favor of concerns next door in eastern Europe, led the Mexican leadership to pursue a strategy of closer ties to the United States, thus ensuring even greater interdependency.

The proximity of the United States to Mexico has affected their relationship in the past, to Mexico's disadvantage, and continues to determine their current relationship. Mexico has always struggled to retain a strong sense of self-identity in the shadow of its more powerful neighbor. Indeed, Mexico's nationalism is in part a response to its experiences with the United States, and Mexico's postrevolutionary foreign policy also, in part, is based on its relationship with the United States. For example, in both international and regional forums, such as the United Nations or the Organization of American States—the preeminent Western Hemisphere organization dominated by the United States—Mexico has tried to become an independent actor in foreign policy matters vis-à-vis the United States. In the 1980s, Mexico offered an important, autonomous voice in Central American politics, especially in regard to the United States' policies toward the civil war in El Salvador and the revolutionary Sandinista government in Nicaragua.

Analysts of Mexican foreign policy have long argued that for many decades the Mexican government's nationalistic foreign policy stance permitted its leadership to grant concessions to the Mexican Left at little political cost. In other words, although the Mexican Left had few opportunities to pursue their agenda in strictly domestic politics, they could claim greater success in the foreign policy arena. Although such concessions created friction with the United States, especially during the Reagan years, it allowed the Mexican leadership to retain strong nationalistic symbols and to reinforce their legitimacy as a protector of Mexican sovereignty. Even in the eyes of Mexico's current administration, sovereignty is the most important foreign policy objective. As President Zedillo declared in a major foreign policy address, "The highest priority of my government will be strengthening and fully exercising national sovereignty. We conceive sovereignty as the exclusive ability of Mexicans to make our own decisions, to define and advance freely and autonomously to our destiny. We do not confuse sovereignty with isolationism."[1]

Because of its historical and geographical circumstances, and the economic and political position of its northern neighbor, Mexico has been forced to consider the United States' policy positions on numerous issues. On the other hand, particularly from the point of view of Mexican policymakers, the United States has essentially ignored Mexico. A former assistant secretary of foreign relations complained:

> As of today, the United States has still not elaborated a coherent policy toward Mexico. This situation, commonly known as "benign neglect," should instead be called "malign neglect," because of its detrimental effects. The U.S. Government has allowed its Mexican policy to be guided strictly by circumstantial interests and criteria, acting only when faced with specific problems.[2]

Some issues, however, do receive attention in the bilateral relations between Mexico and the United States: national security concerns involving drug trafficking, political corruption, and political development; basic economic issues, especially trade, investment, immigration, and debt; and difficult-to-measure cultural influences, especially values, language, and the arts.

NATIONAL SECURITY ISSUES

In its relationship with Latin America, including Mexico, the United States has been primarily interested in political stability, not political liberalization. According to one prominent historian,

> The nondemocratic nature of the Mexican political system has not been a significant factor in Mexican-U.S. relations, with the sole exception of the period in which the Mexican Revolution as an antiauthoritarian revolt coincided with the American reformism headed by President Wilson, and then only for a very short period.[3]

But this pattern began to change in the late 1980s, when Americans in general and some political figures in Congress took a greater interest in what was happening in Mexico's internal politics.

The 1988 presidential elections in Mexico, which captured considerable media attention in the United States, served as a catalyst in making domestic politics an important foreign policy issue. For Mexico, the foreign policy implications were twofold. From the point of view of the opposition parties, and particularly the dissident members of the PRI who sought to defeat their former colleagues, the United States' interest in the elections—given its open support for democratic elections elsewhere in the region—could be used to strengthen the dissidents' ability to win in a "clean" electoral environment. This may be considered a foreign policy issue because many Mexican electoral groups, especially from opposition parties, sought the approval of foreign electoral observers and wanted to guarantee integrity at the ballot box. Mexico's establishment political leadership took the opposite point of view, claiming that such observers were tantamount to foreign interference in Mexican domestic affairs. Despite overwhelming sentiment among Mexican citizens in favor of increasing democratization and free elections, they, too, remained divided on the issue of international observers, with equal numbers for and against their presence in the 1994 presidential elections.

Mexico's foreign policy has become more and more complicated since 1988, as various domestic political groups have traveled to the United States, officially and unofficially, to voice their views and to obtain powerful, political allies. On an official level, spokespersons representing both major opposition parties, the PAN and PRD but particularly the latter, have been successful in gaining a public platform in both the U.S. Senate and House, where foreign relations committees have given them opportunities to testify about the condition of Mexican domestic politics.

These American legislators have not necessarily been interested in the goals represented by Mexican opposition candidates; rather, they have used Mexican testimony to erect obstacles to U.S. presidential policies. For example, as early as 1986 Senator Jesse Helms, who became chairman of the Republican-controlled Senate Foreign Relations Committee in 1995, held hearings demanding free elections as a condition for U.S. assistance to Mexico in renegotiating its foreign debt. This pattern became noteworthy during the Bush and Clinton administrations, specifically in the congressional debate over approving the North American Free Trade Agreement (NAFTA). American opponents of the agreement, which went into effect on January 1, 1994, hoped to use Mexican electoral fraud and political corruption as a vehicle to derail the treaty's approval. In September 1997, Senator Helms again thwarted the president, sinking Clinton's nominee for ambassador to Mexico, moderate Republican William Weld, for being allegedly "soft on drugs."

Beginning with the Bush administration, the American government publicly committed itself to free and fair elections in Mexico, even though its enthusiasm might have waned had Cuauhtémoc Cárdenas won the 1988 elections or regained his strength in 1994. Consequently, in the 1994 presidential elections—but at the very last minute and under intense international pressure—the Mexican government permitted both domestic and international observers. According to an independent observer, "Through its public statements, private diplomacy, and financial support for election-related activities, the Clinton administration went farther than any of its predecessors in setting forth a policy designed ostensibly to support the democratization process. On several fronts, however, this policy fell short of the mark."[4] The author went on to criticize American policy for glossing over major problems in the elections in its public statements; for supporting international observers primarily as a means of legitimizing the elections, rather than making them fairer; and for basing its political development strategy on getting NAFTA approved.

On an unofficial level, Mexicans have involved a plethora of American and international agencies in domestic political affairs since 1988, creating a complex web of external domestic actors in Mexican politics. U.S. human rights and civic organizations' interest and published commentary regarding internal developments in Mexico have further complicated the official bilateral relationship between Mexico and the United States, since their executive branches and foreign relations agencies must consider all these other actors. These unofficial organizations are particularly adept at attracting media coverage.

Perhaps the single most important threat to Mexico's internal security, and that attracting the greatest attention from the United States government, was the uprising led by the Zapatista Army for National Liberation (EZLN) in Chiapas early in 1994. The presence of active guerrilla groups in Mexico not only creates significant national security concerns internally but, because of Mexico's proximity to the United States, also raises grave concerns across the border. The United States thus implicitly became involved in the process by which Mexico chose to confront the rebels. Indeed, the reverberations of such a group extend well beyond traditional national security concerns in both countries, to the economic well-being of both Mexico and the United States. For example, foreign investors' perceptions of the EZLN's continued presence in late 1994 and early 1995 had a significant effect on their confidence in the Mexican economy, continued investment, and the Mexican government's economic policy, leading to the worst crisis in recent Mexican history. The appearance of the Popular Revolutionary Army (ERP) in 1996, although far less visible, reinforces the image of social violence just below the surface of what appears to be a stable polity.

A national security issue of potentially greater significance and of much longer duration in bilateral affairs is that of illegal drugs. The two countries have been collaborating for several decades in the battle against drug production and trafficking.[5] Mexico is not a major source of drugs, although it grows some marijuana that is exported to the United States. But because of the country's geographic location, it has become the major site for the transshipment of drugs from elsewhere in Latin America to the United States. More than 80 percent of the cocaine entering the United States is estimated to pass through Mexico.[6] It is very important to remember—and to stress from an objective as well as a Mexican point of view—that the drug problem originated in the United States, which is the largest illegal drug market in the world, where approximately one of six Americans uses illegal drugs. As George Grayson has argued, "the U.S. government should focus its attention and resources on programs that fight domestic consumption, rather than pressuring Mexico and other nations to pursue policies likely to compromise their armed forces.[7]

Americans' demand for drugs has created many national security problems for Mexico and for Mexican–U.S. relations. Although Mexico has made considerable efforts to stop the shipment and production of illegal narcotics, it has made little headway in stemming the flow of drugs across the border. The implementation of NAFTA has only made this easier.

For Mexico, drug trafficking has had two consequences: First, because of the amounts of money changing hands and the profits to be made, corruption of government officials is inevitable, as is also true in the United States. Because Mexicans' income and standard of living are much lower than in the United States, this corruption has been both broader and deeper here. There is, therefore, widespread concern in Mexico that drug traffickers are establishing stronger ties to government officials. Indeed, in 1995, 42 percent of Mexicans polled believed such a link was strong, and 31 percent, somewhat strong.[8] Recent evidence from new investigations of the political assassinations in 1994—including one that seems to have been engineered by the brother of President Salinas—points to the involvement of drug money. These complex drug-related activities, involving United States actors, are no better illustrated than in the Tijuana border culture south of San Diego, California.[9] Thus, the very security of Mexico's national political life is at stake, and some analysts fear that the country is moving in the direction of Colombia, where drug producers dominate the fabric of political life.

Mexicans also are concerned about issues of sovereignty in relation to combating drug trafficking in Mexico. The United States maintains a drug certification program, which cites those countries that are doing their utmost to support the United States' effort to combat drugs. In April 1998, for example, the Senate actually voted to certify Mexico as making a good-faith effort in combating drugs. Not only do Mexicans see the irony of the United States' making judgments about Mexican efforts—whatever their effectiveness—in confronting a problem created by and originating in the United States, but Mexico also has allowed U.S. drug enforcement agents to operate on its soil. One Mexican analyst pointed out that "from the U.S. viewpoint it would be inconceivable to have Mexican agents traveling freely in their national territory searching for drug users."[10] Not surprisingly, extensive drug use in American society is the behavior that Mexicans find most unattractive about the United States.

What role, if any, should the United States play in Mexican domestic politics? According to a sample of Mexican intellectuals, government officials, opposition-party leaders, and civic organization representatives, the United States government can play a constructive role as an external actor, by continuing to promote political liberalization—while at the same time making it clear that it is supporting the Mexican government and not the PRI—by discouraging the use of violence and human rights abuses; by encouraging a negotiated settlement with the Chiapan rebels, possibly an internationally mediated agreement; and by using its international influence to support Mexico financially toward more equitable economic growth.[11]

CULTURAL INTERFACE

One salient contextual explanation of Mexico's willingness to consider an economic and even a political union with Canada and the United States is that some of the three countries' basic economic and political values are converging. For example, in eleven of fifteen values measured by the *World Values Survey* between 1981 and 1990, Ronald Inglehart and his collaborators discovered that the three countries were simultaneously moving in the same direction.[12] Even though Mexicans admire many qualities of their neighbor to the north, not least its political system, they have many reservations as well (see Table 9-1).

Mexico's distrust of the United States because of the latter's involvement in Mexican affairs is complemented by cultural and economic relationships between the two countries. There is a lively commerce in

Table 9-1 Mexicans' Perceptions of the United States

What Mexicans Like Most	Percentage of Persons Interviewed
Economic opportunities	34
Cultural level	15
Democracy	14
Equality for all	8
Government protects the people	4
Its wealth	4
Good public services	3
Its liberty	2
Other reasons	1
Not sure	11
No answer	4

Source: Los Angeles Times poll, August 1989, courtesy of Miguel Basáñez. This poll is based on face-to-face interviews with 1,835 Mexican adults conducted from August 13th through 15th, 1989, in 42 randomly selected towns and cities throughout Mexico. It has a margin of error of 3 percent in either direction.

ideas, music, art, fashion, and so on. The influence of U.S. culture can be found worldwide, but it is more intense in Mexico by virtue of closeness. Heavy tourist traffic runs in both directions. More Americans report visiting Mexico than any other developing country or region. Of the 62 percent of Americans who traveled outside the United States, 48 percent visited Mexico, or about a third of the U.S. population. Mexico is only second to Canada of all countries visited.[13] Moreover, one-fourth of all foreign visitors to the United States come from Mexico. English is studied and spoken by many Mexicans. Spanish is the foreign language studied most often in U.S. high schools, and Spanish classes from even the smallest rural communities often take field trips to Mexico. American music permeates the airwaves. American performers from rock stars to magicians are headliners in major Mexican cities. Television is saturated with shows and movies from north of the border, and the well-to-do who subscribe to satellite reception have access to a complete range of news and entertainment programs. These circumstances and others have contributed to a condition whereby

> the United States constitutes an almost unavoidable presence in the daily lives of most Mexicans. The music that is heard in the main urban centers of the country, the companies that dominate the billboards and television advertising, the entertainment and new broadcasts of the major media—all of these refer almost by necessity to the United States, creating a sense, however partial and distorted, of familiarity with U.S. society and culture.[14]

Throughout the twentieth century, especially since the 1930s, Mexicans have had to contend culturally and psychologically with American influence, which has had a serious impact on the structure of the intellectual community and on the content of university programs.[15] The proximity of place has also contributed to the fact that more Americans reside in Mexico than in any other Third World country, and more Mexicans reside in the United States than in any other country. Los Angeles has a higher concentration of people of Mexican descent than any city except Mexico City. It can be said that a greater percentage of Mexicans visited a First World country than did the citizens of any other Third World country. By 1989 one in three Mexicans had traveled to the United States, and nearly half said they had relatives living there.[16] Mexicans establish personal links to the United States at a level unmatched by any other country with the possible exception of Israel.

Although we do not have comparable information on how Americans view Mexican values and societal qualities, some data are available on the importance that U.S. citizens accord to Mexico and the issues most important to the two countries' bilateral relations. In general, many Americans have had some firsthand experience with Mexico or Mexicans. This does not necessarily mean that they understand Mexicans better or that it has made them more aware of the importance Mexico plays or might play in their economic and political future. Nevertheless, well before a free-trade agreement was contemplated, Americans understood the potential importance of Mexico's economic development to their own financial fortunes (see Table 9-2). To most Americans in 1990, immigration and political stability were the main issues confronting the United States' relations with Mexico. Today, most Americans, according to a *Wall Street Journal* poll, view Latin America, including Mexico, as a region with a severe drug problem. They not only blame the region for the United States' problem, but consider a reduction in drug trafficking their country's primary foreign policy objective.[17]

Culturally, the relationship is unequal. Because Spanish is the second most frequently spoken language in the United States, and Mexicans— along with Central Americans, Cubans, and other Latin Americans—have spread throughout the United States, their culture influencing the culture of the United States.[18] It can be found in music (for example, in the popular song "La Bamba," of which a hundred versions exist in Mexico), food, and art, and even language (*politico* comes to mind).[19] Some Americans have reacted with a heightened nationalism. The English First movement is an effort to reassert the supremacy of English and of traditional nonminority values in the face of what is deemed to be an onslaught of Hispanic values and language. Oscar Martinez writes,

> Groups such as U.S. English and English First have campaigned hard to convince a large portion of the American public that the use of languages other than English fosters fragmentation in the country and threatens future political stability. Led by California, by the mid-1980s about twelve states had

Table 9-2 Americans' Perceptions of Mexico

Statement Asked	Percentage of Those Agreeing
Mexico's economic problems affect the U.S. economy	77
The U.S. should exert pressure to hold fair elections	54
The U.S. should limit Mexican immigration	43
Mexico is very important to the U.S.	40
Immigration is the most important issue	35
Political stability is the most important issue	32

Source: Data from Christine Contee, "U.S. Perceptions of United States-Mexican Relations," in *Images of Mexico in the United States*, ed. John H. Coatsworth and Carlos Rico (La Jolla, Calif.: Center for U.S.–Mexican Studies, 1989), 17–48.

declared English as their official language, sending a message to Hispanics and other language minority groups that they should rid themselves of their native tongues as quickly as possible. Thus far, similar measures in the legislatures of Texas, New Mexico, and Arizona have failed to pass, but the debate on the issue in these states is bound to increase in the future.[20]

The cheek-by-jowl closeness of Mexico and the United States has given rise to what many observers believe to be a distinct hybrid border culture. The contiguous regions, which share a range of serious problems from unemployment to pollution, have begun to develop local solutions together that reflect the hybrid culture. The borderland has been given the name "MexAmerica" by Lester Langley, who thinks that few in the United States are ready to admit that Mexico might be a determinant of the kind of society we are becoming and the character of our politics.[21]

Politically and culturally it is the United States that exercises the greatest long-term influence. Its position in the world gives it great prestige. This gives its political processes and to some extent its political values a certain degree of legitimacy in the eyes of many Mexicans, including politicians, hence the implicit influence of the United States model—especially as the international trend toward political liberalization, that is, democratization—continues.[22] This influence also generates resentment. Jorge Castañeda argued convincingly that some Mexicans have felt uncomfortable supporting democratization because they sense it is a goal of the United States.[23] Many Mexicans believe the United States exercises a significant influence on Mexican politics, especially those residing along the northern border. (see Table 9-3)

Vexation with and suspicion of their neighbor engender a higher level of nationalism among Mexicans and among their leaders. Accordingly, some political decisions are driven by nationalism. Nationalism in its crudest sense is on the decline, as Mexicans' sense of national identity began gradually in the 1980s to extend beyond their country. Eighteen percent of all Mexicans conceptualize their sense of nationalism as extending beyond

Table 9-3 Mexican Attitudes Towards Foreigners in Mexico

Mexicans Who Believe Foreigners Have a Significant Influence on Domestic Politics:	Percentage Agreeing
Federal District	35
North	63
Center	35
South	36

Source: Este País, June, 1998, 37. National sample of 1,190 of Mexicans older than 18. Margin of error, ±2.9 percent.

that of their own borders, a condition likely to increase with the advent of NAFTA.[24]

ECONOMIC LINKAGES

One of the most sensitive issues in the U.S.–Mexican relationship, because of its prominence as a cause of the Mexican Revolution, is economic imperialism. Even as late as the early twentieth century, some U.S. diplomatic representatives had personal economic interests in Mexico that influenced their recommendations. By the beginning of the revolution, U.S. investment in Mexico had reached staggering figures. Roger D. Hansen remarks that under Díaz, foreign capital (38 percent from the United States)

> flowed into the country in quantities proportionately much greater—in relation to national capital and the natural and human resources of Mexico—than the volume of European capital that entered the United States during its period of most intensive development. Only 100 million pesos as late as 1884, foreign investment rose to 3.4 billion by 1911.[25]

The ideology of Mexicanization, which grew out of the revolutionary struggle, traces its strongest roots to U.S. economic influence and the presence of American businessmen, managers, professionals, and landowners, especially in the north.[26] In formulating its economic development policies, while protecting the sovereignty of its decision making, Mexico has had to consider its economic relationship with the United States. The free-trade agreement will force Mexico to share its economic goals with those of the other two North American nations. Anti-Americanism, which declined under the Salinas administration (1988–1994), intensified sharply in early 1995 as Mexicans learned the contents of a United States–imposed "bailout" agreement to bolster Mexico's sagging peso and rescue it from a serious economic crisis.

The impact of place is no better illustrated than by immigration. It is revealing because its consequences invoke cultural, economic, and political issues. Immigration has a long history, and only in recent years has the United States attempted comprehensively and formally to prevent the flow of Mexican immigrants. Mexicans crossed the border to work for decades after the mid-nineteenth century.

Labor tends to follow capital, especially when unemployment and underemployment reach significant levels. Thus Mexicans went northward during difficult times in search of work. In the past some eventually became U.S. citizens, but most returned to their homeland after short stays. At other times when the United States faced labor shortages, especially of unskilled workers, it promoted controlled flows of such workers, which happened during World War II. What are the economic consequences of this relationship? For Mexico, it has meant increased economic opportunities for its people, in some cases the potential for learning new skills. Also, their wages in large part have been remitted to their places of origin, thereby creating local sources of capital. It has been estimated that emigrants sent as much as $7 billion dollars back to Mexico.[27] For the United States, the economic benefits have been substantial. Historically, most of the migrants have worked in agriculture, providing cheaper foodstuffs than would have been otherwise available. In recent years, Mexicans have contributed many workers to the service sector.

The political consequences of the relationship are numerous. For example, during periods of economic crisis in the 1980s in Mexico, millions of Mexicans sought employment in the United States, revealing the inability of the political model to manage the economy. Indirectly, then, the United States aided Mexican domestic stability by channeling discontent northward. Yet Mexican nationalism—given the historical relationship discussed previously—forces Mexico to express concern over the migration. It is an embarrassment to Mexico. Some Mexicans have been maltreated in the United States or in crossing the border. Their exploitation pressures Mexico to place the issue on the agenda of Mexican–United States relations.

For the United States, the economic implications are obvious. Although the demand for unskilled workers now extends into a variety of occupational categories, critics charge that American workers go unemployed. Some groups in the United States resent what they see as their displacement by immigrant labor from Mexico. Moreover, employers are accused of hiring Mexican workers in order to avoid paying certain benefits and taxes. Finally, middle-class taxpayers have begun to view immigrants as a tremendous drain on welfare resources and public education, leading to the passage of California's Proposition 187 in 1994.

Proposition 187 is essentially anti-immigrant legislation designed to exclude Latinos from California's social services, specifically to remove children from public school classrooms and to prevent their parents seeking health care and unemployment benefits from the state. More than half of all Mexicans view this legislation as racist, and nine out of ten Mexicans strongly oppose similar legislation elsewhere in the United States.[28]

Culturally, immigration spills over into many of the issues affecting U.S.–Mexican relations. The English First movement came about largely through the rapid expansion of the U.S. Latino population, and the visible immigration of Mexicans and Central Americans into the Southwest. Immigration is a perceived cultural threat, which translates into local and state policy debates, often placed before voters. In Mexico, on the other hand, whole villages are literally ghost towns, as younger men and women leave for the United States. Children are often left in the hands of the mother alone or grandparents, breaking down the traditional family structure. Discouraged by the violence of U.S. cities, many migrant Mexicans who have children in the United States send them back to their home communities. But these children bring American values with them, threatening the integrity of the local culture.[29]

Foreign investment, external debt, and trade also affect the bilateral relationship directly and indirectly. The economic linkage between Mexico and the United States is so substantial that its impact on the formal linkages between the two countries—on the everyday lives of many citizens, especially Mexicans, and on sovereignty issues—is unavoidable. For many decades, the United States provided 60 to 70 percent of the merchandise imported by Mexico. In fact, by 1993, before its economic crises, Mexico was buying $42 billion of goods from its northern neighbor, or one-fourth of all goods sold by the United States in the Western Hemisphere. By the end of 1996, the United States sold $67.5 billion in exports to Mexico, 9 percent of all its exports worldwide. Forty-four of fifty states experienced growth in export sales to Mexico from 1995 to 1996.[30] It is figures like these that justify establishing a free-trade agreement between the two countries and Canada. Sidney Weintraub pointed out that

> world trade, in both goods and services, is growing more rapidly within major world regions than between them. For the United States, this reality emerges most clearly in trade with its two land neighbors, Canada and Mexico. The United States, therefore, has a major stake in the economic health of its neighbors; and not just Canada and Mexico, but also the rest of the Western Hemisphere, where the United States is the leading supplier of the region's exports, as it is not for the other major regions, either Asia or Europe.[31]

The anticipation and negotiations surrounding a free-trade agreement between Mexico and the United States dominated their bilateral agenda throughout the Bush and Salinas administrations, becoming a salient political issue in the 1992 United States presidential election. The main impact of NAFTA on bilateral relations before its passage in Congress and its implementation in January 1994 was the greater ability of the bilateral agenda in both countries, but especially in the United States, to frame many other issues in terms of their effect on the trade agreement and to increase speculation on how the completion of such an agreement might affect internal issues in both countries in the future, including those already on the bilateral agenda. President Salinas himself formulated much of his domestic program around the concept of NAFTA and its ultimate approval. Although Mexico's decision to internationalize its economic development strategy and to form closer economic ties with its neighbors was seen by many in the United States international community as bringing Mexico closer in line with their own economic philosophy, thereby decreasing the potential for conflict on economic matters, at least from an ideological perspective. The actual linkages themselves highlighted other issues extending well beyond those purely "economic.".[32]

The North American Free-Trade Agreement is a complex document with implications for member countries' social policies. Management–labor relations provide a useful example of how a foreign economic policy agreement can have broader political implications domestically. In Mexico, most organized labor is co-opted by government-controlled unions. Moreover, the structural and legal pattern of labor-business relations enables the government to provide the decisive vote in arbitrated disputes. One of the most controversial side agreements in the NAFTA requires Mexico to conform to its own laws in protecting labor rights. The U.S. labor movement, though it opposes NAFTA, succeeded in obtaining certain agreements, which, if enforced, would strengthen workers' rights in Mexico. In April 1995, U.S. labor unions and human rights groups persuaded Robert Reich, the secretary of labor, to discuss with his Mexican counterpart the specific issue of workers in a Sony factory in Nuevo Laredo who had been prevented from establishing an independent union, thereby violating Mexico's own labor code.[33] The reverse is also true. In May 1998, four Mexican unions, with the support of the American teamsters union, filed a complaint against the Washington State apple industry for violating migrant worker rights, including safety and pay issues. The significance of this and other NAFTA side agreements is that they provide an important legal vehicle for American groups to become involved in numerous Mexican domestic issues, among them labor and environmental concerns, and for Mexicans to do the same in the United States.

The broader issue that economic and commercial agreements emphasize for both countries, but especially Mexico, is nationalism. Some analysts have gone as far as to argue that not only has NAFTA shrunk Mexican national sovereignty but a decline in state sovereignty, engineered through international agreements, limits the country's ability to protect ordinary citizens' interests.[34] Although this interpretation can be disputed,

NAFTA and the increasing economic dependency of the two countries have determined other major policy decisions. The most striking example of such a consequence is the Clinton administration's financial rescue package offered in early 1995 after the devaluation of the peso led to extensive capital flight. Indeed, the size of the United States and international agency aid, some $49 billion, was in part based on Mexico's membership in NAFTA.[35] The package itself, because it required Mexico to guarantee repayment of its loans to the United States ($20 billion of the total), generated further concern in Mexico, because numerous Mexicans viewed the aid as further evidence of the United States' infringement on their sovereignty.[36]

Immigration, trade, and investment have many more ramifications, both subtle and obvious. The point is that their proximity makes both countries prisoners, to some extent, of each other's problems. And although Mexico labors under a much greater dependency and subordination, it affects the United States. For example, the United States experienced an unexpected and immediate increase in its trade deficit in the months immediately following the devaluation of the Mexican peso in 1994 as United States exports became excessively expensive and Mexican imports relatively cheap. Mexico's political system must consider carefully the domestic issues and associated policies that bear on this relationship. The United States has no direct veto power over Mexican politics, but its presence casts a permanent shadow that the Mexican political leadership cannot ignore.

CONCLUSION

As this chapter makes clear, it is obvious that the United States exercises a significant role in Mexico, not only in its dominance over the focus of Mexican foreign policy, but in numerous other facets, social, cultural, and economic. The North American Free Trade Agreement only has reinforced a level of influence long apparent, implicitly and explicitly, in the relationship between Mexico and the United States. While it is true that Mexico's strong sense of nationalism was a natural response to its historical experience with the United States, Mexico has found it necessary, for important economic and social reasons, to modify its traditional posture in return for identifying its future development more closely with the fortunes of the United States.

Numerous issues affect the bilateral relationship between these two neighbors. This chapter touches only on those that are most prominent, particularly in the 1990s. The national security agenda between the two countries increasingly has taken precedence over other traditional issues, but the scope of national security concerns, because of increased linkages practically and formally, has broadened and deepened. Issues such as combating drug trafficking have gone well beyond social agendas typically associated with such problems to become inextricably intertwined with the very legitimacy of Mexican political institutions and the stability of its political system.

The intensity and breadth of the bilateral agenda, often involving issues affecting the domestic policy perspectives and postures of the two countries' voters and politicians, complicate their foreign relations.[37] Some of these issues, such as corruption and illegal immigration, evoke heated, emotional responses on both sides of the border. A strong temptation exists, particularly in the United States, for national legislators to impose moral and philosophical judgments on Mexico's political model, and specifically on its path and pace of political and economic development. The increased involvement in Mexican domestic affairs by the U.S. media, and civic organizations such as human rights groups, ensures the U.S. government's continued and heightened involvement in Mexican matters. At the same time, the expanding pluralization of Mexico's political process and the contentiousness of its differing political actors, nationally and regionally, further complicate relations between both countries, a situation unlikely to change into the next century.

NOTES

1. "Excerpted Remarks by Ernesto Zedillo, Address on Foreign Policy," June 26, 1994.

2. José Juan de Olloqui, "On the Formulation of a U.S. Policy Toward Mexico," in *Mexico in Transition, Implications for U.S. Policy*, ed. Susan Kaufman Purcell (New York: Council on Foreign Relations, 1988), 107. This can be seen in a more practical circumstance, when the Clinton administration allowed its ambassadorship to Mexico to remain vacant for nearly a year in 1997–1998 after its first nominee was rejected by the Senate Foreign Relations Committee.

3. Lorenzo Meyer, "Mexico: The Exception and the Rule," in *Exporting Democracy, the United States and Latin America*, ed. Abraham Lowenthal (Baltimore: Johns Hopkins University Press, 1991), 228.

4. Jared Kotler, *The Clinton Administration and the Mexican Elections* (Albuquerque: Resource Center Press, 1994), 28.

5. See "The Fight Against Drugs," Mexico, Office of the President, September, 1997; *US/Mexico Bi-National Drug Strategy*, High Level Contact Group for Drug Control, U.S.–Mexico, February, 1998; and Executive Office of the President, Office of National Drug Control Policy, *Report to Congress* (Washington, D.C.: September, 1997).

6. Silvana Paternostro, "Mexico as a Narco-democracy," *World Policy Journal* 12 (Spring 1995), 44.

7. "Mexico's Future Is Up for Grabs," *Orbis* 41 (Winter 1997), 100.

8. "Encuesta Metropolitana," *Este País*, April 5, 1995.

9. Sebastian Rotella, *Twilight on the Line, Underworlds and Politics on the Mexican Border* (New York: Norton, 1998).

10. José Luis Reyna, "Narcotics as a Destabilizing Force for Source Countries and Non-source Countries," in *The Latin American Narcotics Trade and United States National Security*, ed. Donald Mabry (Westport, Conn.: Greenwood Press, 1989), 126.

11. Washington Office on Latin America, Delegation Report, "Peace and Democratization in Mexico: Challenges Facing the Zedillo Government," January 12, 1995. The linkages between national and international actors are discussed by Denise Dresser in her comprehensive "Treading Lightly and Without a Stick: International Actors and the Promotion of Democracy in Mexico," paper presented at the Latin American Studies Association, Atlanta, March 1994; and by Beth Sims, *Supporting Mexican Democratization, Issues and Challenges for Foreign Actors* (Albuquerque: Resource Center Press, 1994).

12. Ronald Inglehart, Miguel Basáñez, and Neil Nevitte, *Convergencia en Norte América, comercio, política y cultura* (Mexico City: Siglo XXI, 1994), 190–91.

13. Christine E. Contee, "U.S. Perceptions of United States–Mexican Relations," in *Images of Mexico in the United States*, ed. John H. Coatsworth and Carlos Rico (La Jolla, Calif.: Center for U.S.–Mexican Studies, 1989), 30.

14. Coatsworth and Rico, *Images of Mexico in the United States*, 10.

15. See Roderic Ai Camp, *Intellectuals and the State in Twentieth Century Mexico* (Austin: University of Texas Press, 1985), 79.

16. *New York Times* poll, October 28–November 4, 1986; *Los Angeles Times* poll, August 1989.

17. *Wall Street Journal*, April 16, 1998; and the original data, courtesy of Miguel Basáñez.

18. For excellent background on these issues, see Jaime Rodríguez and Kathryn Vincent, eds., *Common Border, Uncommon Paths* (Wilmington: Scholarly Resources, 1997).

19. For numerous examples of these special influences, see Tom Miller, *On the Border: Portraits of America's Southwestern Frontier* (Tucson: University of Arizona Press, 1985).

20. Oscar Martínez, *Troublesome Border* (Tucson: University of Arizona Press, 1988), 97.

21. Lester D. Langley, *MexAmerica: Two Countries, One Future* (New York: Crown Books, 1988), 7.

22. For an excellent discussion of the dilemmas facing the United States government in the promotion of the liberal model in Mexico, see Sergio Aguayo, "Mexico in Transition and the United States: Old Perceptions, New Problems," in *Mexico and the United States: Managing the Relationship*, ed. Riordan Roett (Boulder, Colo.: Westview Press, 1988), 157.

23. Jorge G. Castañeda, "The Choices Facing Mexico," in *Mexico in Transition: Implications for U.S. Policy*, ed. Susan K. Purcell (New York: Council on Foreign Relations, 1988), 26.

24. Inglehart et al., *Convergencia*, 177.

25. Roger D. Hansen, *The Politics of Mexican Development* (Baltimore: Johns Hopkins University Press, 1971), 15–17.

26. For its evolution, see Robert Freeman Smith, "The United States and the Mexican Revolution, 1921–1950," in *Myths, Misdeeds, and Misunderstandings*, ed. Jaime Rodríguez and Kathryn Vincent (Wilmington: Scholarly Resources, 1997), 181–98.

27. Sam Quiñones, "Dream Houses," *US/Mexico Business*, May 1998, 72.

28. MORI de México weekly poll for *Este País*, November 9 and November 23, 1994.

29. A vast literature exists on this topic. Some of the best recent work, for example, is that of Jorge Bustamante, "Undocumented Immigration: Research Findings and Policy Options," in *Mexico and the United States*, ed. Riordan Roett (Boulder, Colo.: Westview Press, 1988), 109–32. For a comprehensive earlier account, see Wayne A. Cornelius, *Mexican Migration to the United States: Causes, Consequences, and U.S. Response* (Cambridge, Mass.: MIT Center for International Studies, 1978).

30. "NAFTA, the Standard for Free Trade," Mexico, Office of the President, September 1997.

31. Sidney Weintraub, *NAFTA: What Comes Next?* (Westport, Conn.: Praeger, 1994), 108.

32. For two excellent interpretations of the domestic political implications of NAFTA in Mexico, see Guy Poitras and Raymond Robinson, "The Politics of NAFTA in Mexico," *Journal of Inter-American Studies and World Affairs* 36 (Spring 1994): 1–35; and Jorge Castañeda, "Can NAFTA Change Mexico?" *Foreign Affairs*, 74 (September–October 1993): 66–80. A discussion of the implications and perceptions on both sides can be found in Ricardo Grinspun and Maxwell Cameron, eds., *The Political Economy of North American Free Trade* (New York: St. Martin's Press, 1993). Background on the negotiating and the side agreements is provided in George Grayson's excellent *The North American Free Trade Agreement, Regional Community and the New World Order* (Lanham, Md.: University Press of America, 1995).

33. Robert Bryce, "Gripe on Mexican Labor to Get NAFTA Hearing," *Christian Science Monitor*, April 26, 1995, 6.

34. Julie A. Erfani, *The Paradox of the Mexican State, Rereading Sovereignty from Independence to NAFTA* (Boulder, Colo.: Lynne Rienner, 1995), 178–79.

35. Sidney Weintraub, "Prospects for Hemispheric Trade and Economic Integration," CSIS Policy Paper on the Americas, 1995, 5. Also see Weintraub's "Mexico's Devaluation: Why and What Next?," CSIS, January 4, 1994, for an insightful explanation of how the devaluation came about. Mexico actually borrowed $13.5 billion, and repaid the amount in full, with interest, by January 1997.

36. Precise details of the agreement are provided in "Statement of Treasury Secretary Robert E. Rubin, Mexico Agreement Signing Ceremony," *Treasury News*, February 21, 1995. Nearly two-thirds of Mexicans polled at the time the peso-rescue package was announced thought that it greatly compromised their sovereignty. MORI de México poll for *Este País*, February 1, 1995.

37. An insightful inside analysis of some of these problems, including recommendations for solving some difficulties, is provided by Arturo Valenzuela, former Deputy Assistant Secretary of State for Inter-American Affairs, in *The Challenge of Mexico to U.S. Foreign Policy*, Occasional Paper Series, Overseas Development Council, Washington, D.C., June 1997.

10

Political and Economic Modernization: A Revolution?

> [E]ven though democratic rules are necessary conditions for political alternation, they do not necessarily result in an alternation in power, unless we resort to non-democratic "corrective" actions.
>
> Nevertheless, as long as the government continues to be seen as the only agent capable of managing and making decisions on electoral results, and as such, as the only interlocutor of contending political parties, a view inherited from years of centralized decisions, the electoral process will remain a source of public skepticism.
>
> ROBERTA LAJOUS, *Examen*

The political question foremost in the minds of most observers and Mexican citizens alike is, What will be the influence of liberalism, economic and political, on Mexico's governmental model and its economic future? Many of the political and economic changes that have taken place in Eastern Europe since 1989 have far exceeded the expectations of most experts. Boundaries have been redrawn; political processes have been turned upside down; regional stability has been rendered problematic; and economic structures have collapsed or are tottering. Mexico has not been immune to the winds of change. Some analysts argue that international influences and world public opinion have strongly affected Mexico. Mexican architects of recent reforms, including former Treasury Secretary Pedro Aspe, consider Mexico to be part of "this vast process of world institutional evolution."[1]

BASES FOR ECONOMIC MODERNIZATION

For the average Mexican, the most important economic issues are employment and level of income. In 1997, Mexicans considered more sources of employment and better wages to be the most significant pending issues.[2] Mexico, like many other Third World nations, faces numerous challenges in stimulating economic growth, regardless of the strategy it chooses to pursue. Mexico's economy has changed significantly since the 1940s, in both size and the composition of its workforce. In the 1990s, Mexico has four times as many people in the economically active population as it did after World War II. From 1970, when Echeverría became president, to 1996, midway through the Zedillo administration, Mexico nearly tripled its workforce, from 12.9 million to 35.2 million. As the data in Table 10-1 demonstrate, Mexico has moved away from an agriculturally dominant society to an economy represented by manufacturing, commerce, and services. Mexico witnessed an increasing growth in ranching and agricultural workers from 1900 through 1960. As of 1960, such workers accounted for 54 percent of the economically active workforce, and until the mid-1980s, they were the single largest sector of the economy. But by the mid-1990s, agricultural employees represented only 23 percent of the workforce, half the total workforce in 1960. Although they have grown only slowly in number since 1960, proportionately their reduction has been dramatic. In the past two decades, most of the new jobs in Mexico were in the manufacturing, commerce, construction, and transportation sectors. In volume, the service industry provided the most new jobs, 8.1 million, equal to the total population employed in agriculture. Today, services account for the largest single sector of the economy.

Table 10-1 Mexico's Economically Active Population, by Economic Sector

Sector	1950	1970	1996	1950/1996 % Change
Agriculture	4,823,901	5,103,519	7,921,700	64.2
Petroleum and extractive	97,143	180,175	190,200	95.8
Manufacturing	972,542	2,169,074	5,721,700	488.6
Construction	224,512	571,006	1,796,700	701.8
Electric energy	24,966	53,285	202,200	708.0
Commerce	684,092	1,196,878	6,116,100	794.2
Transportation	210,592	368,813	1,310,000	523.8
Services	879,379	2,158,175	10,210,200	1,061.5
Government	—	406,607	1,576,900	—
Other	354,966	747,525	180,300	344.2
Total	8,272,093	12,955,057	35,226,000	325.8

Source: David E. Lorey, *The Rise of the Professions in Twentieth-Century Mexico, University Graduates and Occupational Change Since 1929,* 2d ed. (Los Angeles: UCLA Latin American Center, 1994), 137; and Mexico, Presidencia de la República, *Ber Informe de gobierno, Anexo,* September 1, 1997, 41.
[a]Although no figures are available for 1950, the growth in government employees from 1940 through 1996 was 546.3 percent.

One social issue with important political ramifications is the ability of a country's economy and its economic model to produce upward social mobility and to increase the size of the middle class. A great danger in the austerity program introduced by President Zedillo is that measured by their income, many Mexicans may lose their status as members of the middle class and, even more likely, will be unable to move from the working class into the middle class. The data in Table 10-2 illustrate several features of the Mexican class structure. Most important, the middle class has witnessed stable growth and, from the 1950s to the 1990s, doubled. Although the percentage of working-class Mexicans continues to fall, the decline has been slow, particularly in the 1970s and early 1980s. The most dramatic change has been among Mexico's upper classes, which have tripled in size since 1950. What these figures do not reveal are two patterns. First, the rapid growth of the Mexican population, especially since the 1950s, has created a working class and a marginal population, which in absolute numbers are far larger today than they were in the early part of the century. For example, of Mexico's current population, nearly 96 million, 55 percent, or 52.8 million, are in the lower class, a figure larger than Mexico's entire population in 1960. What these figures also fail to show is the increasing concentration of wealth, as is true in the United States as well, among upper-income Mexicans. Thus even though the size of the lower class has continued to shrink, the quality of their life has worsened, not improved.

An important change that de la Madrid introduced and his successors have aggressively pursued is an increase in foreign investment. A major basis for the economic liberalization program is the generation of capital for the Mexican economy, especially foreign investment. The data in Table

Table 10-2 Mexico's Class Structure from 1895 to 1990

Year	Class (%)					
	Upper	Change	Middle	Change	Lower	Change
1895	1.5	—	7.8	—	90.7	—
1940	2.9	93.3	12.6	61.5	84.5	−6.8
1950	1.7	−41.4	18.0	42.9	80.3	−5.0
1960	3.8	123.5	21.0	16.7	75.2	−6.4
1970	5.7	50.0	27.9	32.9	66.4	−11.7
1980	5.3	−7.0	33.0	18.3	61.8	−6.9
1990	6.8	28.3	38.2	15.8	55.0	−11.0

Source: Howard F. Cline, *Mexico: Revolution to Evolution, 1940–1960* (New York: Oxford University Press, 1963), 124; Stephanie Granato and Aida Mostkoff Linares, "The Class Structure of Mexico, 1895–1980," *Society and Economy in Mexico*, ed. James W. Wilkie (Los Angeles: UCLA Latin American Center, 1990); David Lorey and Aida Mostkoff Linares, "Mexico's Lost Decade," *Statistical Abstract of Latin America*, vol. 30, pt. 2 (Los Angeles: UCLA Latin American Center, 1994), 1339–60.

Table 10-3 Foreign Investment in Mexico

Administration	Totals (U.S. $ millions)	% Change
1970–1976	1601.4	
1976–1982	5470.6	241.7
1982–1988	13,455.4	146.0
1988–1994	60,565.5[a]	350.1
1994–1997	29,891.2	—

*Source: Crónica del gobierno de Carlos Salinas de Gortari, síntesis e in-
díce temático* (Mexico City: Presidencia de la República, 1994), 441; and
Mexico, Presidencia de la República, *3er Informe de gobierno, anexo*, September 1, 1997, 119.
[a]Beginning in 1989, investment figures included those in the Mexican
Stock Exchange; the data for 1997 are estimates only.

10-3 show the growing importance of this variable in Mexico's economic
development strategy. From 1988 to 1994, foreign investment increased
fourfold. In 1993 alone, in anticipation of the North American Free-Trade
Agreement, foreigners invested $15.6 billion, with U.S. investors account-
ing for 59 percent of investments since 1991.

ECONOMIC LIBERALIZATION

Whether the source of economic change in Mexico is international or domestic or both, there is no question that the administration of Carlos Salinas de Gortari instituted major economic reforms indicative of an altered
government economic philosophy. As we argued earlier, the relationship
between the state and the private sector has long been symbiotic and contentious. Its features emerged from a hybrid economic philosophy extending back to nineteenth-century laissez-faire liberalism and to social responsibility themes incorporated into the 1917 constitution.

For most of the twentieth century, the government offered a mixed
private–public economic model, in which the state played a decisive, sometimes overpowering role. In the 1970s, under President Luis Echeverría
(1970–1976), the legitimacy of the political model increasingly came into
question. Echeverría's difficulties stemmed in part from the events of 1968,
during which the army violently suppressed a student demonstration in the
capital. He pursued various social and economic strategies to enhance presidential legitimacy and the political model's prestige.[3] Public employment
was used to foster economic growth and stability, increasing opportunities

for many Mexicans. One social scientist remarked, "Even though the public sector had had a relatively dynamic growth throughout the previous decade, during the first half of the 1970s it broke all precedents."[4]

During Echeverría's tenure, large reserves of petroleum were discovered. The government began exploiting those reserves and, on the basis of oils sales abroad, secured international loans to finance development projects.[5] During the early 1970s the government bought or gained control of hundreds of businesses and industries, placing more economic and human resources in the hands of government managers than at any time before. At the end of his administration Echeverría further alienated the private sector by attempting to expropriate valuable lands in the northwest.

Echeverría's successor, José López Portillo, a politician-technocrat experienced in the government financial sector, attempted to mend relations between the private and public sectors. Initially successful, he continued the pattern of borrowing large sums of money to invest in Mexico's economic infrastructure and development. When the oil boom abruptly ended and prices at the barrelhead plunged, the country found itself in serious trouble. It was hugely indebted to domestic and foreign bankers and was paying extraordinarily high interest.[6]

Instead of putting the brakes on the state's economic expansion, López Portillo actually stepped on the accelerator. In his last year in office, without warning or consultation, he announced the nationalization of the domestic banking system.[7] With a single decree, the president increased state control over the economy, of which bank-held mortgages increased it to somewhere between 75 and 85 percent. The move exacerbated the business community's lack of trust in the government and strongly encouraged the flight of capital from Mexico, primarily to the United States.[8] When López Portillo left office a few months later, the presidency was at its lowest ebb in decades; the business–government relationship was in great disrepair; and Mexico was in economic crisis.

López Portillo's successor, Miguel de la Madrid (1982–1988), like his mentor, was a product of the public financial sector, having worked in Mexico's equivalent of the U.S. Federal Reserve Bank, in the Secretariat of the Treasury, and as secretary of planning and budgeting. His economic philosophy, however, represented a different ideological wing of the government leadership. Essentially, he believed that the best strategy for rescuing Mexico from economic woe was to follow the strict, orthodox economic guidelines recommended by the International Monetary Fund (IMF): reduce government expenditures and impose controls on salaries, prices, and inflation.[9]

De la Madrid also introduced the most important element in Mexican economic liberalization: privatization. He actually wanted to undo the nationalization of the banks—which in itself would have had an immediate impact on government ownership—but believed that the mid-1980s were not a politically propitious time for the move.[10] Instead, he took several moderate steps that enabled joint private-public ownership of certain financial institutions. At the end of his administration, it became clear that some government-owned firms would be sold back to the private sector.

De la Madrid ensured the importance of privatization specifically and economic liberalism generally in selecting Salinas to follow him. The 1988 presidential succession took on great significance in the political leadership. In one sense, competition among contenders within the PRI represented a conflict between a more traditional economic philosophy, which favored state control and deficit-spending budget strategies, and the more orthodox private-sector emphasis that de la Madrid had reintroduced.[11] Although de la Madrid had improved the relationship between the private sector and the state, Salinas, by his second year in office, had established a clear-cut policy incorporating many ingredients of international economic liberalism.

It is very important to take note of U.S. influence on the Salinas policy. The United States did not play a direct role in the formulation of Mexico's economic policy. Nevertheless, both Reagan and Bush pushed a more orthodox economic policy domestically and similar policies elsewhere, including that toward Mexico. Throughout the 1980s the United States expressed serious concern about Mexico's stability and its economic and political future. The American financial community, which held large portions of the Mexican government's debt portfolio, echoed this concern. Default might well have initiated a Latin American domino effect, with drastic consequences for the already shaky U.S. financial structure and the U.S. economy.[12] Salinas saw capital as essential to Mexico's economic recovery in the short term and international competition in the long term. When he realized that European governments and lenders were preoccupied with Eastern Europe, he turned to a free-trade agreement with the United States and Canada. Bush, who had close ties to Salinas, committed himself and the United States to approve such an agreement and encouraged Salinas to move ahead on it. In anticipation, Salinas and his economic team, most of whose members had studied in the United States, began to put many government-owned firms up for sale and to cut tariffs dramatically—many dropped from as high as 200 percent to an average of only 9 percent in 1992. The initiatives led to the return of some domestic capital and to new foreign investment—more than $60 billion by 1994 (see Table 10-3).

In late 1991 and early 1992 the government began to sell off the banks it had nationalized a decade earlier. It also put on the market several major corporations owned by the government, including Teléfonos de México (Telmex), which had a monopoly on telephone communications in Mexico, and Mexicana Airlines, one of the two major domestic lines. In fact, of the 1,155 firms that the government owned as late as 1987, it retained control of only 286 in 1992, a drop of 80 percent. Critics also charged that the primary beneficiaries of the privatization program were friends of the president, including prominent businessmen who served on his campaign finance committee.[13]

The U.S. financial community responded favorably to these dramatic changes from a state-led to a free-market economy. Editorials in business-oriented publications like the *Wall Street Journal* praised Salinas and his collaborators. Other periodicals, such as *Business Week*, predicted a boom period for Mexico, making it attractive to investors. The Mexican government repeatedly cited its positive press as evidence supportive of its policies.

Yet critics charged that the state-controlled sector remained bloated. They argued that twelve of the twenty largest firms in terms of employees were still under state control. Indeed, state-owned firms employed 79 percent of all workers, and the size of the bureaucracy was not much reduced from what it had been in 1987—from 4.4 to 4.1 million, largely the result of the sale of banks and government-owned companies.[14]

Parallel to his commitment to privatize and open up the economy to international competition, Salinas in 1992 startlingly proposed to overhaul the *ejido* land structure, a system of small-property holding controlled by each village. After the revolution, successive governments gave lands to individually operated *ejidos*, whose owners received use-right titles but not actual ownership from their local villages. Critics of agrarian reform charge that insufficient credit stems from an *ejidatorios*'s lack of collateral. Salinas's new legislation granted actual ownership and contract rights to these farmers. To keep farmers on the land and to assist in the transition to a more competitive market with U.S. imports, the government introduced Procampo, a program designed to eliminate its price supports for food by giving stipends (which would begin to drop after ten years and end in fifteen) directly to producers.[15]

Salinas introduced one other major social-economic policy soon after taking office, one closely linked to political liberalization. Known as the National Solidarity Program (Pronasol), or popularly as "Solidarity," it provided government seed money for local projects. Ostensibly, the philosophy behind the program was to encourage grassroots organization and local leadership. Thousands of farmers received loans; communities established rural medical clinics and renovated schools; and scholarships were awarded to promising students. By 1993 the government had spent 33 billion pesos on the program. Its supporters assert that it promoted grass-roots organization and leadership because local residents chose and prioritized the programs. Critics in opposition parties and some independent observers view Pronasol as a sophisticated, centrally controlled funding agency that has built considerable electoral support for the government party since 1989. Procampo was accused of the same partisan linkage in the 1994 election. Still others believe that it was a means of enhancing the president's personal power and political influence.[16] The president institutionalized this new program, giving it cabinet status in the new Social Development Secretariat and appointing the former head of the PRI, Luis Donaldo Colosio, to direct it. There is no question that this position was central to Colosio's becoming the PRI's presidential candidate in 1994.

Regardless of the weaknesses and strengths of Salinas's economic policies, he pursued a consistent economic strategy, composed primarily of privatization, internationalization, and foreign investment. As part of his overall strategy to modernize Mexico, he was personally much more committed to economic than political liberalization. In fact, as he made clear, he intended to pursue modernization and, implicitly, the interrelationship of the two components. Not wishing to make the same errors as the former Soviet Union had, Salinas declared:

> Freedoms of what you call the glasnost kind have existed for decades in Mexico. What hasn't existed is the freedom of productive activity, because the government owned so many enterprises.
>
> So, actually, we have been more rapidly transforming the economic structure while striking along many paths of reform on the political side.
>
> But, let me tell you something. When you are introducing strong economic reform, you must make sure that you build the political consensus around it. If you are at the same time introducing additional drastic political reform, you may end up with no reform at all. And we want to have reform, not a disintegrated country.[17]

Salinas carefully planned his economic strategy and, more important, gave particular attention to the constituencies to whom it was addressed. His prudence paid off in considerable domestic and foreign support. He also used his economic successes—higher capital investment, lower inflation rates (reduced from 52 to 8 percent between 1988 and 1993), and increased dollar reserves—to mollify some of his domestic and many of his international critics, especially the United States.[18]

What sort of a legacy did Salinas leave for President Zedillo? In his last state of the union speech, delivered shortly before he left office, Salinas pointed proudly to the statistical achievements of his administration. Some of his accomplishments were a 2.9 percent growth rate in the gross domestic product; a decline in public-sector expenditures of 25 percent in real terms, tied largely to a decrease in interest payments on the public debt; an increase in the number of taxpayers, from 1.76 million to 5.66 million, which raised revenues by 32 percent; a reduction in state-owned enterprises by 67 percent (415 companies); an expenditure of $2.7 billion yearly on 523,000 Solidarity projects; and a dramatic increase in public health expenditures.[19]

When Zedillo became the PRI candidate, he promised a ten-point program as his strategy for building on and continuing his predecessor's program. While praising the achievements of the preceding administration, Zedillo identified a number of problems that economic liberalization had not eliminated: insufficient jobs (with a 3 percent annual growth rate in the workforce, an average of 1 million new jobs are needed), a flat rate of productivity (only one-third of the population is economically active), and regional and sectoral inequities. Zedillo proposed boosting investment—public, private, and foreign—to increase money for education, altering the fiscal system to promote investment, encouraging saving, hastening deregulation, expanding new technological applications, broadening foreign competition, strengthening Procampo, and protecting the environment. Zedillo wanted an economic growth rate in 1995 twice that of the population growth rate, that is, 3.8 percent.[20]

But instead of having an opportunity to build on the economic structure left by his predecessor and to concentrate on political liberalization, Zedillo was confronted with a major economic crisis in the first month of his administration, the magnitude of which Mexico had not experienced even in the difficult days of the 1980s. Zedillo's economic team decided to devalue the Mexican peso against the dollar—a serious problem ignored by his predecessor—allowing it to float free.[21] Rather than the peso's stabilizing at a new exchange rate, which Mexican economists expected to be only 15 to 20 percent lower than the old rate, there was a run on the peso. According to some analysts, the New York financial community shares the responsibility for Mexico's crisis, having pressured the Mexicans—with the threat of withdrawing their investments—into issuing billions of dollars worth of dollar-denominated, short-term bonds, *tesebonos*, as a substitute for the peso-denominated investments, *cetes*. Although investors liked the higher returns on the *cetes* before 1994, the political situation in Mexico during 1994 and the declining dollar reserves made fund managers in New York worry about the security of Mexican peso bonds. Indeed, the

Mexican government issued so many of the devaluation-proof *tesebonos* that ten billion became due between the end of December 1994 and March 1995.[22] Although it was able to meet its short-term obligations with the help of public, international financing, its level of debt remains a concern to analysts.[23]

The result of the crises caused by the devaluation of the peso is that Mexico faced negative economic growth in 1995, a loss of somewhere between 250,000 and 1 million jobs before the end of the year, a reversal of foreign investment and capital flight, a dramatic rise in inflation exceeding 50 percent yearly, an extraordinary rise in private-bank interest for mortgages and loans far above the inflation rate, and numerous business closures and bankruptcies, including the threat of important state governments' declaring financial insolvency.

After pursuing a severe austerity program for two years, and achieving a GDP of 7.5 percent and an inflation rate of 15.7 percent in 1997, Zedillo introduced PRONAFIDE, a medium-term economic program pursuing strategies designed to promote public and private savings and investment. The president introduced his own social programs, Progresa and Salud 2000, committed to increased spending in social development and health care. The federal budget's largest outlay in 1997, 56 percent, was for social programs.[24]

To what extent has economic liberalism, as pursued by each administration since 1982, improved the standard of living for most Mexicans? Despite economic statistics showing improved productivity and growth, the record is not very encouraging. The distribution of income continues to favor wealthy Mexicans (see Table 10-4). Two-thirds of all income is distributed to 30 percent of the population. (In the United States, the top 20 percent of the population receive 55 percent of the national income.) The lowest 30 percent of the population, as measured by income, receives only 8 percent.[25] Furthermore, real salaries have continued to fall in Mexico since 1975, whether one looks at the minimum wage, which in 1993 was less than half of what it was in 1975, or contractual and assembly plant salaries. Per capita income in 1993 was $3,993. The United Nations estimated that the number of Mexicans living in conditions of poverty, moderate poverty, and extreme poverty totaled 51 percent, 30 percent, and 16 percent of its population, respectively. Fifteen percent of Mexico's population earns less than a dollar a day.[26]

The pattern in Mexico's standard of living can also be examined from a more sophisticated perspective, more revealing than that of per capita income alone. The National Bank of Mexico, one of the country's most

Table 10-4 Distribution of Income in Mexico, 1984–1992 (in percent)

Family Income by Deciles, Lowest to Highest	1984	1989	1992
1	1.72	1.58	1.56
2	3.11	2.81	2.75
3	4.21	3.74	3.70
4	5.32	4.73	4.70
5	6.40	5.90	5.70
6	7.86	7.29	7.11
7	9.72	8.98	8.92
8	12.16	11.42	11.57
9	16.73	15.62	16.02
10	32.77	37.93	38.16

Source: Fernando Pérez Correa, "Modernización y mercado del trabajo," *Este País*, February 1995, 27.

prominent financial institutions, has generated a Well-Being Index, composed of many variables related to an individual person's standard of living. Using their index, and statistics from the national census, they have constructed comparable data from the 1920s through the 1990s (see Table 10-5). Their data convincingly demonstrates strong growth from 1950 to 1980, and especially in the 1960s, with a 3.7 percent increase, but an extremely low level of well-being has been achieved since 1980.

Table 10-5 Mexico's Well-Being Index, 1925–1995 (in percent)

Year	Index[a]	Annual Growth Rate
1925	60.6	0.6
1930	62.3	1.6
1940	73.2	0.7
1950	78.5	2.4
1960	100.0	3.7
1970	144.1	2.3
1980	181.5	0.5
1990	190.5	1.0
1995	198.0	—

Source: Review of the Economic Situation of Mexico, March 1995, 83.
[a]The well-being index refers to basic necessities; it is an aggregate measure of prosperity using nineteen factors related to income, food consumption, health, education, clothing, and urbanization.

DEMOCRATIZATION

In Mexico, as elsewhere in the world, political liberalization has meant democratization. Thus, the international winds of change indicated a combined political-economic model, incorporating political democracy on the one hand and economic capitalism on the other. Mexicans had long expressed an interest in democratization, which flared up after independence, in the 1860s and 1870s, at the time of the revolution, and then again in the 1960s and 1970s.

As was true with the movement toward economic liberalization, President de la Madrid paved the way toward recent political events. Soon after taking office, as part of a moral renovation, he promised cleaner elections and decentralization of the candidate selection process within the government party. Initially, the promises translated into actual improvements, and opposition parties, especially the National Action Party, won many local elections in the mid-1980s.[27] Surprised, government officials reversed the apparent opening by resorting to the "doctoring" of vote counts. The practice roused the Catholic hierarchy and the country's leading intellectuals to proclaim disbelief in government vote counts in the 1986 elections in Chihuahua.

Within the government leadership, a debate ensued as to future political and economic strategies. The debate centered on two primary, interrelated issues. First, should the government expand its commitment to the economic programs introduced gradually under de la Madrid, programs that reduced the standard of living of a fourth of Mexico's economically active population, or should it resort to spending programs to moderate the drastic effects of austerity and resist paying the international debt? Second, should the leadership open up the political system to widespread competition and report electoral results honestly or continue along the same road?

The political figures who wanted to return to deficit spending, economic nationalism, and strong state leadership, combined with electoral honesty, lost out in the internal battles for the presidency. In 1987 when they tried, particularly on the issue of democratizing the PRI, to pressure the leadership from within, they were summarily dismissed from PRI party ranks. Their decision to form an opposition movement under Cuauhtémoc Cárdenas provided a catalyst for the most important election in recent Mexican political history.

The presidential election of 1988 was a test of the legitimacy of the establishment leadership. Although preelection polls indicated the strength of Cuauhtémoc Cárdenas, most analysts underestimated his appeal to the electorate. It was clear that Salinas was the least popular choice among his own party rank and file, and he personally generated little additional support during the campaign. The official results show that Salinas won 50.74 percent of the vote; Cárdenas's alliance, 31.06 percent; and Manuel Clouthier, the National Action Party's candidate, 16.81 percent.

The official results were widely disputed in the media. As noted in the previous chapter, many independent observers and critics believe the figures were fraudulent, and many suggested that Cárdenas may actually have defeated Salinas. Most Mexicanists contend, and they are borne out by survey research, that Salinas won but with a much smaller margin than actually reported.[28] Even accepting the official results, the PRI and the establishment leadership gave up more seats in the Chamber of Deputies and, for the first time, in the Senate than at any other point up to then.

The election of 1988 had numerous consequences. Among them, it provided a catalyst for the development of a new opposition party, the Democratic Revolutionary Party (PRD), which slipped from second to third place in 1991 but restored its strength in 1997, and remains an important alternative to the PRI and PAN. The PRD was formed in 1988 after the demise of a temporary electoral alliance under Cárdenas. Second, the election gave greater prominence to the Chamber of Deputies, in which nearly half of the seats, proportional and district alike, went to the opposition. Third, it brought the democratic desires of the populace to the fore and gave much greater visibility to desires that had been expressed electorally on the district and regional levels since the 1940s but never so dramatically in a national election.[29] Fourth, it contributed to new political alliances, notably between the PAN and the PRD in the electoral arena and between the PAN and the PRI in the policy arena. Fifth, it paved the way for a series of gubernatorial elections, directly or indirectly leading to opposition victories in 1989, 1991, and 1992. Finally, it forced the government leadership to reformulate its political constituencies and, in doing so, introduced political changes as dramatic as those in the economic sphere.

Salinas took office in December 1988 with only a minimal level of political legitimacy. Having won or imposed the disputed election results, he faced—as no president in recent memory had faced—inauguration with very little public support. But Salinas confounded his detractors and supporters alike, moving quickly to establish a reputation as decisive. Instead of depending on the presidency to increase his political influence, Salinas enhanced the prestige of the presidency with his own power and strength. He did this in a series of deft decisions, including using the army to arrest a corrupt union leader and to seize a major drug trafficker, as well as arresting and prosecuting a well-known businessman for financial fraud.

Throughout his tenure Salinas used the presidency as the leading institution to implement his policies and to centralize control of decision making. One of the more interesting ironies of his administration was the concentration of decision-making authority in the presidency.[30] He streamlined the workings of the cabinet, removing the agency that both he and his mentor, de la Madrid—and his disciple, Zedillo—had used to rise to the top of the political ladder. Salinas eliminated programming and budgeting by joining it with the Secretariat of the Treasury. He further coordinated cabinet policymaking by expanding interagency planning through subcabinet groups.

At first glance, Salinas's promise of freer elections appeared to be translated into victories for the opposition. In Baja California, where opposition parties had dominated in the 1988 presidential election, the PAN won its first gubernatorial contest in 1989. No opposition candidate had been permitted to win since the 1930s. It became clear, however, that the government was not committed to political modernization to the same degree as economic liberalization.

In 1991 two important elections took place in San Luis Potosí and Guanajuato. Both states have long histories of support for opposition parties, notably the PAN, but San Luis Potosí generated its own opposition movement in the 1950s.[31] In both cases, the elections were contentious, but the PRI claimed overwhelming victory in each. What most observers found difficult to credit was the *level* of the PRI victory. In San Luis Potosí the PRI gubernatorial candidate took office but was shortly removed by the president, who replaced him with a national PRI leader as the interim governor. In Guanajuato the president removed the PRI candidate before he was installed, substituting a mayor from the PAN. In 1992 state leadership claimed victory in elections in Tabasco; this too led to the removal of the governor.

Each of the three elections had something in common: The opposition planned a protest march to Mexico City, objecting to the alleged fraud. The president of Mexico intervened in all three states, forcing the governor or governor-elect from office. In fact, by 1992 Salinas had removed eight governors, more than any other president in forty years,[32] which points up two important patterns in his administration. First, the president made the decisions, and the president extralegally brought about resolution of the disputes. Second, Salinas legitimized opposition protests as a viable means of expressing demands. Each time he reacted by removing a governor, he encouraged protests in the future, a pattern Zedillo inherited in his presidency, in both Chiapas and Tabasco.

There is a certain irony in Salinas's liberalization philosophy. Economically, he tried to demonstrate that Mexico is decentralizing, allocating decision-making authority to numerous independent enterprises. Politically, although he said he wanted liberalization for his own party leadership and in national politics, the results demonstrate otherwise: As the government decentralized economic decision making, it actually centralized political decision making even more.

Other characteristics of Salinas's political strategy illustrate the complexity of his policies and the contradictions in his goals. The most radical political policy of his administration involved long-standing church–state relations. Early on Salinas announced his desire to "modernize" church–state relations. He invited church leaders to his inauguration, an unprecedented gesture, and followed this by appointing a personal representative to the Vatican.

In December 1991 Salinas proposed changes in the constitution in regard to church–state relations. Among the changes later approved by the Chamber of Deputies were recognizing all churches as legal entities; allowing priests and ministers to vote and to run for political office if they had resigned from their clerical offices five years earlier; permitting churches and religious officials to offer primary and secondary education as long as they respected government-approved plans of study; allowing public celebrations of religious ceremonies; granting churches the right to own property; and explicitly separating churches from the state.

Although clergy traditionally violated some constitutional provisions in practice, the president confronted a highly emotional issue with deep roots in Mexican political liberalism. The proposals, however, not only modernized the relationship between religion and the state but they also conformed to explicit principles of democracy, particularly concerning the right to vote. On the other hand, Mexico's general record on human rights has contradicted many of the goals implicit in democratization (see Table 10-6).

Again, as in the case of economic liberalization, the United States has been an important, if indirect, actor in Mexico's internal political affairs. In testimony before the House Committee on Foreign Affairs, leaders of international human rights organizations described many human rights abuses. Specifically, Amnesty International's representative, the deputy director of its Washington, D.C., office, stated, "Mexico is a country with staggering levels of political violence."[33] In 1997, the most severe abuses occurred in Chiapas, Guerrero, Oaxaca, and the Federal District.

Table 10-6 Sources of Human Rights
Abuses in Mexico, 1997 (in percent)

Responsible Party	1997
Army	27
State Judicial Police	14
Local Police	14
Local Authorities	11
Public Security	9
Undetermined	9
Paramilitary Groups	7
Secretariat of Government	5
Attorney General	4

Source: Comisión Mexicana de Defensa y Promoción de los Derechos Humanos, *Guión* (January, 1998), 31, based on 485 reported violations,
January–December, 1997.

Thus human rights abuses in the criminal justice system were identified as endemic in many international and domestic reports, and some government officials intimidated political opponents and independent observers
connected with the media. Reporters were beaten, kidnapped, threatened,
pressured, and deported for articles critical of the president, his family, and
his policies. A closed, not an open, climate for public discussion of important issues exists in Mexico.[34]

International pressure forced Salinas to establish the National Commission for Human Rights, initially presided over by Jorge Carpizo, a highly
respected jurist and supreme court justice.[35] The president's primary motivation was to temper worldwide disapproval of Mexico's human rights
record in anticipation of public discussion and congressional hearings in
the United States on the proposed free-trade agreement. The commission
has been able to investigate some complaints and protect the rights of some
abused citizens, but the government's commitment to full investigation and
vigorous prosecution is questionable. The most notorious example of the
Mexican government's commitment occurred in the late fall of 1991. In a
confrontation between Mexican army troops and agents of the federal attorney general's office, the troops, protecting a landing strip in Veracruz
for drug traffickers, killed seven agents. A chase plane pursued the drug
plane, and U.S. drug enforcement agents filmed the encounter. The president gave the Commission for Human Rights Commission responsibility
for investigating. Although it issued a 104-page report and the army tried
and convicted the zone commander and other officers, neither the report
nor the trial gave an explanation for the murders.[36]

The influence of independent domestic and international human rights groups played a crucial role in reversing the government's policy in Chiapas, where Salinas initially pursued a repressive policy against the indigenous uprising on January 1, 1995, led by the Zapatista Army of National Liberation (EZLN), which seized several towns and attacked troop encampments in the region of San Cristóbal de las Casas. Human rights observers and newspaper reporters documented cases of summary executions, physical abuses, and general mistreatment at the hands of government troops. Their allegations and reports figured significantly in motivating public opinion against the government's use of troops, leading instead to the establishment of a peace commission. They, along with the Catholic Church, were again crucial in bringing the 1997 murder of forty-five indigenous peasants in Acteal, Chiapas, by a paramilitary group to the public's attention.

National, state, and local election results from 1990 to 1993, presidential intervention in electoral disputes, and failure to respond fully to human rights abuses revealed the slow pace and incompleteness of political reform and democratization in Mexico. Electoral integrity is not the only test of the government's commitment to democracy. The public's cynicism about government institutions is also a consequence of pervasive corruption in public life. It is not just obvious forms of corruption that detract from the integrity of the institutions and the leadership but also corruption's detrimental effects on the sense of community interest and trust. Thus, pervasive corruption complements the belief that public life provides opportunities to benefit family and friends rather than to serve the interests of all Mexicans. This is not to say that all public officials in Mexico are dishonest but to suggest that an ambience favorable to self-interest, dishonesty, and favoritism prevails in many areas and at numerous levels of the public sector. The Mexican public itself believes that corruption is widespread.[37]

Corruption, however, has taken a greater toll on society, as events in Mexico make clear the country's involvement in drug trafficking, primarily in transporting illegal drugs from Latin America through Mexico into the United States. The political assassinations in 1994 and the reinvestigations under the Zedillo administration point to drug-related involvement in several notable murders, specifically those of Cardinal Juan Jesús Posadas in Guadalajara in May 1993, of presidential candidate Luis Donaldo Colosio in March 1994 (as well as that of the Tijuana police chief investigating his murder), and of the PRI secretary general José Francisco Ruiz Massieu in downtown Mexico City in September 1994. Some analysts fear that the levels of corruption in Mexico have reached deeply and broadly into the highest levels of government and the military and that Mexico is on the verge of a "Colombianization" of political life. There is no better example of these conditions than in Tijuana, the important border city near San Diego, California.[38] The pervasiveness of this corruption was brought home to the Mexican people when Ruiz Massieu's brother Mario, the assistant attorney general in charge of anti-drug-related activities and of the investigation of his brother's murder in 1994, was arrested in early 1995 after the government discovered that he had deposited millions of dollars in U.S. bank accounts. Indeed, the extent of money-laundering operations among prominent banks in the United States and Mexico, and worldwide, is an issue of global importance. As one report concluded, "Mexico's banking and financial sector lacks adequate controls on money laundering and has become one of the most important money laundering centers in the western hemisphere."[39] Although Zedillo has promised to battle this debilitating influence, there is little evidence to support a marked reduction in drug-related corruption.

MEXICO'S FUTURE

Mexico today faces a democratization challenge to its semiauthoritarian political model emanating from its citizenry and from dissident and opposition elites. The challenge is formidable and has many consequences for the leadership in both the short and long term. It is also clear that the economic strategy pursued by the government, especially since 1988, is affecting and will be affected by the tends in political liberalization.

If Mexico is undergoing a slow, tortuous process of democratization, what exactly does that imply? As several analysts have shown, democracy incorporates the following: policy debates and political competition, citizen participation, accountability of the rules to law and representative mechanisms, civilian control over the military, and respect for the views and rights of others.[40]

It is not enough to introduce the mechanisms or processes of democracy; in this respect, Mexico has already achieved certain facets of a democratic system. What is equally important but more difficult to accomplish is a certain level of societal trust, which in turn encourages people to respect the political views of others.[41]

The Mexican government has chosen to pursue economic and political liberalization. Although Salinas argued for the necessity of economic liberalization first, followed by a more evolutionary political liberalization, there are no guarantees that economic decentralization and foreign invest-ment will automatically produce democratic political tendencies. There is no doubt that the two trends are intertwined and that certain aspects of Mexico's economic liberalization strategy will enhance political develop-ments, including the decentralization of economic authority, competition, the introduction of international influences, and the exchange of ideas.[42] Most observers believe, for example, that the free-trade agreement by Canada, the United States, and Mexico will have certain consequences and benefits for democratization.[43]

In a comprehensive analysis of transformation in state–society rela-tions focusing on the Solidarity program, John Bailey, a leading observer of Mexican politics, concluded shortly before Zedillo took office that

> the presidency and executive structures benefit from Pronasol rather to the exclusion of legislatures and political parties, even including the PRI. Thus, rather than strengthening institutional pluralism, Solidarity reinforces presi-dentialism. It would appear that efforts to reform the official party reached their peak in this particular *sexenio* in the party's 14th Assembly held in Sep-tember 1990.[44]

Basically, the government's strategy was to win grassroots support for the PRI by building on the traditional corporatist structures. Although some of the traditional structures were changed in the process, they did not change the source of political influence, the executive branch, by 1994.

To what degree does Mexico promote policy debate and political com-petition? Since the 1980s, political competition has greatly increased, mea-sured in terms of opposition successes in the voting booths. Competition initially reached a high point in the 1988 presidential election. Although its meaning is confused because many citizens voted against the PRI rather than for a specific alternative, the fact is that half the voters, according to the official statistics, voted for a nongovernment candidate, and in reality probably more than half voted for other parties. Three years later the 1991 elections revealed an entirely different situation: Opposition strength ap-peared to have vanished into thin air. Despite allegations of widespread fraud by opposition parties, empirical survey research pointed to a revival of PRI strength and appeal while support for the newest party, the PRD, waned. Nevertheless, the desire of the government party to overwhelm its opponents and to claim a sweeping victory negated any interpretation that viable political competition existed. As one critic suggested, Mexico cre-ated electoral pluralism *without* competition.[45]

The presidential elections of 1994 returned Mexico to the electoral context of 1988 in regard to the level of support for the opposition. But as has been argued earlier, the outcome of the 1994 elections changed all previous patterns, including those recorded in 1988, in two potentially significant ways. First, the turnout was extraordinary and introduced a large minority of Mexicans directly into the political process. If they continue to participate in the political process, even if only electorally, they could provide a base for future opposition growth. Second, although the proportion of voters casting their ballots for the PRI remained unchanged from 1988, the composition of the voters was quite different, especially in state income levels, rural and urban patterns, and region. Mexico is witnessing an important change among the types of voters who support opposition-party candidates. For example, the opposition demonstrated a substantial increase in support among rural voters and voters in the south, two traditionally "safe" groups for PRI.

The midterm elections in 1997 reinforced the patterns which became apparent in 1994. The scope of opposition victories was sustained, and PRI declined from a majority to a plurality party. Not only could competitiveness be measured between the PRI and the opposition collectively, but the PRD and PAN became more closely balanced among the leading opposition parties.

Electoral contests have always received most of the attention in the media and in analyses of political competition. Perhaps the most obvious weakness in measuring Mexico's democratic achievements is in the policy arena. The argument in the past has been that political leadership and the governing party representing that leadership were sufficiently broad, ideologically speaking, to incorporate opposing points of view. Although policy debates rarely spilled over into public view, there was considerable give-and-take within the top executive-branch echelon. In recent years, however, although this pattern was still the norm, presidents narrowed the range of acceptable policy alternatives, especially in the economic realm, forcing dissident members of their own party from leadership posts.

From 1988 to 1991, for the first time in recent Mexican history, the opposition acquired sufficient strength in the Chamber of Deputies to give the lower house a strong voice in the policy process—especially when the government desired constitutional amendments, for which it lacked a sufficient proportion of PRI legislative votes. Debate over significant policy issues opened up when the government party sought allies to support constitutional legislation. The 1991 elections damped this departure, reducing public debate, but this practice was revived in 1994 and accentuated in the austerity measures proposed by the Zedillo administration. Even within its own ranks, the government tried to maintain very strict discipline, not permitting officials to speak out on controversial policy issues. When two PRI legislators joined opposition deputies in voting against the austerity package, loyal PRI deputies proposed removing them from the party. After 1997, the opposition actually took charge of the legislative branch, in effect giving them control over the legislative agenda.

Citizen participation has undergone several changes in recent years. The 1988, 1994, and 1997 electoral contests generated considerable interest and hence participation. But in the recent past, participation declined as cynicism toward the electoral process burgeoned. Still, it would be fair to say that the development of a viable third party in 1989 reflected new levels of citizen participation. Perhaps more important, grassroots organizations have flourished. They encompass a broad spectrum of citizens and interests. These are positive signs, yet the ability of citizens to participate in the decision-making process or to have their interests directly represented at policymaking levels is minimal. This is due in part to the structure of the relationship between the legislative and executive branches and the continuing dominance of the latter over the policy process.

The most remarkable change resulting from the elections is the experience that Mexicans obtained at the local and state levels. Not only did the PAN and, to a lesser extent, the PRD defeat the PRI in numerous mayoral and gubernatorial races, but Mexicans are being exposed to alternative styles of executive-branch decision making on the local level. A major consequence of these experiences can be linked to a deconcentration of authority and a decentralization of political power. For example, after 1996, two-thirds of the social development budget, Mexico's largest line item, was devolved to municipal coffers.[46] Opposition victories do not mean necessarily better government or more successful government. But a prominent emerging pattern is a revival of autonomy and independence at the local level.[47] This is demonstrated in the fact that local leaders, typically from opposition parties, are demanding more control over financial resources, the crucial variable in determining political influence. The mayor of Ciudad Juárez, Mexico's fourth largest city, demanded that the federal government turn over $4.9 million in revenues from tolls taken at the international bridge to its sister city, El Paso, Texas. The mayor, a PANista, set up municipal toll booths to take the money away from federally operated toll collectors.[48] Popular postures taken by local opposition-party leaders are being emulated by members of the government party in similar posts.

A second consequence is that state legislative bodies are acting more boldly, best represented by the PANista-controlled Jalisco congress, which on March 23, 1995, rejected an essential component of President Zedillo's economic austerity package: a 50 percent increase in the value-added tax. According to local experts, this is the first time that a federal policy of this magnitude was rejected by a local legislature.[49]

To most Mexicans, the accountability of their leadership is a moot point. Although individual citizens can and do use the legal system to protect themselves from abuses by the executive branch, including the presidency, they are few in number. Actions of the executive branch, even when carrying out policy decisions favored by most Mexicans, often contradict legal guidelines or ignore institutional channels. Many of Salinas's decisions were not legally implemented, whether they involved criminal matters, such as arresting a drug dealer, or were purely political, like his removals of state governors.

The continued use of the presidency to resolve political questions when legal channels are at hand, has numerous consequences. It puts the presidency above all other institutions, giving it extraordinary powers in practice and in the eyes of the citizenry. Hence, when the president exercises authority extralegally, he creates expectations on the part of the average Mexican. Even when the president intervenes to overturn elections and to support politically liberalizing trends, the intervention itself contravenes these goals. The justification that the ends justifies the means is contradictory to democratization.

The presidency is the most important institutional force in Mexican society and, as such, serves as the leading model for other forms of political and social behavior. If the president behaves in a paternalistic, interventionist, and authoritarian manner, he will set the tone for the rest of the political system and society. Although Zedillo has pledged, according to one leading analyst, "nothing less than the end of presidentialism," his attempts to implement such a strategy, at a time of extreme crisis, have been nearly futile.[50] His actions during the first two-thirds of his presidency provide evidence of both a withdrawal from and a continuation of, interventionism. But overall, despite his inconsistency, Zedillo has reduced presidential power, and increased the pace of federalism and decentralization.

The rule of law has yet to develop substantial prestige in Mexico. Analysts argue that the influx of foreign businesses and greater international competitiveness will encourage heavier reliance on the legal system to resolve disputes, given that these new phenomena traditionally used similar channels in their own cultures. This may well be the case, but for the average Mexican, the law provides few guarantees of equal treatment. As the human rights literature make clear, the criminal justice system is often the abuser of human rights, not their protector. The level of corruption also influences the legal system and the law's applicability to all citizens.[51]

For much of Latin America and many other Third World countries, civilian control over the military has rarely existed. The Mexican civilian sector, however, has had an exceedingly successful relationship with the military, especially since the 1930s, and has unquestionably maintained its supremacy. Even so, the relationship is quite complex and contains many variables. To achieve civilian supremacy, civilian leadership gave up a part of its autonomy regarding military matters, including promotions and the internal allocation of funding. As the event in Veracruz illustrated, civilian leadership, including the president, placed self-imposed limits on their ability to discipline errant and corrupt behavior by members of the armed forces. Civilian leadership retained its position in part by never publicly criticizing the armed forces—actually by heaping praise on its institutional integrity even when that may not have been the case.[52]

Finally, as our earlier analysis of citizen political values and attitudes showed, many Mexicans share beliefs conducive to democratic behavior. However, large portions of the populace and of the leadership, opposition and establishment alike, have not yet accepted the obligations of a democratic culture, one of which is tolerance of opposing political and social views. Establishment leadership's positive actions toward its own members and toward members of the opposition can encourage this value. The degree to which the electoral process remains open and highly competitive also encourages this value.

Mexico's political development has taken some interesting turns in the 1990s. Its politicians and political process labor under a special burden with which few countries have had to cope: proximity to the United States. As noted in the discussion of the historical evolution of Mexico's political characteristics, just the geographic nearness of the United States and its historic involvement in internal Mexican affairs were part of Mexico's earlier history.

The United States continues to exercise considerable influence on Mexico's leadership, albeit usually implicit and indirect. In fact, if the United States were to attempt to influence Mexican political affairs directly, the effort would surely backfire. Nevertheless, the influence is obvious and many actors are involved. For example, U.S. media often criticize Mexico for its political failures, focusing in recent years on electoral fraud, corruption, and human rights abuses.[53] Mexicans often resort to nationalism to deny the veracity and importance of the criticism. On the other hand, opposition leaders cite the reports to justify their own criticism and to take the leadership to task. Also, in a search for greater legitimacy, establishment leadership and the Salinas administration particularly used favorable reports in the international press to gain credibility within Mexico and abroad.

The United States has exercised an indirect influence since the 1980s on many aspects of government policy through its drug interdiction program. Drug enforcement agents have worked closely with their Mexican counterparts to stanch the northward flow of drugs. The involvement of U.S. representatives in matters pertaining to Mexican national security often raises important political issues. It is very unlikely that the confrontation between the army and agents of the attorney general's office in late 1991 would have become a public issue involving the National Commission for Human Rights, the Secretariat of National Defense, and the president if agents of the U.S. Drug Enforcement Agency had not been present.

The posture of the U.S. government toward various Mexican policies can flavor the political environment. This is not to suggest that the United States alone can or does determine political decisions in Mexico, but it may well bear on their outcome. For example, until 1988 some U.S. officials were unceasingly critical of Mexico's failure to increase electoral competitiveness and to provide honest vote counts. Some observers noted, however, that after 1988 such criticism was tempered or dropped altogether. The change was motivated, it was suggested, by U.S. support for Salinas's economic strategy and by the perception that the populist Left, which opposed these policies, would be the primary beneficiaries of a political opening.[54] It is obvious, however, that before, during, and after the implementation of NAFTA, as highlighted in the U.S. loan package in 1995, severe criticism of Mexican political corruption continues unabated.

Whether or not Mexico's leadership is truly committed to democratic reforms, the fact is that many forces within and outside Mexico are pushing it in the direction of greater democracy, with all that entails.[55] Although the contradictions between strong state-led economic liberalization and political democracy abound, it is not likely that the leadership can sustain the separation indefinitely. Democratization is rapidly eating away at the framework of authoritarianism in Mexico, creating the hybrid political model of the future. Whatever path it takes, Mexico will carry its own special politics into the twenty-first century.

NOTES

1. Pedro Aspe, "Thoughts on the Structural Transformation in Mexico: The Case of Privatization of Public Sector Enterprises," speech to the World Affairs Council, Los Angeles, June 21, 1991, 6.

2. "Social and Political Perceptions," *Review of the Economic Situation in Mexico*, June 1997, 242–45.

3. Samuel Schmidt, *The Deterioration of the Mexican Presidency: The Years of Luis Echeverría* (Tucson: University of Arizona Press, 1991).

4. Luis Rubio and Roberto Newell, *Mexico's Dilemma: The Political Origins of Economic Crisis* (Boulder, Colo.: Westview Press, 1984), 134.

5. George Grayson, *The Politics of Mexican Oil* (Pittsburgh: University of Pittsburgh Press, 1980), 119.

6. Sidney Weintraub, *A Marriage of Convenience: Relations Between Mexico and the United States* (New York: Oxford University Press, 1990), 134ff.

7. Sylvia Maxfield, "Introduction," in *Government and Private Sector in Contemporary Mexico*, ed. Sylvia Maxfield and Ricardo Anzaldúa Montoya (La Jolla, Calif.: Center for U.S.–Mexican Studies, UCSD, 1987), 18.

8. Daniel Levy and Gabriel Székely, *Mexico: Paradoxes of Stability and Change* (Boulder, Colo.: Westview Press, 1987), 157.

9. Wayne A. Cornelius, "The Political Economy of Mexico Under de la Madrid: Austerity, Routinized Crisis, and Nascent Recovery," *Mexican Studies/ Estudios Mexicanos* 1 (Winter 1985): 83–124.

10. Personal interview, Mexico City, July 20, 1984.

11. Peter H. Smith, "The 1988 Presidential Succession in Historical Perspective," in *Mexico's Alternative Political Futures*, ed. Wayne A. Cornelius, Judith Gentleman, and Peter H. Smith (La Jolla, Calif.: Center for U.S.–Mexican Studies, 1989), 402.

12. Tom Barry, ed., *Mexico: A Country Guide* (Albuquerque: Inter-Hemispheric Education Resource Guide, 1992), 86.

13. *Mexico Report*, February 10, 1992, 6; and Judith Teichman "Dismantling the Mexican State and the Role of The Private Sector," in *The Political Economy of North American Free Trade*, ed. Ricardo Grinspun and Maxwell Cameron (New York: St. Martin's Press, 1993), 177–92.

14. *Mexico Report*, February 10, 1992.

15. Sidney Weintraub, *NAFTA: What Comes Next?* (Washington, D.C.: CSIS, 1994), 53–54.

16. Raymundo Riva Palacio, "Mexico Is Not an Island," *El Financiero International*, February 24, 1992, 17; Sergio Sarmiento, "Solidarity Offers Hope for Votes," *El Financiero International*, September 30, 1991, 12.

17. "A New Hope for the Hemisphere," *New Perspective Quarterly*, 8 (Winter 1991): 128.

18. For some unusual insights into his strategy, see Robert A. Pastor, "Post-Revolutionary Mexico: The Salinas Opening," *Journal of Inter-American Studies and World Affairs* 32 (Fall 1990): 1–22.

19. "Salinas' Economic Tally," *El Financiero International*, November 7–13, 1994, 15.

20. Ernesto Zedillo, "A Strategy for Mexico's Economic Growth," June 6, 1994.

21. The clearest explanations of the devaluation decision and the mistakes made by both Salinas and Zedillo are explored briefly in Sidney Weintraub's "Mexico's Devaluation: Why and What Next?" (Washington, D.C.: CSIS, January 4, 1994), 1–7; Francisco Gil Díaz and Agustín Carstens, "Some Hypotheses Related to the Mexican 1994–1995 Crisis" (Mexico City: Bank of Mexico, 1996); and Nora

Lustig, "Mexico in Crisis, The U.S. to the Rescue" (Washington, D.C.: Brookings Institution, 1996).

22. Douglas W. Payne, "Wall Street Blues," *The New Republic*, March 13, 1995, 20, 22.

23. Claire Poole, "Beast of Burden," *Mexico Business*, December 1996, 30, cites Carlos Marichal, an economic historian who argues that "Mexico's foreign debt load is the biggest ever in the history of Latin America, or for that matter, of any developing country."

24. Ernesto Zedillo, "Social Policy, a Committment to Mexicans," September 1997.

25. For a discussion, see John Sheahan's excellent "Effects of Liberalization Programs on Poverty and Inequality: Chile, Mexico, and Peru," *Latin American Research Review* 37, 3 (1997): 7–37.

26. "Anti-poverty Program," *Review of the Economic Situation of Mexico*, September 1997, 369–72.

27. John Bailey, "Mexico," in *Latin American and Caribbean Contemporary Record, 1985–86*, ed. Jack W. Hopkins (New York: Holmes & Meier, 1987), B355–58; Wayne A. Cornelius, "Political Liberalization in an Authoritarian Regime: Mexico, 1976–1985," in *Mexican Politics in Transition*, ed. Judith Gentleman (Boulder, Colo.: Westview Press, 1987), 15–40.

28. For various analyses of the results, see Edgar W. Butler and Jorge A. Bustamante, eds., *Sucesión Presidencial: The 1988 Mexican Presidential Election* (Boulder, Colo.: Westview Press, 1991).

29. Roderic Ai Camp, "Mexico's 1988 Elections: A Turning Point for Its Political Development and Foreign Relations," in *Sucesión Presidencial: The 1988 Mexican Presidential Elections*, eds. Edgar W. Butler and Jorge A. Bustamante (Boulder, Colo.: Westview Press, 1990), 104–8.

30. For interesting insights into the issue of leadership, from the point of view of a Mexican intellectual, see Federico Reyes Heroles, "De la debilidad al liderazgo," *Este País*, September 1991, 3–10.

31. Robert R. Bezdek, "Electoral Opposition in Mexico: Emergence, Suppression, and Impact on Political Processes" (Ph.D. diss., Ohio State University, 1973).

32. Ted Bardacke, "Another Governor Bites the Dust," *El Financiero International*, February 10, 1992, 13. No more were removed after 1992, but the same pattern almost prevailed in Tamaulipas in 1993.

33. House Committee on Foreign Affairs, *Hearing Before the Subcommittee on Human Rights and International Organizations, and on Western Hemisphere Affairs, September 12, 1990* (Washington, D.C.: GPO, 1990, 31.

34. For a short list, see Andrew Reding and Christopher Whalen, "Fragile Stability, Reform and Repression in Mexico Under Carlos Salinas, 1989–1991" (New York: World Policy Institute, New School for Social Research, 1991), 12ff.

35. See National Commission for Human Rights, *Third Report, June–December, 1991* (Mexico city: 1991), for details.

36. *Washington Post*, January 14, 1992; *Los Angeles Times*, January 15, 1992, and December 7, 1991.

37. Stephen D. Morris, *Corruption and Politics in Contemporary Mexico* (Tuscaloosa: University of Alabama Press, 1991), 103. Morris provides the most detailed analysis of corruption and politics in print.

38. Sebastian Rotella, *Twilight on the Line, Underworlds and Politics at the Mexican Border* (New York: Norton, 1997).

39. Douglas Payne, "Drugs into Money into Power: A Global Challenge," *Freedom Review* 27 (August 1996), 84.

40. See Terry Lynn Karl, "Dilemmas of Democratization in Latin America," *Comparative Politics* 23 (October 1990): 2–3; David Llehmann, *Democracy and Development in Latin America: Economics, Politics and Religion in the Postwar Period* (Philadelphia: Temple University Press, 1990), 206.

41. For arguments in support of this interpretation, see Roderic Ai Camp, "Political Liberalization: The Last Key to Economic Modernization in Mexico," in *The Politics of Economic Liberalization in Mexico*, ed. Riordan Roett (Boulder, Colo.: Lynne Rienner, 1993), 17–34.

42. See Luis Rubio, "Economic Reform and Political Liberalization," in *The Politics of Economic Liberalization in Mexico*, ed. Riordan Roett (Boulder, Colo.: Lynne Rienner, 1993, 35–50.

43. For an excellent presentation of possible alternative scenarios involving the impact of free trade on Mexican politics, see Peter H. Smith, "The Political Impact of Free Trade on Mexico," *Journal of Inter-American Studies and World Affairs* 34 (Spring 1992): 1–25.

44. John Bailey, "Centralism and Political Change in Mexico: The Case of National Solidarity," in *Transforming State–Society Relations in Mexico*, ed. Wayne A. Cornelius, Ann L. Craig, and Jonathan Fox (La Jolla, Calif.: U.S.–Mexican Studies Center, 1994), 118.

45. Juan Molinar Horcasitas, *El Tiempo de la legitimidad, elecciones, autoritarismo y democracia en México* (Mexico City: Cal y Arenas, 1991), 247. As Wayne Cornelius concluded: "For the entrenched PRI bureaucracy, governability—not election fairness and democracy—is the central political problem." See "Mexico's Incomplete Democratic Transition," paper presented at the International Studies Association, Acapulco, March 1993, 47.

46. Víctor A. Espinoza Valle, "The New Federalism and Institutional Change in Mexico," *Enfoque*, Fall 1996, 13.

47. The best case study is that of Chihuahua. See Victoria E. Rodríguez and Peter M. Ward, *Policymaking, Politics, and Urban Governance in Chihuahua, The Experience of Recent PANista Governments* (Austin: LBJ School of Public Affairs, University of Texas, 1992); and their more comprehensive work, especially Part 3, *Opposition Government in Mexico* (Albuquerque: University of New Mexico Press, 1994).

48. Carlos Vigueras, "Juárez Charges Own Border Tolls," *El Financiero International*, April 10–16, 1995, 1.

49. Javier Hurtado, "El derecho de la oposición," University of Guadalajara, March 28, 1995, 1–5.

50. John Bailey, "The 1994 Mexican Presidential Election Post-Election Report" (Washington, D.C.: CSIS, 1994), 12.

51. One of the most informative and pragmatic discussions of the linkage between economic reform and political practices is presented in Luis Rubio, "The Mexican Democratic Quandary" (New York: Salomon Brothers, 1994), 40–43. The best comparative study is that by Judith Gentleman and Voytek Zubek, "International Integration and Democratic Development: The Cases of Poland and Mexico," *Journal of Inter-American Studies and World Affairs* 34 (Spring 1992): 59–109.

52. For details about this relationship, see Roderic Ai Camp, "What Kind of Relationship?" in *Generals in the Palacio: The Military in Modern Mexico* (New York: Oxford University Press, 1992), 212ff.

53. Delal Baer, "Misreading Mexico," *Foreign Policy* (Fall 1997): 138–50.

54. For a sophisticated presentation of this argument, see Lorenzo Meyer, "Mexico: The Exception and the Rule," in *Exporting Democracy: The United States and Latin America*, ed. Abraham F. Lowenthal (Baltimore: Johns Hopkins University Press, 1991), 227.

55. For an excellent overview of what has occurred and the dilemmas it poses for Mexico, see John Bailey and Leopoldo Gómez, "The PRI and Political Liberalization," *Journal of International Affairs* 43 (Winter 1990): 291–312; Adolfo Gilly, "The Mexican Regime in Its Dilemma," *Journal of International Affairs* 43 (Winter 1990): 273–90.

Bibliographic Essay

For the student initially exploring Mexican politics, a voluminous literature exists in both Spanish and English. The purpose of this essay, however, is only to list sources that can lead to more detailed analyses. Such
sources are those readily available, generally in English, and published in
the last decade.

For Latin American politics and Mexican politics specifically, an excellent place to start is David W. Dent, *Handbook of Political Science Research on Latin America, Trends from the 1960s to the 1990s* (Westport,
Conn.: Greenwood Press, 1990), which includes chapters on various countries, several thematic topics, and two chapters on Mexico covering domestic and international affairs. For a more complete survey of recent material on Mexico, in all languages, with brief annotations, see my
"Government and Politics, Mexico," in vol. 55 of *Handbook of Latin American Studies: Social Sciences*, ed. Dolores Moyano Martin (Austin: University of Texas Press, 1997), 387–404, as well as previous volumes. The
Handbook is now accessible through CD-ROM at many research libraries,
or on the internet at the Library of Congress, at www.leweb2.loc.gov/hlas.

There also are some excellent broad surveys of various facets of Mexican politics, decision making, and political economy. A good first source
is John Bailey, *Governing Mexico, the Statecraft of Crisis Management*
(New York: St. Martin's Press, 1988), which examines the administrative
and structural capabilities of the party and the state in the context of recent
reforms. For a broad political, social, and economic overview, the best general survey is Daniel Levy and Gabriel Székely, *Mexico: Paradoxes of Stability and Change*, 2d ed. (Boulder, Colo.: Westview Press, 1987), which
also focuses on Mexico's relationship with the United States, providing a
joint Mexican and North American interpretation. George Grayson offers
a more recent but less in-depth appraisal, with a corporatist flavor, in *Mexico, From Corporatism to Pluralism?* (New York: Harcourt Brace, 1998).
A Mexican view from a political-economic perspective can be found in

254   BIBLIOGRAPHIC ESSAY

Roberto Newell and Luis Rubio, *Mexico's Dilemma, the Political Origins of Economic Crisis* (Boulder, Colo.: Westview Press, 1984); and in Julie A. Erfani, *The Paradox of the Mexican State, Rereading Sovereignty from Independence to NAFTA* (Boulder, Colo.: Lynne Rienner, 1995), which concentrates on the evolution of the state. Another valuable interpretation, particularly of the Luis Echeverría (1970–1976) and José López Portillo (1976–1982) administrations, is Judith Hellman's, *Mexico in Crisis*, 2d ed. (New York: Holmes & Meier, 1983). For a recent Mexican perspective, see Miguel Basáñez, *La lucha por la hegemonia en México, 1968–1990*, 8th ed. (Mexico City: Siglo XXI, 1990).

Several edited collections provide recent, up-to-date interpretations of developments immediately before the 1988 presidential election and consequences since 1988. These include Judith Gentleman, ed., *Mexican Politics in Transition* (Boulder, Colo.: Westview Press, 1987); Wayne A. Cornelius, Judith Gentleman, and Peter H. Smith, eds., *Mexico's Alternative Political Futures* (La Jolla, Calif.: Center for U.S.–Mexican Studies, UCSD, 1989); Maria Lorena Cook, Kevin J. Middlebrook, and Juan Molinar, eds., *The Politics of Economic Restructuring, State–Society Relations and Regime Change in Mexico* (La Jolla, Calif.: Center for U.S.–Mexican Studies, UCSD, 1994); and Wayne A. Cornelius, Ann L. Craig, and Jonathan Fox, eds., *Transforming State–Society Relations in Mexico, the National Solidarity Strategy* (La Jolla, Calif.: Center for U.S.–Mexican Studies, UCSD, 1994). These works contain some of the best interpretative essays on recent Mexico by North American and Mexican scholars.

The only extensive comparative analysis of Mexico and another country is that of Brazil and Mexico, found in Sylvia Ann Hewlett and Richard S. Weinert's excellent *Brazil and Mexico, Patterns in Late Development* (Philadelphia: ISHI, 1982). For more focused comparisons see an excellent work on labor by Karen E. Joyner, "Labor and Development in Poland and Mexico" (Master's thesis, Tulane University, 1993); and Edward L. Gibson, *The Populist Road to Market Reform: Policy and Electoral Coalitions in Argentina and Mexico* (Buenos Aires: Universidad Torcuato Di Tella, 1996). Of course, various edited collections include Mexico as part of a larger regional approach. Among the best are Daniel Levy and Kathleen Bruhn, "Mexico: Sustained Civilian Rule and the Question of Democracy," in *Democracy in Developing Countries: Latin America*, 2nd edition, ed. Larry Diamond, Seymour Martin Lipset, Juan Linz, and Jonathan Hartlyn (Boulder, Colo.: Lynne Rienner, 1998); and Lorenzo Meyer, "Mexico: The Exception and the Rule," in *Exporting Democracy, the United States and Latin America*, ed. Abe Lowenthal (Baltimore: Johns Hopkins University Press, 1991), 215–32.

The historical literature on Mexico is extensive and detailed, although there are gaps for many topics and periods. The best comprehensive survey of Mexican history is that by Michael Meyer, William L. Sherman, and Susan M. Deeds, *The Course of Mexican History*, 6th ed. (New York: Oxford University Press, 1999), which lists readings for various periods and subjects, many of them classics. A Mexican perspective is available in Héctor Aguilar Camín and Lorenzo Meyer, *In the Shadow of the Mexican Revolution, Contemporary Mexican History, 1910–1989* (Austin: University of Texas Press, 1993). For a historical survey focusing on popular culture and the perspective of the masses, see Colin MacLachlan and William H. Beezley, *El Gran Pueblo, A History of Greater Mexico* (Englewood Cliffs, N.J.: Prentice-Hall, 1994). For a broad overview of political characteristics stemming from the colonial system, see Colin M. MacLachlan, *Spain's Empire in the New World* (Berkeley and Los Angeles: University of California Press, 1991). For the late-nineteenth-century political heritage, Lorenzo Meyer, The Origins of Mexico's Authoritarian State, Political Control in the Old and New Regimes," in *Authoritarianism in Mexico*, ed. Luis Reyna and Richard Weinert (Philadelphia: ISHI, 1977), 3–22; and Charles A. Hale, *The Transformation of Liberalism in Late Nineteenth Century Mexico* (Princeton, N.J.: Princeton University Press, 1989), provide helpful interpretations. From a Mexican point of view, especially for understanding the political development and the importance of culture for politics, it is helpful to read Justo Sierra, *The Political Evolution of the Mexican People* (Austin: University of Texas Press, 1969); Samuel Ramos, *Profile of Man and Culture in Mexico* (Austin: University of Texas Press, 1962; and Octavio Paz, *The Labyrinth of Solitude, Life and Thought in Mexico* (New York: Grove Press, 1961).

A broad understanding of the theoretical debates concerning Mexico's unique political model can be found in a revealing discussion in the now-classic by Carolyn Needleman and Martin Needleman, "Who Rules Mexico? A Critique of Some Current Views of the Mexican Political Process," *Journal of Politics* 31 (November 1969): 1011–34. For a variety of interpretations of authoritarianism in Mexico, see José Luis Reyna and Richard Weinert, eds., *Authoritarianism in Mexico* (Philadelphia: ISHI, 1977). An interpretation stressing the corporatist flavor of the regime is lucidly conveyed by Ruth Spalding, "State Power and Its Limits: Corporatism in Mexico," *Comparative Political Studies* 14 (July 1981): 139–64; and John W. Sloan, "The Mexican Variant of Corporatism," *Inter-American Economic Affairs* 38 (Spring 1985): 3–18. For a review of some of the recent literature on an eclectic approach, see Viviane Brachet-Márquez, "Explaining Sociopolitical Change in Latin America: The Case of Mexico," *Latin American Research Review* 27 (1992): 91–122.

The subject of contemporary Mexican political culture has received more attention from Mexican than from U.S. analysts. The comparative classic on this topic, although flawed in places, is by Gabriel Almond and Sidney Verba, *The Civic Culture; Political Attitudes and Democracy in Five Nations* (Boston: Little, Brown, 1965); and the even more useful follow-up analysis in their edited work, *The Civic Culture Revisited* (Boston: Little, Brown, 1980). Another work, again comparing Brazil and Mexico, although having less to do with political values, is that by Joseph A. Kahl, *The Measurement of Modernism, a Study of Values in Brazil and Mexico* (Austin: University of Texas Press, 1974). The most recent comparative study, although focusing on international linkages, is that by Ronald Inglehart, Neil Nevitte, and Miguel Basáñez, *Convergencia en Norte América, comercio, política y cultura* (Mexico City: Siglo XXI, 1994). Several excellent works have appeared in Mexico that provide data on changing Mexican social and political values. The two most comprehensive surveys are by Alberto Hernández Medina and Luis Narro Rodríguez, eds., *Como somos los mexicanos* (Mexico City: CREA, 1987); and Enrique Alduncín, *Los valores de los mexicanos* (Mexico City: Fomento Cultural Banamex, 1986). A much less comprehensive update can be found in Ulises Beltrán, *Los Mexicanos de los noventa* (Mexico: UNAM, 1996).

On the relationship between cultural values and democracy, a good place to begin is Ronald Inglehart, "The Renaissance of Political Culture," *American Political Science Review* 82 (November 1988): 1219. For some useful comparisons with Mexico, see Mitchell Seligson, "Political Culture and Democratization in Latin America," in *Latin American and Caribbean Contemporary Record*, ed. James Malloy and Eduardo A. Gamarra (New York: Holmes & Meier, 1990), A49–65; and the multi–Latin American survey by Miguel Basáñez, Marta Lagos, and Tatiana Beltrán, *Reporte 1995: encuesta latino barómetro* (1996). For Mexico, the best analysis is that by John Booth and Mitchell Seligson, "The Political Culture of Authoritarianism in Mexico," *Latin American Research Review* 19 (1984): 106–24. Other recent views, based on survey research and public opinion polls, can be found in Roderic A. Camp, ed., *Polling for Democracy: Public Opinion and Political Liberalization in Mexico* (Wilmington, Del.: Scholarly Resources, 1996).

In regard to the more specific issue of how values affect partisanship, alienation, and tolerance, there is very little literature on Mexico. One major study is that by Rafael Segovia, *La politización del niño mexicano* (Mexico City: El Colegio de México, 1975), which analyzes data on Mexico City schoolchildren, offering many useful comparisons with similar studies of the United States. Other than the Almond and Verba book, the most important analysis, a case study, is by Richard Fagen and William Tuohy,

Politics and Privilege in a Mexican City (Stanford, Calif.: Stanford University Press, 1972), which explores citizens' attitudes in the Veracruz capital of Jalapa. The best general analysis of this subject is still that by Ann Craig and Wayne Cornelius, "Political Culture in Mexico, Continuities and Revisionists Interpretations," in *The Civic Culture Revisited*, ed. Gabriel Almond and Sidney Verba (Boston: Little, Brown, 1980), 325–93.

For specific groups or issues tied to political behavior, few studies are available in English or in Spanish. On partisanship, some of the best work is that by Joseph Klesner, "Changing Patterns of Electoral Participation and Official Party Support in Mexico," in *Mexican Politics in Transition*, ed. Judith Gentleman (Boulder, Colo.: Westview Press, 1987), 95–127. Excellent new interpretations of specific elections are available in Jorge I. Domínguez and James A. McCann, "Shaping Mexico's Electoral Arena: The Construction of Partisan Cleavages in the 1988 and 1991 National Elections," *American Political Science Review* 89 (March 1995): 34–48; Joseph Klesner, "The 1994 Elections, Manifestation of a Divided Society?" *Mexican Studies* 11 (Winter 1995): 137–49; and Joseph Klesner, "Democratic Transition? The 1997 Mexican Elections," *PS* 30 (December 1997): 703–11. For the impact of religion, see my "The Cross in the Polling Booth: Religion, Politics, and the Laity in Mexico," *Latin American Research Review* 29 (1994): 37–68; and Charles L. Davis, "Religion and Partisan Loyalty, the Case of Catholic Workers in Mexico," *Western Political Quarterly* 45 (March 1992): 275–97. On the subject of gender, the only analysis specifically on this topic is that by William J. Blough, "Political Attitudes of Mexican Women, Support for the Political System Among a Newly Enfranchised Group," *Journal of Inter-American Studies and World Affairs* 14 (May 1972): 201–24.

Three general works are available on political recruitment: Peter H. Smith, *Labyrinths of Power, Political Recruitment in Twentieth-Century Mexico* (Princeton, N.J.: Princeton University Press, 1979), which explores these patterns from 1900 through the Echeverría administration; Roderic A. Camp, *Political Recruitment Across Two Centuries, Mexico, 1884–1993* (Austin: University of Texas Press, 1995), which looks at these patterns from the time of Porfirio Díaz to the present, analyzing opposition as well as establishment politicians; and Miguel Centeno, who examines younger, lower-level technocrats in his revealing *Democracy Within Reason, Technocratic Revolution in Mexico*, 2nd edition, (University Park: Pennsylvania State University Press, 1997). For recent trends, see Roderic Ai Camp, "Camarillas in Mexican Politics, the Case of the Salinas Cabinet," *Mexican Studies* 6 (Winter 1990): 85–108; "The Zedillo Cabinet: Continuity, Change, or Revolution?" Western Hemisphere Election Studies Series

(Washington, D.C.: CSIS, January 5, 1995); and "Technocracy a la Mexicana, Antecedents to Democracy," in *The Politics of Expertise in Latin America*, ed. Miguel Centeno and Patricio Silva (New York: St. Martin's Press, 1997), 196–213. For an understanding of the role of informal groups and upwardly mobile political careers, see Merilee S. Grindle, "Patrons and Clients in the Bureaucracy: Career Networks in Mexico," *Latin American Research Review* 12 (1977): 37–66; and Luis Roniger, *Hierarchy and Trust in Modern Mexico and Brazil* (New York: Praeger, 1990).

One area in domestic politics that has received considerable attention, theoretical and substantive, is the relationship between the government and important interest sectors. The theory of corporatism, which has been most often used to analyze this relationship in Mexico, has been well described in the articles cited by Sloan and Spalding. For a useful historical view, set earlier in the twentieth century, see Nora Hamilton, *The Limits of State Autonomy, Post Revolutionary Mexico* (Princeton, N.J.: Princeton University Press, 1982). For an interpretation of the changes that took place in the late 1980s, see Howard J. Wiarda, "Mexico: The Unravelling of a Corporatist Regime?" *Journal of Inter-American Studies and World Affairs* 30 (Winter 1988–1989): 1–28. Important new explorations of these and related issues can be found in the Maria Lorena Cook, Keven J. Middlebrook, and Juan Molinar volume just mentioned, as well as in two excellent books, Diane E. Davis, *Urban Leviathan, Mexico City in the Twentieth Century* (Philadelphia: Temple University Press, 1994); and Viviane Brachet-Marquez, *The Dynamics of Domination, State, Class, and Social Reform in Mexico, 1910–1990* (Pittsburgh: University of Pittsburgh Press, 1994). The most insightful recent analysis is Blanca Heredia's "Clientelism in Flux: Democratization and Interest Intermediation in Contemporary Mexico," paper presented at the National Latin American Studies Association, Guadalajara, 1997.

To understand policymaking generally in Mexico, the best sources include John Bailey's *Governing Mexico;* and Judith A. Teichman, *Policymaking in Mexico, From Boom to Crisis* (Boston: Allen & Unwin, 1988). For specific case studies dealing with the bureaucracy, see Susan Kaufman Purcell, *The Mexican Profit-Sharing Decision, Politics in an Authoritarian Regime* (Berkeley and Los Angeles: University of California Press, 1975); Peter Ward, *Welfare Politics in Mexico, Papering over the Cracks* (London: Allen & Unwin, 1986); Merilee Grindle, *Bureaucrats, Politicians, and Peasants in Mexico: A Case Study in Public Policy* (Berkeley and Los Angeles: University of California Press, 1977); and Diane Davis, *Urban Leviathan.* For decision making in new opposition-controlled settings, but at the state and local levels, see Victoria Rodríguez and Peter Ward, *Pol-*

icymaking, Politics, and Urban Governance in Chihuahua, the Experience of Recent PANista Governments (Austin: LBJ School of Public Affairs, University of Texas, 1992); and their edited *Opposition Government in Mexico* (Albuquerque: University of New Mexico Press, 1994).

For specific groups and their relationship to the state, several studies are available. In the context of the relationship to the military, see Roderic Ai Camp, *Generals in the Palacio, the Military in Modern Mexico* (New York: Oxford University Press, 1992), especially the final chapter for a broad overview from the 1940s to the present; Stephen J. Wager, "The Mexican Army, 1940–1982: The Country Comes First" (Ph.D. diss., Stanford University, 1992), an insightful institutional analysis; Michael J. Dziedzic, "The Essence of Decision in a Hegemonic Regime: The Case of Mexico's Acquisition of a Supersonic Fighter" (Ph.D. diss., University of Texas at Austin, 1986), an excellent case study of Mexico's decision to acquire fighter planes from the United States; Phyllis Greene Walker, "The Modern Mexican Military: Political Influence and Institutional Interests" (Master's thesis, American University, 1987), based on numerous interviews, which explores the topic generally; Stephen J. Wager, "The Mexican Military Approaches the 21st Century: Coping with a New World Order," *Special Report* (Carlisle, Pa.: Strategic Studies Institute, U.S. Army War College, 1994); and David Ronfeldt, ed., *The Modern Mexican Military: A Reassessment* (La Jolla, Calif.: Center for U.S.–Mexican Studies, UCSD, 1984), a collection of pieces by leading students of the military.

For business and politics, the best work on industrial groups is that by Dale Story, *Industry, the State, and Public Policy in Mexico* (Austin: University of Texas Press, 1986). For the broad relationship between businesspeople and the state, see my *Entrepreneurs and the State in Twentieth Century Mexico* (New York: Oxford University Press, 1989). An excellent case study, although having important theoretical implications, is Douglas C. Bennet and Kenneth E. Sharpe, *Transnational Corporations Versus the State, the Political Economy of the Mexican Auto Industry* (Princeton, N.J.: Princeton University Press, 1985). A broad collection, incorporating Mexican and North American scholarship is Sylvia Maxfield, ed., *Government and the Private Sector in Contemporary Mexico* (La Jolla, Calif.: Center for U.S.–Mexican Studies, UCSD, 1987). The best recent works are those of Yemile Mizrahi, on the relationship between entrepreneurs and the PAN; her "A New Conservative Opposition in Mexico: The Politics of Entrepreneurs in Chihuahua (1983–1992)" (Ph.D. diss., University of California at Berkeley, 1994); and Carlos Alba Vega, "Los empresarios y el estado durante el Salinismo," *Foro Internacional* 36 (January 1996): 31–79.

The most neglected link in this relationship is that between church and state. The most comprehensive work is Roderic Ai Camp, *Crossing Swords: Politics and Religion in Mexico* (New York: Oxford University Press, 1997). For a Mexican view, see Roberto Blancarte, *El poder salinismo e iglesia católica, una nueva convivencia?* (Mexico City: Grijalbo, 1991). In English, useful descriptions of this relationship are Allan Metz, "Mexican Church–State Relations Under President Carlos Salinas de Gortari," *Journal of Church and State* 34 (Winter 1992): 111–30; Roberto Blancarte, "Religion and Constitutional Change in Mexico, 1988–1992," *Social Compass* 40 (1993): 555–69; Michael Tangeman, *Mexico at the Crossroads, Politics, the Church, and the Poor* (Maryknoll, N.Y.: Orbis, 1995); and Paul J. Bonicelli, "Testing the Waters or Opening the Floodgates? Evangelicals, Politics, and the 'New' Mexico," *Journal of Church and State* 39 (Winter 1997): 107–30.

Labor's relationship to the Mexican government has received more attention than the church or the military. The best general interpretation can be found in Kevin J. Middlebrook, ed., *Unions, Workers, and the State in Mexico* (La Jolla, Calif.: Center for U.S.–Mexican Studies, UCSD, 1991), especially his introductory chapter, "State–Labor Relations in Mexico: The Changing Economic and Political Context," 1–26. A short but helpful overview is also provided in George Grayson, *The Mexican Labor Machine: Power, Politics, and Patronage* (Washington, D.C.: CSIS, 1989). The most significant theoretical examination is by Ruth Berins Collier, *The Contradictory Alliance, State–Labor Relations and Regime Change in Mexico* (Berkeley: International and Area Studies, University of California, 1992).

The other group whose relationship is analyzed is intellectuals, a more amorphous sector institutionally. Various studies explore the development and contributions of individual intellectual groups, especially writers, but the literature is sparse on the issue of broad intellectual–state relationships. But see Roderic A. Camp, *Intellectuals and the State in Twentieth Century Mexico* (Austin: University of Texas Press, 1985). For an important analysis of dissent in Mexico, see Evelyn P. Stevens, *Protest and Response in Mexico* (Cambridge, Mass.: MIT Press, 1974). This subject is also examined by Judith Hellman, the Levy and Szekely work, and Basáñez's book. Dissenting groups, in the form of nongovernmental organizations and popular organizations, are discussed in Joe Foweraker and Ann L. Craig, eds., *Popular Movements and Political Change in Mexico* (Boulder, Colo.: Lynne Rienner, 1990); Douglas A. Chalmers and Kerianne Piester, "Nongovernmental Organizations and the Changing Structure of Mexican Politics," in *Changing Structure of Mexico: Political, Social, and Economic Prospects*, ed. Laura Randall (New York: M.E. Sharpe, 1996), 253–61; and

Katherine M. Bailey, "Civic NGOs in Mexican Politics: A New Democratizing Force" (Masters thesis, Tulane University, 1998). Probably no topic on Mexican politics has generated more literature, but few serious, objective analyses, than armed movements. For the EZLN, the most useful works include Thomas Benjamin, *A Rich Land, a Poor People: Politics and Society in Modern Chiapas* (Albuquerque: University of New Mexico Press, 1989); Tom Barry, *Zapata's Revenge: Free Trade and the Farm Crisis in Mexico* (Boston: South End Press, 1995); George A. Collier, "The New Politics of Exclusion: Antecedents to the Rebellion in Mexico," *Dialectical Anthropology* 19 (May 1994): 1–44; and Joseph M. Whitmeyer and Rosemary L. Hopcroft, "Community, Capitalism, and Rebellion in Chiapas," *Sociological Perspective* 39 (Winter 1996): 517–38. A sense of the existence and activities of other armed groups, including the ERP, can be obtained from "Mexico: Armed Insurgent Groups," a report compiled by the Immigration and Refugee Board, Ottawa, Canada, May 1997.

A group which demands increasing analysis, both at the elite and the mass level, is that of women. Women not only have been essential in the rapid expansion of NGOs, but have increased their presence among the three major parties. The most comprehensive books available to date are Victoria E. Rodríguez, ed., *Women's Participation in Mexican Political Life* (Boulder, Colo.: Lynne Rienner, 1998), and Anna M. Fernández Poncela, ed., *Participación política: las mujeres en México al final del mileneo* (Mexico: Colegio de México, 1995). The most comprehensive historical account is Anna M. Fernández Poncela's "La historia de la participación política de las mujeres en México en el último medio siglo," *Boletín Americano* 36, (1996): 111–23. For the importance of feminism generally, see Marta Lamas et al., "Building Bridges: The Growth of Popular Feminism in Mexico," in *The Challenge of Local Feminisms: Women's Movements in Global Perspective* (Boulder, Colo.: Westview, 1995), 324–47. An excellent case study of a feminist public policy issue can be found in Linda S. Stevenson, "Gender Politics in the Mexican Democratization Process: Sex Crimes, Affirmative Action for Women, and the 1997 Elections," paper presented at the David Rockefeller Center for Latin American Studies, Harvard University, Cambridge, 1997.

The branches of government and their relationship to the policymaking process have been neglected completely in the literature on Mexican politics. For the legislative branch, the only comprehensive studies are those by Rudolfo de la Garza, "The Mexican Chamber of Deputies and the Mexican Political System" (Ph.D. diss., University of Arizona, 1972), which, of course, describes features no longer present in this branch, and Alonso Lujambio, *Federalismo y Congreso en el cambio político de México* (Mex-

ico: UNAM, 1995). Richard Bath, "The Mexican Congress: A New Role?"
Proceedings from the 37th Annual Meeting of the RMCLAS, February 1989,
Las Cruces, N.M., 82–90, looks at its changing relationship with the ex-
ecutive branch. For a view of congress in the 1990s, see my "Mexico's
Legislature, Missing the Democratic Lockstep," in *Legislatures and De-
mocratic Transformation in Latin America*, ed. David Close (Boulder,
Colo.: Lynne Rienner, 1995), 17–36. The only analytical work on the ju-
dicial branch is Pilar Domingo, "Democratization Without Separation of
Powers? The Case of the Mexican Supreme Court," paper presented at the
National Latin American Studies Association, Washington, D.C., 1995.

The government party has received more attention than the branches
of government. In English, the best recent analysis is by Dale Story, *The
Mexican Ruling Party, Stability and Authority* (Stanford, Calif.: Hoover Institute, 1986). The most comprehensive historical analysis of the party is
by Javier Luis Garrido, *El partido de la revolución institucionalizada, la
formación del nuevo estado en México (1928–1945)* (Mexico City: Siglo
XXI, 1982).

Opposition parties continue to attract attention in the literature, usu-
ally in an electoral context. The most comprehensive, up-to-date survey of
the opposition role can be found in the previously mentioned *Opposition
Government in Mexico*, edited by Victoria Rodriguez and Peter Ward. For
the National Action Party, the best institutional analysis remains Donald
Mabry's *Mexico's Acción Nacional: A Catholic Alternative to Revolution*
(Syracuse, N.Y.: Syracuse University Press, 1973). Abraham Nuncio, *El
PAN* (Mexico City: Editorial Nueva Imagen, 1986), provides some insights
into the PAN's recent activities, but Soledad Loaeza's "Derecha y democ-
racia en el cambio político mexicano, 1982–1988," *Foro Internacional* 30
(April–June 1990): 631–658, does it more objectively. The PRD has not
received adequate treatment because of its recent origins. However, for
some views of the Democratic Revolutionary Party through its leadership,
see Jesús Galindo López, "A Conversation with Cuauhtémoc Cárdenas,"
Journal of International Affairs 43 (Winter 1990): 395–406; and Carlos B.
Gil, *Hope and Frustration, Interviews with Leaders of Mexico's Political
Opposition* (Wilmington, Del.: Scholarly Resources, 1992). Miguel Angel
Centeno's short *Mexico in the 1990s, Government and Opposition Speak
Out*, Current Issue Brief (La Jolla, Calif.: Center for U.S.–Mexican Stud-
ies, UCSD, 1991), offers some useful insights into differences in their joint
views on policy issues.

Analyses of elections, election data, and the 1988, 1991, 1994, and
1997 elections specifically abound. Some of the better work in English can
be found in Gentleman's *Mexican Politics in Transition;* Cornelius et al.,

Mexico's Alternative Political Futures; and Edgar W. Butler and Jorge A. Bustamante, *Sucesión Presidencial, the 1988 Mexican Presidential Election* (Boulder, Colo.: Westview Press, 1991), the most detailed examination in English of this benchmark election. A more comprehensive analysis leading up to 1988 is Joseph A. Klesner, "Electoral Reform in an Authoritarian Regime: The Case of Mexico" (Ph.D. diss., MIT, 1988); and Arturo Alvarado Mendoza, *Electoral Patterns and Perspectives in Mexico* (La Jolla, Calif.: Center for U.S.–Mexican Studies, UCSD, 1987), containing Mexican and North American interpretations. For a post-1988 analysis, see Keith Yanner, "Democratization in Mexico, 1988–1991" (Ph.D. diss., Washington University, 1992); and Juan Molinar Horcasitas, *El tiempo de la legitimidad, elecciones, autoritarismo y democracia en México* (Mexico City: Cal y Arena, 1991). For the 1991 elections and comparisons between 1988 and 1991, see the excellent work by Jorge Domínguez and James McCann, *Democratizing Mexico: Public Opinion and Electoral Choices* (Baltimore: The Johns Hopkins University Press, 1996); and Joseph Klesner, "Realignment or Dealignment? Consequences of Economic Crisis and Restructuring for the Mexican Party System," in *The Politics of Economic Restructuring*, ed. Cook, Middlebrook, and Molinar, 159–94. For 1994, see Joseph Klesner, "The 1994 Elections, Manifestation of a Divided Society?"; and John Bailey, *The 1994 Mexican Presidential Election Post-Election Report*, Election Studies Series (Washington, D.C.: CSIS, 1994). For 1997, see Armand Peschard-Sverdrup, *The 1997 Mexican Midterm Elections, Post-Election Report*, Western Hemisphere Election Study Series (Washington, D.C.: CSIS, 1997), and Jorge I. Domínguez and Alejandro Poiré, *Toward Mexico's Democratization: Parties, Campaigns, Elections, and Public Opinion* (London: Routledge, 1998).

Political and economic liberalization have received considerable attention since 1987, especially after Salinas's first year in office. A broad, theoretical context can be found in Terry Lynn Karl, "Dilemmas of Democratization in Latin America," *Comparative Politics* 23 (October 1990): 1–21. For highly critical views of Salinas's and Zedillo's political failures, see Andrew Reding's essays, for example, "Mexico Under Salinas: A Facade of Reform," *World Policy Journal* 6 (Fall 1989): 685–729, or "Facing Political Reality in Mexico," *The Washington Quarterly* 20, (1997): 103–16; and Carl J. Migdail, "Mexico's Failing Political System," *Journal of Inter-American Studies and World Affairs* 29 (Fall 1987): 107–23. For more balanced assessments, see John Bailey and Leopoldo Gómez, "The PRI and Liberalization in Mexico," *Journal of International Affairs* 43 (Winter 1990): 291–312; and Riordan Roett, ed., *The Politics of Economic*

Liberalization in Mexico (Boulder, Colo.: Westview Press, 1992), both of which combine Mexican and North American interpretations. Another helpful interpretation is Robert A. Pastor, "Post-Revolutionary Mexico: the Salinas Opening," *Journal of Inter-American Studies and World Affairs* 32 (Fall 1990): 1–22. For a brief historical perspective on political modernization, see my "Political Modernization in Mexico, Through a Looking Glass," in *The Evolution of the Mexican Political System*, ed. Jaime Rodríguez (Wilmington, Del.: Scholarly Resources, 1993), 245–64; and Wayne A. Cornelius, "Political Liberalization in an Authoritarian Regime: Mexico, 1976–1985," in *Mexican Politics in Transition*, ed. Judith Gentleman (Boulder, Colo.: Westview Press, 1987), 15–47. The broad consequences of decentralization are evaluated in Victoria Rodríguez, *Decentralization in Mexico* (Boulder, Colo.: Westview, 1997). Mexican views can be found in Andrea Sánchez et al., eds., *La Renovación política y el sistema electoral mexicano* (Mexico City: Porrúa, 1987); and Soledad Loaeza and Rafael Segovia, eds., *La vida política mexicana en la crisis* (Mexico City: Colegio de México, 1987). The economic side, specifically the potential impact of NAFTA, is analyzed by Ricardo Grinspun and Maxwell Cameron, eds., *The Political Economy of North American Free Trade* (New York: St. Martin' Press, 1993). An insightful comparative approach is offered in Judith Gentleman and Voytek Zubek, "International Integration and Democratic Development: The Cases of Poland and Mexico," *Journal of Inter-American Studies and World Affairs* 34 (Spring 1992): 59–109.

For the implications of recent changes in U.S.–Mexican relations as they relate to Mexican political development, see Susan Kaufman Purcell, ed., *Mexico in Transition, Implications for U.S. Policy* (New York: Council on Foreign Relations, 1988); Riordan Roett, ed., *Mexico and the United States, Managing the Relationship* (Boulder, Colo.: Westview Press, 1988); Bilateral Commission on the Future of United States–Mexican Relations, *Dimensions of United State–Mexican Relations*, 5 vols. (La Jolla, Calif.: Center for U.S.–Mexican Studies, UCSD, 1989); and Riordan Roett, ed., *Mexico's External Relations in the 1990s* (Boulder, Calif.: Lynne Rienner, 1991), especially Part 4. A broader, general interpretation is available in Tom Barry, Harry Browne, and Beth Sims, *The Great Divide, the Challenge of U.S.–Mexico Relations in the 1990s* (New York: Grove Press, 1994); and Arturo Valenzuela, *The Challenge of Mexico to U.S. Foreign Policy*, Occasional Paper Series, Overseas Development Council, Washington, D.C., June, 1997. To understand the economic context, see Sidney Weintraub, *A Marriage of Convenience: Relations Between Mexico and the United States* (Oxford: Oxford University Press, 1990), and his *NAFTA: What Comes Next?* (Washington, D.C.: CSIS, 1994); as well as George

Grayson, *The North American Free Trade Agreement, Regional Community and the New World Order* (Lanham, Md.: University Press of America, 1995). To understand the impact on ordinary Mexicans, see the vivid portrait, in their own words, by Judith Hellman, *Mexican Lives* (New York: New Press, 1994). An insightful examination, which touches on many of the political and cultural differences, can be found in Robert A. Pastor and Jorge G. Castañeda, *Limits to Friendship: The United States and Mexico* (New York: Knopf, 1988). For the U.S. view of Mexico, see Sergio Aguayo, *Myths and (Mis) Perceptions: Changing U.S. Elite Visions of Mexico* (La Jolla, Calif.: Center for U.S.–Mexican Studies, UCSD, 1998).

Finally, on the issue of human rights and corruption, Stephen D. Morris, *Corruption and Politics in Contemporary Mexico* (Tuscaloosa: University of Alabama Press, 1991), is the first book-length work to wrestle with this topic in Mexican politics. To understand the influence of drugs, a good place to begin is Douglas W. Payne, "Drugs into Money into Power," *Freedom Review* 27 (July–August, 1996), 9–104. For the best case study, see Sebastian Rotella, *Twilight on the Line: Underworlds and Politics at the Mexican Border* (New York: Norton, 1997). Human rights continue to be neglected from an analytical point of view, but the recent publications of international and national human rights organizations provide some first-hand data on the Mexican situation. Among the most useful are the Americas Watch Report, *Human Rights in Mexico, a Policy of Impunity* (June 1990) and *Unceasing Abuses, Human Rights in Mexico One Year After the Introduction of Reform* (September 1991); the National Commission for Human Rights, *Second Report*, December 1990–June 1991, and *Third Report*, June–December 1991 (Mexico: National Commission for Human Rights, 1991); Minnesota Advocates for Human Rights, *Harassment of Human Rights Defenders in Mexico*, August 1994, *Stifling Human Rights Advocacy in Mexico*, May 1994, *The Mexican Coordination of National Public Security*, June 1994; Human Rights Watch—Americas, "Mexico: The New Year's Rebellion," (March 1, 1994, 24–26; and Andrew Reding, *Democracy and Human Rights in Mexico* (New York: World Policy Institute, 1995). For regular updates monthly, see *Guión*, a publication of the independent Comisión Mexicana de Defensa y Promoción de los Derechos Humanos.

The internet has become a useful tool for Mexican research, primarily for documentary and bibliographic searches, but also for articles in the media and leading magazines. For on-line addresses to almost every important Mexican magazine and newspaper, and to all other sources organized by category, see www.lanic.utexas.edu/la/mexico. For relevant material in the United States media, as well as related articles, see the *New*

York Times, www.nytimes.com, specifically the Americas directory under contents. By far the most useful governmental documents source is that organized by David Block of Cornell University, available at http://lib1.library.cornell.edu. The documents are organized by branch of government. For electoral results and parties, see www.trace-sc.com/parties.htm. The two best sources for up-to-date articles from the Mexican media are *Reforma*, the influential, independent Mexico City daily, at www.infotel.com.mx/reforma, and *Proceso*, a muckraking political weekly, at www.proceso.com.mx. Census statistics are available through www.ags.inegi.gob.mx.

Index